Pure church

The title reflects my overarching passion being purely church. It reminds us of our great need to see the church in all its fulness as utterly pure and totally holy – the bride of Christ!

ISBN: 978-1-0685587-2-6

Pure Church
Copyright © 2025 John Noble

First published 2025 by Boz Publications Ltd

The right of John Noble to be identified as the author of this work has been asserted by them in accordance with the Copyright, Designs and Patents Act 1988. All rights reserved. No part of this publication may be reproduced, stored in a retrieval system, or transmitted in any other form or by any means, electronic, mechanical, photocopying, recording or otherwise, without the prior written permission of the author.

Permission may be obtained by writing to the author at: noblejs@aol.com

A CIP catalogue record for this book is available from the British Library.

Scripture references are taken from:
The Holy Bible. New International Version, (NIV),
Copyright © 1973, 1978, 1984, 2011 by Biblica.
The Holy Bible. Authorized King James Version, (KJV),
Oxford UP, 1998.

Front cover illustration © N.Sokell.

B
BOZ PUBLICATIONS
Boz Publications Ltd.

71-75 Shelton Street, Covent Garden, London, WC2H 9JQ, United Kingdom.
www.bozpublications.com - office@bozpublications.com

PURE CHURCH

The remarkable story of God's grace at work in an unlikely couple

John Noble

Special thanks

I am enormously grateful to my dear friend Jim Holl who gave himself to the almost endless task of proofreading and checking my manuscript. Jim you're a star – thank you so much!

John

Thanks so much to Aiden, my twelve-year-old great-grandson, who is responsible for the title of this book, 'Pure Church' I had been greatly disappointed to learn soon after I had started to write that the original title I had chosen had already been used. When having a family meal, Aiden asked to sit next to me and, whilst we were waiting for the food to arrive, he asked about the books I had written. I told him about the one I was working on and about my frustration that I couldn't use the title I had chosen.

Immediately, he announced that he was going to have a brain-storming session to think of a new title for me. So he grabbed a serviette, asked his mum for a biro, and went to work. He soon came up with a list of ideas which were great but didn't quite hit the spot. I had no expectation that he would be able to find a suitable replacement as I had spent quite a time wracking my brain but I told him that I really appreciated his enthusiasm. Undeterred, he carried on and there on the serviette he wrote two words, 'Pure Church' That was all I needed, Aiden had done the job and I was delighted!

Great-grandpa

Dedications

Firstly, I dedicate this book to my son Matthew and to his lovely wife Cathy who chose to live with us after their marriage to serve us unwaveringly over all these years. They have run the home and the house and suffered all the ups and downs of our lives and moves without a thought for themselves.

When Christine and I have been off on our travels, they have taken full responsibility, leaving us with the knowledge that everything would be taken care of while we were away. Cathy has cooked, cleaned, typed and latterly they stood with me through the tough times of Christine's dementia and, I must say, that I have tended to take them for granted as there was never a complaint. We could not have asked for a more devoted or loving couple for us to have by our sides through all these years. What can I say but a massive 'thank you' to you both.

Of course, I also must dedicate what I have written to Christine and the lovely family she gave me. The five super children and their partners, the many wonderful grandkids, and the growing number of great grand-children of which I am rapidly losing count. It is particularly the latter that I felt I wanted to read this story. Right now they may not appreciate it, but perhaps later in life they may want to read a little of what their old great-grandma and great-grandpa achieved in life with the help of the one and only Jesus who they loved.

CONTENTS

INTRODUCTION { deep, moving.	7
THE EARLY YEARS	15
LIFE AFTER DAD	33
MARRIAGE AND THE JOURNEY BACK TO FAITH	43
OPEN DOORS AND NEW OPPORTUNITIES	56
FULL TIME AND LIVING BY FATH	68
CHURCH GROWTH AND OPEN DOORS	88
WIDER UK AND US RELATIONSHIPS AND MINISTRY	109
EVENTS AND CONFRENCES, CONFERENCES, CONFERENCES...	131
WARTS AND ALL AND MOVING ON	158
SCANDINAVIA	169
INDIA AND SRI LANKA	184
AFRICA	199
OTHER INTERNATIONAL VISITS	227
FINAL WORDS ON THE LOVE OF MY LIFE	241
APPENDIX ONE	248
APPENDIX TWO	250

INTRODUCTION

- From my perspective -

We all see events and occurrences in our lives from different perspectives. That does not mean that our recollection of what happened is wrong or invalid. Why, even Gospel writers came up with differing reports of the same events which took place before their very eyes. Therefore, I believe that if we are seekers after truth, this may well mean that we have a piece of the jigsaw which reveals something of the mega picture of God's workings to fulfil his purposes through history.

So, this story is my understanding of what the Holy Spirit was doing through my life and that of my darling wife, Christine, and the movements of which we were privileged to be a part. It is a far from complete account but I hope it will increase the understanding of how these movements changed the shape, direction and practice of the church at large. Of course, I am referring to the Charismatic Renewal and the House Church Movements.

In 2016 Christine was taken into care after slowly deteriorating after her diagnosis of frontotemporal dementia in 2011. It is an uncommon type of dementia particularly invasive, causing problems with behaviour and language and there is no treatment to slow the advance of the disease. She was initially taken into care for two weeks in order to adjust the medication she was receiving to help control mood swings and behaviour.

In those two weeks it became clear to her carers that Christine needed more support and supervision than I was able to give. Although I didn't want to accept this, it was true. My health was suffering in my efforts to look after her, even though my daughter, Sharon, gave up her job to come and help me. On one occasion Sharon was taking Christine out in the car and suddenly there she was taking off her seat belt and trying to get out of the car.

Of course, Christine has many friends who were keen to know how she was doing, and after just a few weeks I felt the Lord spoke to me concerning sharing news and stories of Christine's life and our work together. Up to that time, being something of a dinosaur, I had no interest in gadgets, social media or anything which could demand learning new skills or which might steal my valuable time and attention.

So when it was suggested that I should open a Facebook page I suffered an immediate negative reaction and only after much love and gentle persuasion by Sharon and my other daughter Ruth, I succumbed, and my page dedicated to Christine was born. I was utterly amazed at the response to my first post on November 11th 2016 which reached over 50,000 people!

My first post

> *I dedicate this page to the amazing and lovely Christine, my wife of 62 years, who is now in care after suffering from the increasing effects of dementia for some years.*
>
> *I was 80 on Saturday the 15th of October and our family turned up in numbers to celebrate in the local Thai restaurant. It was the last family supper before I had to take Christine into the nursing home on Monday 17th. It was a very mixed blessing as I was so grateful for the love and sympathy poured out towards me and*

INTRODUCTION

Christine by our kids, grand-kids and great grand-kids, but I could not shake off the deep feeling of sadness at what was about to happen after so many years of being together.

Apart from her devotion to me and our lovely family, Christine has faithfully ministered to thousands of individuals and churches here in the UK and around the world with her straight talk, prophetic insights, creativity, writing and humour.

Now, in her strange world which we have little access to, I have seen her grasp the hands of Ivy, a lady full of fear in the home where she is, and assure her with great confidence that she is good and will be fine. Her words transformed Ivy from near tears to a peaceful smile.

Apparently, on the first day we left her in the care home, while we travelled back in buckets of tears, she was trying to hold a healing meeting and encouraged one wheelchair-bound lady to get up and walk. Sadly, no revival in the home as yet, but she has brought some light and fun as on occasions she gets up and dances and in her shuffling way urges others to join her as she did so often in church gatherings large and small.

I have, without doubt, been through the worst time of my life as I have watched my princess go down-hill. I have lost her but she is still here. I have experienced the pain of an on-going bereavement which, I guess, could cause some to stumble or lose their faith. But, in a strange way, the experience has drawn me closer to the Lord as I have cried out to him.

I seem to have received a greater understanding and compassion for the multitudes who have been through, and are going through, what I am experiencing but without the support of a wonderful family and the constant presence of a loving God. This has led me to think about what I can contribute now as I will have a little more time being released from the 24-hour care which has pre-occupied me over recent years.

As I have already said being a dinosaur I have never wanted to get involved in social media and, believe it or not, I don't even own a mobile phone. However, after thoughts, prayers and chatting with the family who have been alongside us through this time, I felt the Lord was nudging me to share some of the ministry and teaching he has given me over the years. My hope is that this Facebook page, managed by our daughters Sharon and Ruth, may be a blessing and encouragement to some who are going through tough times or are just looking to be fed and encouraged.

Then a strange thing happened.

After 3 years Ruth was doing some work on the page and discovered 7 unread emails which had been hidden away all that time. Apparently, when she set up the page, she had to create a new address for some reason and it was never used.

Most of the messages were irrelevant or out of date but one was from a Norwegian Pentecostal minister, Geir Lie, who was researching the UK House Church Movement. He was keen to make contact and was seeking my help as he knew of my work and also my involvement in Norway. It read:

Dear John Noble

You do not know me, even though I wrote you a letter many years ago. My name is Geir Lie, and I am a Pentecostal theologian from Norway.

I would like to try to do my part to preserve as much as possible of Holiness, Pentecostal and charismatic materials (books, letters, diaries, etc). There are several good national depositories in many countries... but as far as I am concerned nothing can compete with Flower Pentecostal Heritage Center in the USA. This is the Pentecostal-related library and archives of the Assemblies of God in Springfield, Missouri. This is the largest Pentecostal library with holdings in almost 150 languages.

The Director, Darrin Rodgers, a good friend for more than 10 years, recently visited me here in Norway in order to get important Norwegian materials for his library. Now he has left and I continue

INTRODUCTION

to gather materials and I was wondering if there is a complete set of Fulness magazines which might be donated to the Centre? Restoration magazine would be equally important.

Unfortunately, I am unaware of other magazine titles within the broader 'House Church Movement', but I am sure Terry Virgo and Gerald Coates had their own journals, and others probably, as well. These would also be important to preserve under one roof.

I was hoping you might help me...

I hope to hear back from you.

Sincerely,

Geir

I replied not really expecting him to respond after so long but I was wrong! Geir put me in touch with Darrin Rodgers at the Flower Pentecostal Heritage Centre, Springfield, Missouri, the largest Pentecostal Heritage site in the world. From here I exchanged correspondence with Darrin for some weeks which resulted in my sending archive materials, books and magazines to him for the site. I also gave him information about events and meetings relating to the beginnings of the House Church Movement and the Charismatic Renewal.

At one point Darrin became quite excited as he was reading Andrew Walker's book Restoring the Kingdom. He wrote:

Dear John,

I have Andrew Walker's book, Restoring the Kingdom, in front of me now. It is a wonderfully detailed account that, from my count in the index, includes your name on over 50 pages (about 20 percent of the book). However, it is limited in that he focuses primarily on the movement and doesn't say much about the people themselves and their backgrounds.

I like Geir's suggestion that you tell your story on paper or even on an audio recording.... Write the basic facts of your life...... and particular things that you think should be communicated to future generations.... things that have probably not been documented well or correctly elsewhere.

Just a thought!

Darrin J. Rodgers, M.A., J.D.
Director, Flower Pentecostal Heritage Center
website: www.iFPHC.org

Following the success of the Facebook page I had received a number of suggestions to the effect that I need to write more of our story. One friend put me in touch with an editor who he felt would help me put together my writings and thus make a start on the book. I downloaded all my posts and duly sent them off.

The editor sent a positive reply as she liked much of what I had written but felt it needed much more work from me before she would consider working on a manuscript. Work was not a word I wanted to hear, I had plenty to do visiting Christine every day and maintaining my philatelic business which was growing though stamp fairs and my ebay shop. I also received a message from Amanda Williams, a close friend who had worked with Christine on a number of creative projects. She was also urging me to write:

My lovely friend John

It is with tears in my eyes that I write this...somehow this morning I was sent a post on Facebook that you wrote in 2017 about the worship and dance you and Chris were involved in from Romford days. Also, Les Moir recently published a book (Missing Jewel) on worship songs, do you remember?

Well, the time is now to write your book. I know that I have said that before many times and I remember cooking a nice meal and then nagging you. John, you have such wonderful memories that come alive on the page which I, and many more, would love to read about to keep in our hearts.

At least pray and ask Father and whilst you can't physically visit your beloved at the moment, you can bring her vitality and life back through the pages of your book.

Much love

Manda xxxxxxxx.

Well, I did say a prayer and even scribbled a few thoughts on a pad but couldn't really bring myself to begin what seemed to me to be a daunting task. And the weeks went by.

Then I woke up early one morning and desperately tried to get back to sleep. One method that seems to work for me at times is to sing hymns to myself in my head but I went through the repertoire a dozen times without success. Then, I have no idea where it came from, but I just knew it was, indeed, time to write.

I ran downstairs to grab a pencil and pad which I pulled out of my file and there right on top was Amanda's email! It had to be God and I could hardly proceed without telling Amanda who was having a break in Spain.

Hi Amanda,

I often think of you and wonder how you're doing.

You might be interested to know that today, for one reason and another, I awoke and couldn't get back to sleep. After singing loads of hymns in my head, no idea how I arrived at it, but my conclusion was that I should start writing the book about my life and the House Church Movement. I came downstairs to get a pad and when I pulled it out of my file out popped one email - your message urging me to write! Is that God or what?

I just didn't like the idea of the work involved and had other things on my mind. Then a few months back, by an amazing set of circumstances, I was put in touch with the director of the largest Pentecostal Heritage site in the world! He was keen to learn more about the House Church Movement and we corresponded and I sent my archive material and books to him. He was delighted and said that I needed to write a book about my experiences. However, I still didn't get the message until, finally, today I think it sank in and I began.

Do pray that I get help from heaven to recall the things that will make it a useful contribution to the narrative.

Love you, John

So begins our remarkable story of God's grace at work in this unlikely couple and we give him all the glory!

CHAPTER ONE

THE EARLY YEARS

- John -

I was born into a Salvation Army family. My parents were active officers and my grandparents on both sides were heavily involved in the early days of the movement. My dad's parents were Lt Colonel & Mrs John Noble, well respected senior officers. My mum's parents were Jo and Emma Bright, Jo being described as a paper hanger on his marriage certificate. I learned much about the *noble* art from him which stood me in good stead over the years.

Emma, my maternal grandmother, was a devoted soldier and told me many stories of the great revival she experienced under William Booth. She remembered how an army, aptly named the Skeleton Army, with their black flag with the skull and crossbones emblazoned on it, was formed to oppose them.

They sought to disrupt the Salvation Army in its efforts to evangelise and care for the poor. They would follow the *Army* around throwing tin cans, paint-filled eggs, dead animals, even burning coals and anything they could lay their hands on. But to no avail as it served to bring more and more attention to these brave warriors who ultimately prevailed.

She told me that in the meeting they would shout and praise God singing, 'So we'll lift up the banner on high, the salvation banner of love; we'll fight beneath its colours 'til we die, then go to our home above'. At which point someone would grab the flag, inscribed 'blood & fire', and they would march out into the street and on to the pub where they would drag the drunkards back to the hall.

Once back in the meeting room they would take the front bench and turn it round calling it the 'mercy seat'. Then they would sing and preach the gospel until the men were sober with many streaming to the front to repent and give their lives to Christ.

It was often mayhem in those gatherings and, at such a time, Booth would call on his daughter, Evangeline to speak. She was *The Evangelist* and her passion-filled words brought conviction and the sure promise of forgiveness as hardened drunks and criminals broke, weeping on their knees. Very often, as these men were *saved*, so powerful was their conversion that the next night they would be in the pub witnessing to the miracles Jesus had done in their lives. Her stories made a lasting impression on me and her prayers for me during my years as a rebellious teenager, undoubtedly, played a major part in my returning to the fold!

Growing up as a child meant I was brought up in a family which was involved in a constant round of meetings. Meetings in which I might be incredibly bored or where I sensed the very real presence of the Holy Spirit.

My favourite meeting was the *wind up* which happened after the Sunday evening gathering. It was a relaxed affair where we sang rousing choruses and people gave testimony as to what the Lord had done in their lives.

Testimony was important as it showed that the Lord was at work in your life. At some point or other in the week you would be expected to take part, either by testifying, praying or maybe singing a solo or playing an instrument. Pretty well everyone was trained musically and either you were in the band or the songsters or both! So you learned to be alert and ready, and I believe this proved to be invaluable to me later in life when the Lord called me into church leadership.

I remember in one meeting, when I was just 5 years old, I was pretty bored and spent much of the time sliding up and down the bench where I was sitting. My father, who was the preacher, gave me a public reprimand. When he finished his sermon, as always, he made the appeal but no one moved. I felt really sorry for my dad, so I stood up and went and knelt at the mercy seat to encourage him. I guess he thought I was repenting for my behaviour. So I was duly prayed for and *saved* for the first time.

In those days serving families were moved from corps to corps every year or so. I think the idea was that you should not become too comfortable or overly familiar with the lower ranks. As a result, I went to seven different schools before I settled at grammar school after I was eleven. I don't think that helped my education and development. Looking back, I believe this meant that I didn't make many friends and was often bullied because of the Salvation Army connections.

Children can be cruel! A favourite chant I often heard as I walked home from school was, 'Salvation Army, all gone barmy. One had a wooden leg, kicked the baby out the bed!' and I learned the classic response, 'Sticks and stones may break my bones, but names will never hurt me!' However, 'will never hurt me' is not necessarily true, as I believe the bullying led to the nervous asthma I suffered as a lad.

I also think it taught me to cope with humour and bravado. Thus, I won favour with some of the boys in my class as my behaviour was less than good. One day I grabbed a friend and we went around the whole school whilst lessons were in progress. I stood on his shoulders and placed a small piece of plasticine between the striker and the bell which signalled the end of the lesson. Obviously, much to our delight there was no bell and confusion reigned. The next morning as usual I was late and had to file in down the aisle with the Jews and the Catholics for the announcements. At the end, Harry, or rather Mr Kenwood the headmaster, said, 'Oh, and would Noble come to my office immediately!'

I had a sinking feeling and, as I guessed, it was indeed six of the best with no time to put an exercise book down my trousers. It was a painful experience and after reflection and trying to work out how he knew it was me, it became pretty obvious. It didn't take him long to make the connection from no bell to Noble and my fate was sealed.

On another occasion, with a group of friends, we decided to begin a life of crime by raiding the Pavilion in the centre of the local park. We all agreed to meet at a spot in the midst of some bushes if there was any trouble. Somehow, we got in through a window and foolishly switched on all the lights only to find a few bags of crisps and a couple of bottles of drink.

Suddenly, we saw a blue light flashing and knew that Mr Plod was on his way. We scrambled out of the window and ran off in different directions. I was foolish enough to go to the spot where we promised to meet but no one else turned up and I realised that it was not only Mr Plod but he had brought his Alsatian dog with him for a walk!

I immediately realised he was there to sniff me out and so I stepped into a pool with a bridge over the water. I'd seen the movies where criminals went into the water and came out in a different spot to put the dogs off the scent! However, I began to sink into the silt up to my waist and the stink was incredible – but it worked!

The policeman and his dog walked over the bridge while I shook with fear underneath. I waited and waited for what seemed an eternity, until I heard the car drive away. Then, slowly and cautiously I emerged. Unconvinced that it was completely clear, I dared not make my way back to the gate where we climbed into the park. I crawled on my belly for ages all the while thinking how ashamed I would be if my dear mum found out. I arrived at the back garden of a house, climbed the fence and ran out into the street and escaped to glorious freedom. That was the beginning and the end of my life of crime, thankfully without prosecution!

- *Dad* -

My dad was an incredibly gifted man. As a musician, he played cornet and squeeze box or concertina, which he used in the open air meetings and on the beach in summer outreaches. However, his first love was the violin and he was good, very good, at 16 he was giving lessons! I used to listen to him mesmerised as he practised one of his favourite pieces, the gypsy dance Czardas.

This an exceedingly difficult piece involving double stopping (playing two notes at the same time), plucking, sliding notes and harmonics and much of it played at breakneck speed! You could hear his fingers as he pounded the strings and I can still hear, pretty well, every note of that piece in my head after all these years.

He was also a talented artist. At dinner with Salvation Army friends, he would often do a lightning cartoon for them on their serviette and he loved doing one of William Booth with his hooked nose and long beard. His watercolour paintings were exquisite but tragically we have only one of these, a beautiful Holy Land street scene which I cherish.

As a young officer he met my mother, Hilda Violet Bright, a beautiful and saintly young woman with a deep faith. I was trawling through mum's effects after she passed away in 1979 and discovered a letter from my dad written to her in 1924 before they were married. Evidently, they had an argument, guess what it was about? Nothing other than the Baptism in the Holy Spirit! I was gob-smacked!

Even at that young age dad clearly reckoned he was a bit of a theologian as, in a somewhat condescending way, he sought to correct my mum's thinking. In retrospect I believe he would have done better to respect mum's views and, perhaps, pray a little more about the subject. Certainly, when my mum became aware of our quest for the Holy Spirit she was delighted and very happy to join with us in our home meetings.

When I look back on my relationship with Christine, I have to admit that I had a similar trait. I often moved too quickly to correct her intuition, only to discover that she was right all along. A lesson that many a husband would do well to learn!

Dad's letter:

24 Corswall Street
Coatbridge

22nd November 1924

My Darling Hilda,

I hope you will not mind me typing this letter to you, but as I was coming back in the bus last night, I thought a little about our argument, and was disappointed that I did not make it as clear as I may have done. However, if you do not mind, I will try to enlighten you a little more.

I do not believe that the Baptism of the Holy Spirit is a third blessing. There are only two blessings, namely – Salvation and Sanctification, or in other words the Baptism of the Holy Spirit.

The cleansing or purifying of the heart and the filling with the Holy Spirit are certainly not separate blessings.

Now, the disciples could not have been sanctified until Pentecost. You will remember that Jesus told the disciples to go to Jerusalem and wait for the promised blessing. They accordingly went and continued in prayer and supplication until the day arrived – then, of course, they all received the blessing. The Holy Ghost sat upon each of them. They were now sanctified and employed their sanctified energies in spreading the fame of Jesus.

While the disciples were in Jerusalem waiting for the descent of the Holy Ghost they must have become entirely emptied of self and fully abandoned to His will. This condition of entire abandonment or consecration to God might be called the human side of sanctification, after which the 'promise of the Father' came and they were filled.

I will admit that there was a waiting of ten days, but that need not be. The moment we feel that we are emptied of self and sin it is our privilege to be then and there filled and possessed by the Holy Spirit. The Lord says, 'Then will I sprinkle clean water upon you, and ye shall be clean from all your filthiness and from all your idols will I cleanse you.... And I will put My spirit within you'. You see – cleansing and filling.

Therefore, Sanctification or the Baptism of the Spirit results in renewal of the heart and power for service. Paul spoke of the near 'Holy Ghost...purifying their hearts by faith' and Jesus promised, 'Ye shall receive power after that the Holy Ghost is come'.

In Isaiah 6th chapter there is the record of the prophet's sanctification, and we find that the cleansing and the filling are at the same time. The cleansing was not before the baptism, but by the baptism. The 'live coal' was placed upon his mouth and his sin was purged. Pour water into a bottle and it immediately takes the place of air.

Someone nicely says that the first blessing in Jesus Christ is Salvation, with its negative side of remission of sins and forgiveness, and its positive side of renewal or regeneration – the new birth – one experience. And the second blessing is entire sanctification with its negative side of cleansing, and its positive side of filling with the Holy Spirit – one whole, rounded, glorious, epochal experience.

Now, as to whether the power will remain with us after we have received it depends entirely upon ourselves – upon our obedience to the known will of God, and our faith in His promises. If we continue to obey and maintain our faith, this then, will bring continual enduement. The disciples were filled again and again with the Holy Spirit, and I think we should wait upon God for a special and definite filling for every new task we undertake for Him.

We can, I think, see clearly that the Holy Spirit imparts 'power', power for service. This power will not manifest itself in precisely the same way in each individual. This is brought out very clearly in 1 Cor. 12:4-13. 'Now there are diversities of gifts, but of the same Spirit' etc. Many will see the baptism expecting power as an evangelist, but God has not called them to that work, and the power that comes from the Baptism with the Holy Spirit manifests itself in another way in them.

To sum up the meaning of the Baptism with the Holy Spirit, I think it is the Spirit of God coming upon the believer, purifying the heart, taking possession of all faculties, imparting gifts not naturally our own, but which qualify us for the service to which God has called us.

Now my precious lassie, this letter seems a very, very cold and unusual affair, but I think you will understand. It may help you a wee bit.

Must hurry off. With all my fond love and sincere prayers.

Your very affectionate sweetheart,

Harry xxxxx

Great letter!

I asked my theologian friend, Richard Roberts, to write a reply to my dad's letter which he kindly did for me. His response appears as *Appendix 1* at the end of the book.

THE EARLY YEARS

In his journey as an officer, dad built an amazing library of over 2000 books and he would challenge our visitors to test his knowledge. 'Open any book,' he would say, 'at any chapter and I will tell you what is in that chapter!' I often joke that I have a photographic memory like my dad but I just can't get the lens cap off! However, it was his books which led to his downfall.

Dad was marked as someone who would achieve high rank in the grand scheme of things, possibly even General. Certainly, his friend and colleague, Fred Griffin, became British Commissioner and he used to pinch my dad's sermons! But it was not to be.

The reality is, that as he was a great speaker and extremely well read, he climbed through the ranks and ended up at the Salvation Army Training College at Denmark Hill in south-east London. He was still studying to improve his knowledge of Greek and Hebrew I believe and Army pay was not great and he needed more books.

His bookshop of choice was Foyles in Charing Cross Road and on one visit dad was caught leaving with two books he had not paid for. This was right out of character and so unlike my father who was a stickler for honesty. I know that, as I suffered at his hand if there was any hint of untruth in my words. Mum believed he was most likely having a breakdown with all the pressure his work placed him under.

I was eleven and was at home when the Foyles men came with their suitcases to take away every book with a Foyles sticker for which dad could not provide a receipt. The Army insisted that he should not offer any form of defence as they did not want their *good* name dragged through the press. The judge chose to make an example of dad and he was given 6 months in prison!

Mum wrote to General Albert Osborne without my dad's knowledge saying, 'My poor darling lad will, I am afraid, pay a greater price than his mistake demands'. She also explained that when that 'terrible moment' came when she had to leave him, he said, 'Hilda, I have let down the man I love and respect, the one who has helped me most in my life – the General!'

Mum went on to give a full account as to how the appeal failed on the grounds that he did what he was told to do when he pleaded guilty. She was advised that she could speak up for dad but the judge ignored her. The General replied with a fairly short sympathetic letter assuring mum that she would come through her trial with 'courage and equanimity'. And with that the Army, apart from a few understanding friends, effectively abandoned dad and left him to his own devices.

He came out of prison a broken man but told mum that he had 'peace in his heart that he had never experienced in his life before'. He said this came, 'chiefly through the kindness and sympathy shown by those rough men in the prison'. I know they listened to him playing his violin. I guess the response from those men must have seemed in stark contrast to the treatment he received from the Salvation Army.

Amazingly dad got a good job working at Peter Robinson's, the prestigious fashion store in Oxford Circus. It was part of the Burton group and I believe, in a strange way, it was the Lord's plan as it was to play a part in my return to the spiritual life. But more of that later.

Dad worked in London for a couple of years but then suffered a heart attack from which he was recovering but then he contracted pneumonia and died on October 21st 1952 after a fairly lengthy illness. Mum said that his last words were, 'I am entering a new and happy relationship', and then he was gone.

- Mum -

I'm sure that from what I have shared about my father's story, you will already have a pretty good insight into my mother's character. She was strong, faithful, loving and very supportive of my dad. She took the strain running the family in a very demanding situation and was always there for us. She welcomed all visitors to our home and there were many! She was always ready with her caring and consoling words and generous hospitality even though we lived on a slim financial budget - and remember, through the war years and after, there was rationing!

I noticed that on the back of dad's letter to her she had written a note in pencil, 'Filled with the Spirit' Rev Ernest Boys MA. So it seems to me that the discussion or, at least my mother's interest, continued. One thing is sure, the fruit of the Spirit was continually manifested throughout my mother's life.

Like her mother Emma, she also shared stories of what took place in meetings and also out in the open air. Concerning the outpouring of the Holy Spirit, she said that it was not uncommon for people to have what they called *glory fits* as they fell under the power of the Spirit speaking in strange tongues. Shades of Toronto?

I'm not sure if it was mum, grandma or something I read, but in the early days many used to break bread using water rather than wine because so many had been set free from alcohol. Apparently, the Pentecostals had not invented Ribena at that time! The practice was clearly not continued.

Sometime after my father died, mum reconnected with an old sweetheart, Fred Grigg, and she remarried in 1958. This gave her security and companionship but Fred also passed away in 1966 at the age of just 64 and she was alone again. I knew she was lonely and, unlike my mum, was feeling a little sorry for herself. I remember giving her a good talking to and telling her to sell up and move into our close-knit church community.

At the time there were around 200 of us living within 400 yards of one another and I said, 'Mum, we need grandmothers with us and your presence will be invaluable'. She accepted my challenge, moved down to Romford and was loved by everyone! She moved in with us and was a blessing to us all with her unwavering faith in God's love. Her house sold really quickly as there was usually someone waiting for a property to come and join us in the area.

A few years later in 1979 she was diagnosed with inoperable cancer and was not given too long to live. As testimony to the kind of woman she was, when she came back from the doctors to break the news to us, she said, 'Oh, you poor darlings, I am so sorry you'll have to look after me'. No thought for herself. The end came quite unexpectedly as when I came down in the morning and went into her room it was clear that she had been very unwell and didn't even call us in the night. She had hung on waiting to say goodbye. Her last words were the understatement of the century, 'I've had a bit of a bad night!' I called our kids into the room and they each said their farewells. Then I said, 'Goodbye mum, and tell them we're coming too!' She obediently closed her eyes and was gone. I was devasted but so proud of her. I like to think that I might have such a good passing when the time comes.

- Margaret -

My sister, Margaret, is 6 years older than me which meant we didn't share the same friends. In the summer holidays I spent much time with my grandad Jo and grandma Emma. They lived in Hadleigh, Essex and had a large newt pond in the garden which kept me busy with worms on a string pulling them out. Margaret was elsewhere with her friends so we didn't spend much time together.

She was the brainy one but, as I recollect, she went to 13 schools before landing a place at university in St Hild's college in Durham. She survived all the changes of schools to do very well in spite of the challenges. She also met her husband to be there and remained up north when she had completed her degree and married.

THE EARLY YEARS

My abiding memory of Margaret was from our time in Brighton at the end of the war where my dad was commanding officer of the Salvation Army corps. Margaret would have been 16 and was asked to recite a poem she had learned – Longfellow's *The Vision Beautiful*.

It's the story of a monk who had a heavenly visitation from the Lord which captivated and enthralled him until he heard the poor ringing at the gate for their daily food. He chose to respond and leave his cell to feed the hungry. On his return, to his amazement, the vision remained and the poem starts with that profound utterance, which has stayed with me ever since:

> *'Hads't thou stayed, I must have fled!*
> *That is what the Vision said.'*

Those words had a profound effect on me and have remained with me ever since. In retrospect, I guess I saw how easy it is to get so wrapped up in our spiritual experiences that neglect the very things the Spirit would have us do.

I later picked up that my sister's time at university led her in a different direction to the path that mum and dad hoped she would take. I believe that this caused a certain amount of tension when Margaret was home during the holidays and challenged my dad's faith. However, I was a little too young to get involved in those debates.

My other memory of Margaret is of us huddled together with mum in the Morrison shelter, under a metal table designed to give protection during the bombing. Brighton was in a direct route over which the doodle bugs flew in their journey towards London and many of these evil contraptions didn't make it to their destination.

After the sirens went warning us of a pending invasion, we would rush into the shelter and listen for the throbbing sound of the engines. When that sound stopped, we would count to 15 waiting for the dreaded explosion. If we heard the bang, we were safe, if not....

As an aside, when the war ended there were great celebrations and my dad went down to the area around the pier in full uniform in case there were people needing help. At some point he put his cap down and when he went to retrieve it, it had disappeared. The next day he went back to look around after all the mayhem and discovered the cap on the head of a statue. I don't recall how he got it down but I wouldn't put it past my dad to have climbed to get it back.

I am sad that I don't get to see my sister these days, she is way up north and being well looked after in care and I just can't face the journey. We occasionally speak on the phone but I notice she says the same thing over and sometimes rings me back having forgotten that she had already spoken to me. It seems she has a much less invasive type of the same illness as dear Christine.

I can't leave my reflections on Margaret without mentioning another incident which had serious impact on my life. She came back from a party she had been to with friends where they played the occult game Ouija often called, talking board. The letters of the alphabet with the numbers 1 to 9 are arranged on a board or shiny table. A glass is placed upside down on the surface and each player puts their finger on the glass which then moves around the table spelling out words and numbers to bring messages from *the other side* or the spirit world. Margaret was sceptical at first believing that someone was deliberately pushing the glass around. However, her scepticism melted away as the glass went on spelling out things about her life and family which no one else in the room could possibly know. This intrigued me and I determined to play this game with my friends with dire consequences which I will return to in the next chapter.

- *Christine* -

I am sure you, my readers, are well aware that many of the things that happen to us in our early years can be a real blessing or even a tragic curse. This is the reason I share some of the events and experiences which Christine and I went through as we grew up. Some of the blessings helped to shape us in positive ways, other things needed to be dealt with in the name of Jesus.

For example, one simple thing which I overheard my father say to a friend about me as a boy was, 'John has his buttons sewn on the right side!' I took that to be a compliment which I have never forgotten. Conversely, in my account of Christine's childhood I will tell of an experience which seriously damaged her without her realising. This had to be brought out into the light and broken off her.

Christine's mother, Florence or Florrie, as everyone called her, was one of fourteen boys and girls in the large family. They lived in the East End of London in a close community and, Christine, being born within the sound of Bow Bells, is able to say that she is a true Cockney. Mind you, you would never know it as every trace of the accent went with her love of acting and elocution.

She always said that the closeness within the family and in the wider community made her feel safe and secure and was the source of her love for living and sharing her home with others. Whilst I was happy with my own company, she was gregarious and was never happier than when our home was full of people and that worked well for us. Because her family lived so close together her mum never worried that she had not come home from visiting one of her aunts, as she would just be put down to sleep with one of her cousins, top and tailed if necessary.

It was wartime and that part of London suffered terribly in the blitz. On one occasion she remembered a bomb blast which fractured the sewer and her grandma simply picked her up and waded through the smelly mess to take her home.

When the war ended, Christine's side of the family moved out into Essex along with many other East Enders and Florrie bought a shop. She was a canny sales woman, and Christine said that she could sell snow to

Eskimos and sand in the desert! Her dad, Stan, had a responsible job on the railways and was often called out at night to resolve problems or even oversee a train crash. He also travelled overseas to observe the way things were done in other countries.

It was around this time that one of the life-changing events I mentioned earlier took place. Apparently, Christine fell down some kind of hole and grazed her leg, not a serious problem and the wound soon healed. Sometime later Christine complained to her mum that her leg was painful, but for some reason her dad got the idea that she was not telling the truth. Maybe he thought she was trying to get out of doing something she didn't like at school.

She continued to complain as the pain got worse and her dad became angry and punished her. This caused her to close down on the matter and lie when asked if she was still in pain. Days later her mum saw her legs side by side and screamed - one leg was clearly thinner than the other! Her parents rushed her to see the doctor who confirmed that Christine had the serious bone disease osteomyelitis.

At that time such a diagnosis would have resulted in amputation. However, the surgeon had experience during the war of treating soldiers coming home from the front with serious injuries and he had undertaken pioneering bone-grafting work. He said that he was willing to try to save Christine's leg and thus followed months in hospital and two breakages. While we can look back and thank God for the incredible patience and success of the surgeon, at the time it left scars, not only on Christine's body but also on her mind.

Moving forward briefly to our relationship after marriage, it was not long before we found that we were experiencing difficulties communicating with one another. If, in any way, I appeared to threaten Christine, she retreated into herself and it was impossible to reach her. This left me frustrated and upset. Of course, this happens in marriages but we felt this was more sinister, so we prayed and my daughter Sharon has a vivid recollection of what Christine saw in a vision.

In her vision, mum looked around and saw a totally desolate valley. It was desert-like with absolutely nothing growing in it. Looking closer she noticed that there were small shoots of green life sprouting up here and there.

Suddenly, the valley darkened and a sense of dread descended on her. The sun was blotted out and a huge shadow fell across the valley. She cowered afraid to look but she heard a blood curdling squawk and looked up to see a huge bird with a sharp, evil metal beak. As she watched, the bird dived upon the shoots and gobbled them up until the valley was picked clean, then the bird flew off.

As mum surveyed the desolate scene and examined the destruction, she saw a large wooden box she had not noticed before. The box emanated foreboding and mum felt great dread every time she looked at the box.

Then she heard a voice gently say to her that she needed to face her fear and open the box and look inside. Mum instinctively knew that if she wanted to be set free, this was what she had to do. It took all her courage to walk over to the box and in fear and trembling, open it. As she lifted the lid the huge bird flew out and came towards her and she clearly saw it had her father's face. It was the memory of his actions in the past that was stripping the valley clean of every bit of new growth. The bird shrieked in fear and left the valley.

Well, we prayed, rejoiced and thanked the Lord as Christine was wonderfully delivered! That is not to say that we didn't have our differences after that but life was lived on an entirely different plain thanks to the revelation of the Holy Spirit. Furthermore, Christine went on to manifest a remarkable authority to deal with similar situations in other people as we shall see as we continue our story.

Christine returned to school after her surgery and went on to win a scholarship to study at one of the leading drama colleges in the UK, if not the world, at the time – RADA, The Royal Academy of Dramatic Art!

- Christine's brother, Roger -

Roger was nine years younger than Christine, so whilst he was lots of fun, we didn't have a great deal to do with him. However, when he was ready to start work after leaving school, I got him a job in the company I was working for at the time and we used to drive into London together in my Mini Minor. That is, until he learned to drive and acquired his own Mini Minor. After that we used to leave home at the same time and see who could get to work first. This resulted in one or two near brushes with some nice policemen as we cut corners, drove along cycle tracks and through garage forecourts. Not something I would recommend doing today!

We love Roger, and have enjoyed our relationship with him over the years

CHAPTER TWO

LIFE AFTER DAD

I was 16 when dad passed away and coming up was the big decision, to continue my studies and go into the 6th form or leave and get a job. Actually, I liked school and was quite popular. I had a good group of friends who enjoyed my antics. However, although I was in the A stream (no idea how I managed that) and was often top in a new subject, that lasted about 3 months and I spent the rest of my time in the bottom three. I was voted form captain and also our house football captain, this in spite of the fact that my football skills were very limited. I believe I had some leadership qualities and as a result could get help from the brighter lads with homework, sometimes in a pretty good copy of my own fair hand but this didn't help when it came to exams. When the GCSE results came back most boys in my form had between 8 and 12 passes, many with A's all round.

I managed a miserable 3 ordinary passes and when I went for my interview with the careers master and asked him what he thought I might do for a living, he said that I would make a good teacher. I asked him what subjects he suggested? There was a pause before he replied, 'I see what you mean!' It was then that I realised further education was not my best option and decided it was time to find a job. I talked it through with mum and she had the bright idea of getting in touch with the director dad worked for at Peter Robinsons in Oxford Circus.

Dad was well liked there and seemed to have earned their respect. I had an interview with Mr Palfreyman and was duly appointed to the grand position of 'Assistant to the advertising manager'.

The position carried great responsibility which mainly consisted of scouring the newspapers for our advertisements, sticking them in a scrapbook and recording the number of garments sold from each ad. This important information was necessary to determine if we should run further ads or ditch the item. I also did a certain amount of floor walking, checking and signing sales bills. This made me feel quite important especially as I looked the part in one of the suits dad used to wear to work.

I enjoyed working in London and the new found freedom which my small income, £4.10/-, provided. It meant I could pursue my interest in young ladies and enjoy a few pints, sometimes more than a few, with my friends. We occasionally played the Ouija game with some fascinating results. I also began to smoke, after all I worked in an office with a chain smoker. Time merrily slipped by until suddenly, one morning, I was brought up with a jolt! There, in the post, were my call up papers for National Service and my time to enter her majesty's pleasure had arrived.

- *National Service* -

Obviously, like all young men of my age, I was asked to attend an interview and medical examination which, in itself, was a bizarre experience. I was told to strip off and, totally naked, was given an eye test. Then I sat a brief intelligence test and they questioned me to see if I had any preference as to which part of the armed forces I would like to join.

Having watched the coronation of Queen Elizabeth ll, I had been pretty impressed by the performance of the Guards on parade and, without thinking, suggested that the Guards might be a good option. I was immediately given a place in the Irish Guards and looking back wondered if that had anything to do with my intelligence test. If so, I pondered what that said about me and, more importantly, what did it say about the Irish Guards? I was to find out soon enough as I arrived at the Guards barracks in Caterham, Surrey on the 10th of March 1955.

The first couple of days were basically preparation as we queued up to get our uniforms, boots, a rifle and a haircut. The haircut was more like sheep-shearing, short back and everything! That was a bit of a shock as gone were my lovely locks. For the rest, we attempted to clean our boots and iron our uniforms with varying degrees of success. We looked a pretty sorry bunch compared to the guys who were marching up and down on the parade ground.

March the 12th was St Patrick's Day, and in the morning we were woken up by the sergeant who brought us warm beer in a tea bucket to fill our mugs whilst we were still in bed. Ah this is the life we thought! What a nice sergeant! Little did we realise this was a tradition of the day and was not to be repeated for another year!

The next morning, as we sought to snuggle down as we heard that nasty bugle blowing reveille, the barrack room door crashed open and there was the *nice sergeant* screaming, 'Get out of bed!' at the top of his raspy voice! Thus, we were introduced to the nightmare of life in the Irish Guards which was to play out for the next two years!

During the next six months of basic training we learned that complete, unquestioning, obedience was required so that in battle we would do whatever we were told without hesitation. This was said to be for our own good, as fast action saves lives. However, it also ensures that you will rush to any situation where even angels fear to tread!

We painted coal white, cut grass with scissors, polished the soles of our boots and picked up fallen leaves in autumn one by one, when a perfectly groomed brush stood erect in its place in the shed untouched!

We marched endlessly up and down banging our feet shouting, 'One, two, three – one'. We threw our rifles about from shoulder to ground and up again until we could do it with the precision of synchronized swimmers in the Olympics.

The assault course looked like fun until we put on full kit loaded up and had to carry our rifles. Although you did get to smile if you were ahead of the overweight and less fit guys who failed to swing across the mud pond on the knotted rope. Pendulum-like they went back and forth until, finally, they lost their grip and slid down into the slimy depths. Oh, those poor shiny boots and all that laundry!

I think it was fear that dealt with my dyslexia. I had a problem with 'right' and 'left', and 'east' and 'west'. I usually said one when I meant the other or responded the wrong way when told to turn. This often led to frustration especially when someone was trying to give me directions.

However, my initial failure came whilst drilling and threw the whole squad into total confusion. The sergeant screamed, 'leeaft - turn!' and I managed a sharp right as the rest correctly turned left, this meant we ended up in a heap. This, in turn, led to the *nice sergeant* asking questions concerning my birth and parenthood, after which I somehow managed to get it right for a whole two years. That is, until I was demobbed, when I reverted back to my old problem which occasionally still haunts me even to this day!

I also had to learn the language. For some time I struggled to understand the broad Irish accent but, in the end, came to love it. However, I never managed to master the blarney. Occasionally, for example, I was late getting back into barracks after a night out along with some of my Irish compatriots, thus we were marched into company orders to explain our lateness and to make our case, otherwise it was extra drills or even time in a punishment cell.

We stood in line waiting for our names to be called, 'O'Brian'. O'Brian stepped forward banging his right foot down, 'Sir!' he shouted with a pleasant lilt. 'Well?' queried the officer waiting to hear the reason for his lateness. 'To be sure it was this hay lorry sir, right in front of the bus and....' 'Dismissed!' said the officer. 'Noble.' 'Sir!' shouted I, banging my foot equally hard and trying for that pleasant lilt. 'Well Noble?' 'Sir, the bus company had cancelled the 7.45am bus and the queue was....' Drat, I forgot the, 'To be sure!' That must have made the difference I thought, as the officer barked, 'Two extra drills!'

Our pay was not what you would call adequate, twenty eight shillings a week to be exact. And that was before haircuts (I once had two in one day) and barrack room damages were deducted. A packet of 5 filter tipped Woodbine cigarettes cost one shilling and a ha'penny, so that, together with a pint and a ticket to the Orchid Ballroom in Purley, was a rare treat. So in the dark winter nights there wasn't much to do and I introduced the guys to the Ouija game. This provided some scary moments as the glass spelt out things which no one could have guessed and I earned the name, 'the ghost man!'

One evening a burly Irishman mocked us from the door of our barrack room and I challenged him to put his finger on the glass. He was reluctant so I said, 'You're scared!' That brought him in and he touched the glass, then leapt into the air, screamed and ran out. Looking back and reflecting on this, I have to say that I am not proud of what I did and would never suggest that anyone gets involved in that kind of thing as you will see the effects it had on me later.

In spite of playing this dangerous game, from time to time I had feelings that somehow God was with me and there was a real purpose to my life. I had no idea what he might have in store for me but one evening, as I was walking back to barracks from a visit to the cinema in Purley, I looked up to see the heavens ablaze with the light of a trillion stars. I was so impressed with the wonder of what God had created and, in that moment, I just knew that I had a destiny to find and fulfil.

After we finished our training my leadership ability was recognised and I was immediately promoted to trained soldier, the equivalent of lance corporal in the Guards. This meant I would be responsible, under the sergeant, for a new squad to get them up to standard, particularly in connection with their tidiness in the barrack room and their appearance, shiny boots, and all. I had one problem - I was too nice!

I would share my cigarettes with them and couldn't bring myself to shout or turn their beds over when they weren't made up properly. I didn't throw their kit out of the window into the rain if it wasn't up to standard. As a result, they failed their passing out and had to do some extra work. I lost my job and was sent to work in the cookhouse serving meals and washing up for 200 men, but I got to go home some weekends. Sometimes my dear old mum would come all the way from Ilford to Caterham to pay for an evening out at the cinema.

- *Enter Christine stage left* -

Mum had become friends with Sheila, one of the nurses who looked after my dad when he was ill. Unbeknown to me, mum shared a concern that my girlfriend back home was not right for me. It was very unlike my mother but with Sheila they cooked up a plan to introduce me to a young lady who Sheila suggested might be someone who could lure me out of the offending relationship. So on one of her trips to come and take me to the cinema mum asked if she could bring this young lady to meet me. I made no objection to such an idea and a date was set for me to meet Christine Barnard!

I was bowled over and very impressed. It was 1956 and this young lady was in the star class at The Royal Academy of Dramatic Art. With her in that star class was Rodney Bewes, Peter Bowles, Albert Finney and Valerie Singleton. In the same year was Richard Briers, Jack Hawkins and Glenda Jackson and in the class of 1955 was Peter O'Toole. To top it all one of her teachers was Peter Ustinov!

The thing is, I aspired to be an actor and my main claim to fame was that I played Mark Anthony in Julius Caesar in the final school play before I left. Well, I played him for one of the three nights as Mark Anthony was ill and would miss the first performance. Foolishly, he had no understudy and someone said to the director, 'Sir, Noble has learned a couple of scenes for some work we did in class!' A couple of scenes is not the whole play! Nonetheless, Noble was roped in on the basis that much of the latter part of the play he had to read the lines whilst acting at the same time.

This was not the best way to start an acting career! I did my utmost to swat up on the lines the night before, but only discovered the full extent of the problem at the dress rehearsal next day. Trying to remember lines at the same time as working out where your next move is supposed to be, whilst wrestling with your sword and attempting to see from the book when your next line is due, is actually impossible. Looking back, I guess that the pain and embarrassment of that experience squashed any thought of going the drama school route that this young lady had travelled. I had huge admiration for what she had achieved.

A few months back I was rooting round in a drawer and found the first letter I wrote to Christine after our second meeting. It clearly refers to an occasion I very well remember as we played the Ouija game.

23121141 T/S Noble.
No 5 Company Irish Guards,
Guards Depot,
Caterham,
Surrey.

My dear Christine,

Please forgive me for writing to you like this it probably seems rather strange, but I must be that kind of person. For that reason,

I don't want you to take this letter too seriously (not that you would anyway).

A couple of days back we met for the first time and I eyed you with the usual eye that men eye a pretty woman who crosses their path (if you see what I mean). No? Never mind! Now this second time that we met things happen fast. I say things... I mean... things happen with cards and on tables that completely confuse me, and yet I knew exactly what everything was leading up to almost before we started.

When I say leading up to – it seemed as if each word or action or turn of a card was part of a plan which was not allowed to reach its climax and yet made quite clear its meaning.

Even now it all seems so clear and yet I have never been so confused. Although we only met for a few hours and any attraction you had for me could not have had time to sink in – I miss you!!! Not desperately mind you, but quite enough. I feel as if I've known you for quite a time.

Well, that's enough of that, I'm relieved to write although I don't know whether I should have done so or not. I must admit you have been on my mind most of the day. Sixteen hours ago, we were all keen to find out what the glass had to tell and you should know that at least I am anxious to see if it is true.

I do hope you have recovered from your sleepless nights and startling discoveries. If the worst comes, I'm not such a bad bloke and I reckon I could just about put up with you. No further comment.

In approximately one and a half hours I will commence my recovery by going to bed at 8.30pm, as you were, 7.45 pm.

I really must close now, don't feel obliged to write but I think I would appreciate it. In fact, I know I would appreciate it.

Various attempts at ending crossed out:

All my love; love: sincerely: faithfully: I'm not quite sure which but any way it's John.

Xxxxxx

I must say, reading this letter today, I am surprised that Christine bothered to write back. As not only did my writing skill desperately need honing, but my attempts to impress Christine were also seriously lacking. But reply she did and thus began a relationship which, at the time of writing, has lasted over 65 years!

I think from the letter it is pretty obvious that at this second meeting we were playing the Ouija game with some friends and something unusual happened. Christine was well versed in the occult as her mother used to attend the Spiritualist Church and take Christine with her.

The short story is, that on this particular evening, Christine saw a vision and went into a trance and then did automatic writing. That is, writing whilst in the trance state with her eyes closed. In addition, from the messages which came through as the glass moved round the table, it was clear that it was foretelling our marriage.

Again, I have to stress that this activity is not a game. Indeed, it is a very dangerous pastime and not to be recommended as, ultimately, it led to both of us needing deliverance and the Lord's gracious intervention.

From this point, for the rest of my time in the Guards, I focused on keeping out of trouble so that nothing caused me to lose my quota of free weekends. I kept my head down and the mess room spotless. I was well turned out; boots with a shine you could see your face in; sparkling brass and trousers with a crease sharp as a knife. Though I say it myself, I looked quite dashing in my dress uniform and evidently Christine thought so too.

Finally, on the 30th March 1957, the day of my discharge arrived and I was once more a free man! My discharge paper reported: Military

Conduct *very good* - the highest standard awarded - and I quote the testimonial I was given, signed by our Commanding Officer, Lt Colonel J Bowes Lyon:

> *'A clean soldier and hard-working man who has carried out his duties very well. He has an honest, sober and thoroughly reliable character and a pleasant personality.'*

Not sure about the *sober* bit, but it was back to work in civvy street and no more short back and sides for me! The folk at Peter Robinsons had kept my job open and with a testimonial like mine how could they refuse? Christine had finished her course at RADA and, apart from a brief time in repertory theatre, she decided her future was with me. She found a job at Dollond and Aitchison in Oxford Street. just up the road from where I was at Oxford Circus.

So, with my mother and her nurse friend having achieved their objective to prise me out of the relationship with my other girlfriend, they now had to cope with the new situation.

I quickly slotted back into life with my old school friends but now with Christine by my side. It was work hard during the week and party hard over the weekend and, although I had not jettisoned my belief in God, it played no significant part in the way I behaved. Except that is, unless anyone challenged my belief that God created the world in which we live. Then I would dive in and make my case, otherwise it was wine, woman (Christine) and song all the way!

Actually, that is not completely true. I am not sure how it came about but at work I took on the role of chairman of the Christian Union. This was a small group that met regularly to discuss matters of faith and belief and this proved to be an important factor in my journey back to the Lord as we shall see.

Chapter Three

MARRIAGE AND THE JOURNEY BACK TO FAITH

After I proposed to Christine and she accepted, I was told that it was the custom to ask her dad for her hand in marriage. I quite liked her father, Stan, but he was a big guy and a senior inspector overseeing work and repairss on the railway system and, as such, he was quite an imposing figure.

As it happened, working on the railways gave Stan unlimited travel anywhere in Europe free, or very reasonably priced for family and friends. So he and Florrie invited me to join them along with Christine and their son Roger on holiday to Majorca. I jumped at the chance and determined to pop the question one evening after he'd had a few drinks.

It worked! And although I was extremely nervous, Stan didn't seem to notice and he readily agreed that we could go ahead with our plans to tie the knot! I was elated and Christine was quite pleased too. A date was set for a service at the Anglican church which Florrie used to attend from time to time. Being a belt and braces kind of person, she kept her options open - Spiritualist, Anglican you never know what credentials you might need when you arrive at the Pearly Gates.

March 1st 1958 couldn't come too soon for me but St Clements, Balfour Road, in the parish of Great Ilford, being an Anglican church, there were things that had to be done before the great day. I was expected to be confirmed for a start, that was no big deal for me. I knew that I had been dedicated as a baby in the Salvation Army and another blessing would not go amiss. Then, of course, there were banns to be read and halls to be booked and Florrie was in her element. She would invite her large family and multitudes of friends from among the customers who bought from her shop. We compiled a large present list with high hopes of generous responses.

I wasn't greatly impressed with my confirmation classes as I seemed to learn quite a bit about the structures of the Church of England but very little about Jesus. My sister, Margaret, and cousin, Ann, along with the three girls of mum's nurse friend were booked as bridesmaids and my good friend from school days, Don Falconer, was my best man. I don't remember much about my stag night except that the next morning when I enquired how I received the nasty gash on my forehead, Don confessed that they had dropped me on the way home from my stag party!

Finally, the day arrived and there we all were in the church in our Sunday best waiting for the lovely Christine to arrive. Being somewhat overwhelmed by the enormity of the situation, I turned to Don and said, 'I'm just going to pray mate!' and fell on my knees to ask God's blessing! Don was dumbfounded as he had never heard anything like that from me before. However, it was probably good I did pray, as afterwards I heard that when Christine and her dad arrived at the church, he took her by the hand and said, 'Are you sure about this? You don't have to go through with it, we can turn round and go home now!'

Naturally, my bride was late and a great feeling of relief and excitement came over me as the mighty organ thundered out Handel's Wedding March. And there she was, in stunning beauty, gliding down the aisle on Stan's arm, my Christine! Hymns were sung, words were said, vows were made, the bride was kissed and the register signed, the cameras clicked, and before we knew it, we were whisked away to the reception.

MARRIAGE AND THE JOURNEY BACK TO FAITH

Don't ask me why, but I had booked a houseboat on the Thames for our honeymoon. You might say, 'Ah, that was nice!' but it was March 1st and heavy rains caused flooding on the river! Thankfully, our break was cancelled. And as I look back, I think it must have been the Lord as we were saved from what would have been a rather bleak and chilly week moored up in the middle of nowhere. To the rescue – Butlins! Yes, Butlins Honeymoon Hotel in Brighton. You can imagine, after it was all over there were the many questions from interested friends about how it all went and then the inevitable ask and no way it could be avoided. 'Where did you say that you went for your honeymoon?' 'Oh, Butlins?!' Well, it didn't matter to us, we had each other and that was all that did matter. We had made it and our new life together had begun but it was not all sweetness and light.

When we came home to our newly decorated and furnished flat upstairs in my mum's house in Goodmayes, I had set up my small slate-bed billiard table in the centre of our lounge. It was not, perhaps, the most sensitive thing I could have done as it was all very quiet apart from the clicking of the balls as I played while Christine watched. Later she confessed that she almost screamed and went home to mum. You see, she had lived all her life in a busy house with constant visits from friends and family and now a lonely future appeared to stretch out before her.

So began a sharp learning curve for me, as I guess it did for many freshly married young men who have only had themselves to think about. Christine was strongly opinionated and to use that description of me would be to grossly underestimate the nature of my opinions. Stan saw this and as we left the wedding reception, he shook me firmly by the hand and said, almost with compassion, 'I'll give you six months!'

More than once, he was almost proved right but he had not understood one thing, God was on our case. There was no way he could have known the Holy Spirit was watching over us and was going to become our great teacher as we commenced our journey. We can see now that at key moments He led significant people to cross our path to help us find our true destiny and calling in Jesus.

One such person was Michael Harper, a young curate who, in 1958, was called to the great John Stott's church, All Souls in Langham Place, just up the road from Peter Robinsons where I worked. Another, was Lily Allder, who worked at Dellin's, the local grocery shop at the top of Ashgrove Road in Goodmayes, where our flat was situated. I have absolutely no doubt that the Holy Spirit gently guided these two wonderful people, so very different from one another, into our lives.

Part of Michael's role as a curate was to serve as a chaplain to the stores in Oxford Street and Peter Robinsons was the nearest one to All Souls. So, naturally it was to PRs that he came first. After enquiring in the Personnel Department, he was delighted to find that there was a functioning Christian Union and came to seek me out as the chairman. It was only years later that he confessed how his delight turned to disappointment after we chatted. He was expecting to meet a live evangelical Christian with a heart to see people blessed and helped and he found me – a likely lad who loved his pint and to party!

However, give him his due, he did his best to engage with me and invited me and Christine back to his flat where he and his wife gave us tea - cucumber sandwiches as I remember. Then they endeavoured to entertain us. I don't think he had quite got the measure of us though, as whilst Jeanne played the piano Michael sang, *Three Little Maids Are We* from Gilbert and Sullivan! We would have felt much more at home a few hundred yards up the road at 100 Oxford Street in Humphrey Lyttelton's Jazz Club.

Nevertheless, we continued to meet up and he kindly risked inviting the two of us to attend a weekend conference with some army major who apparently was a fine bible teacher. We enjoyed the ministry and the discussions and were hugely impressed with the large black leather bibles that everyone carried. And so our relationship continued to develop apace.

Meanwhile, back in Goodmayes, Christine was shopping in Dellin's for our weekly shop. This was quite a different experience to visiting a supermarket today as she sat on a high stool next to a marble slab where the cooked meat and ham was sliced and served. She had her shopping list which she read out item by item whilst the lady serving ran round the shelves bringing back what was required.

At the checkout there was Lily, always ready with a smile and a chat. On this occasion she must have seen something in Christine as she invited the two of us to her home for a meal with her and her husband, Len. We accepted, and so began a deep friendship which was to last for many years and helped us to discover the next step in God's amazing plan for our lives. We see now that the Holy Spirit was working a pincer movement, with Michael and Jeanne in town where I worked and with Len and Lily on the ground at home.

Len was a lovely man and he and Lily attended a local Baptist Church and he suggested that we might like to go along with them one Sunday. We took them up on the offer and were blessed, although having experienced those *wind up* meetings in the Salvation Army I felt there must be more. We chatted about the early church and the outpouring of the Holy Spirit and Len also expressed a longing for something more.

Len helped to run an independent Sunday school and, having heard about my Salvation Army background, asked if I would be willing to take on the boys' bible class, which was very brave of him knowing that I was still a bit of a lad. I said I would have a go and started off by sharing my story which went down a storm. Each week we would meet together and I would share something from the bible and tell some more stories which usually ended with my saying something like, 'But don't do as I do, do what the bible says!' It was not ideal but we were on a journey and the Lord was with us.

In the midst of all that was going on, and I can't recall exactly when, we had one of our Ouija seances and something happened which seriously troubled me. In amongst all the messages that were coming through, the glass spelled out a request for us to say the Lord's Prayer backwards! I was brought up with a start and couldn't bring myself to even attempt that. We immediately stopped what we were doing and from that point on I began to read the bible again and that was the last time we played that game.

- Come Holy Spirit -

As I read the bible and talked with Len and Lily it was clear that we were developing a longing for the kind of church experience which we read about in the Acts of the Apostles. Then it came to our attention something of significance was happening in little mission in Bethnal Green, where the pastor and his youth group met every Thursday evening to pray.

News got out that there had been an outpouring of the Holy Spirit and the young people were blessed and speaking in tongues. Christians were drawn to join them from various parts of the UK, and even missionaries who were on furlough came and left rejoicing after receiving the Baptism of the Holy Spirit. I encouraged Len to come with me and see for ourselves.

We entered The Good Shepherd Mission in Three Colts Lane, Bethnal Green and were welcomed by Pastor Ray Shaw. It was only afterwards I discovered that this was in the very street where William Booth opened his first Salvation Army corps! As we knelt with those young people, there was an intensity as they prayed, messages in tongues came forth and interpretations were given and then Pastor Ray laid his hands on us and the rest is history!

I laughed, I cried and walked around speaking in tongues full of overwhelming joy. I just felt I had walked right back into the arms of Jesus and he had welcomed me home. Len was also blessed and we knew that the Lord had started something special in our lives and that we would never be the same again. We returned again and again to that mission and, as the weeks went by, we learned that over 600 people from the UK and different parts of the world were filled with the Spirit in that Thursday night young people's prayer meeting! And that was just the beginning.

On returning to work, which was around an hour's journey each way, I devoured my bible on the train and in my lunch hour. I underlined all the verses that were familiar to me and also the verses that immediately impressed me. I made an appointment to meet up with Michael Harper at St Peter's Church, in Vere Street, to share my story. He was gracious but not greatly impressed. He explained that he believed in the gift of healing for today but the gifts of prophecy, tongues and interpretation had been withdrawn as we now have the bible.

It was around three months later when the Spirit fell on Michael as he was praying and he began reciting Psalms by heart which he had never learned. He also spoke in tongues, all of which put him at odds with John Stott and other evangelical leaders. So in 1964 he left All Souls and started The Fountain Trust, and thus the Charismatic Renewal was well under way and I had the privilege of working with him in many situations here in the UK and around the world but more of that later.

Apart from the influence of Michael and other gifted bible teachers in the Renewal, there were several books which were extremely helpful as we were seeking to understand and confirm what we were seeing in scripture. The simple nature of church, relationships and ministry challenged much of what we saw in the traditional models. I believe three of these books are worthy of particular mention, Watchman Nee's *The Normal Christian Church Life*, *The Churches of God* by G H Lang and Roland Allan's *Missionary Methods – Paul's Ways or Ours?*. I remember that this book was first published in 1912 and was rediscovered in the 1960s fifty years later – something which Allan predicted would happen.

By this time Christine had stopped working in London and started work as a teacher in a pretty rough girls' school in Dagenham with year five which she was entirely suited for. In those days there was no demand for us to be politically correct, in fact at the time we had never heard the term. So it was that she grabbed one foul-mouthed girl and dragged her off to the changing rooms where she washed her mouth out with soap. This suitably impressed the other girls and Christine had them eating out of her hand from then on.

With her drama degree she was teaching English and drama and, to the amazement of all, she had the girls doing Shakespeare as the school play - *Twelfth Night* - as I remember. Everyone was extremely pleased but Christine was now pregnant with our first child and it was soon time to leave. On the day of her departure, she was quite moved as the girls turned up with all kinds of pretty presents for the new baby. However, her pleasure was short-lived when a local shopkeeper turned up at the school with a policeman to collect up many of the gifts which had been obtained without a receipt!

Up to this point, while Christine was deeply interested in what had happened to me, she had made no commitment to Jesus. So, when Len suggested that we should all attend a tent crusade meeting with evangelist David Shepherd speaking, I jumped at the chance. It was a lively event and a good message and when the appeal came Christine stood up and went forward to receive Jesus as her saviour.

We were absolutely delighted and when we asked her what happened, she said that she decided to go forward and give Jesus a whirl! And, if she was in a position to answer that question today, she would say exactly the same thing but with a postscript, 'That day I decided to give Jesus a whirl and I have been whirling with him ever since!' Later, she was also Baptised in the Holy Spirit and in water at the Good Shepherd Mission just before, Sharon, our eldest daughter, was born on the 23rd of June 1960.

- Kids galore! -

After Sharon our family grew quite rapidly. Matthew, our eldest boy, was born on the 11th of August 1961. He was our miracle boy as he suffered from asthma and at one point went down with pneumonia. He was seriously ill and our doctor, who I believe was a godly man, said that he was not sure that Matthew would make it through. He recommended that Matthew should stay at home rather than be hospitalised as he felt he would not cope if he was taken from us.

We were shattered but immediately began to fast and pray and cry out to the Lord for Matthew's healing. Within five days there was a remarkable turn around and we were overwhelmed with thankfulness to God. When the doctor arrived, he was stunned and wrote one word on Matthew's medical card – 'miracle!'

The lovely Ruth arrived on the 14th of June 1965 and the handsome John on the 20th of September 1966. After Matthew was born, I well remember how Christine struggled with motherhood and one day I found her crashed out on the bed sobbing as she felt unable to cope with two young children. I did my fair share of walking up and down in the night, patting and rocking to give Christine some relief, whilst wondering how I could become God's man when I couldn't manage my family.

However, being the kind of person she was, she was soon looking after other people's kids as well and it seemed that suddenly she moved up a gear. It was as if she tapped into a hidden reservoir of maternal ability and nothing was too much trouble. One such child she took on was Karen, a girl two years of age, whilst her mother went out to work. She seemed undernourished and often had bruises. She would sit in a chair with a book on her lap and immediately cry if you tried to engage with her in any way. One day her mother failed to turn up to collect her daughter and social services asked if we would take her on while they tried to sort out what had happened.

To cut quite a long story short, Christine began to work with Karen in an endeavour to help her out of her withdrawn state. It was a slow and challenging process but the time came when Karen was to be put up for adoption. After prayer we felt that we could not let her go into another home, as that might be a further setback for her. Her birthday was the 15th of October, the very same day as mine and we took that as a sign that we should go ahead to adopt her into our family.

So Karen became Sarah and slotted in between Matthew and Ruth. We were told by the psychiatrist who was looking into Sarah's case, that she would always need specialist help and we should not expect her to go to a normal school. But Christine would have none of that and persevered working with Sarah to help her recover from the neglect of her early years. By the time she was five she took her place with Sharon and Matthew at the same school.

- Prayer and fasting -

Meanwhile, I discovered a little old Salvation Army hall with a corrugated iron roof which was open in Seven Kings, just a stone's throw from where we lived. It was very convenient for me and the young lady officer was lovely and, although there was only around seven or eight in attendance, I regularly found that God met me there when I knelt to seek him at the mercy seat.

Later, I was able to use the hall for nights and half-nights of prayer, where a group of us met to cry out for revival. On cold winter nights the coke boiler was stoked and glowed red hot at times as did our prayers.

I was so keen I started fasting twice a week as I had read that was what John Wesley did. I was not always wise in my enthusiasm and decided to fast for five days from Monday morning to Friday evening with no food or drink!

Remember, I was working in London and had a busy job, not now at Peter Robinsons but at a small advertising agency just off Regent Street. It was a busy job and I stood by my pledge not to eat or drink.

One Wednesday evening when I arrived home, I went into the bathroom and having a dry mouth I rinsed it out with water and spat blood. My feeling was that this was not good, so from that point on I sipped water but carried on with the fast.

Having continued with the boys' bible class, I added a weekly social evening for them and their friends using the Salvation Army hall. We played games and ended with a *God slot* and we grew as others came along and joined in. I arrived at the club on the Friday evening of my fifth fasting day and at sunset my fast ended and I sent one of the lads out to buy me a bag of chips and a can of coke! Not the best way to end any fast!

I thank the Lord that he preserved me through those early days and, ultimately, gave me spiritual fathers who nurtured and encouraged me without putting me down. Furthermore, if anyone is thinking of seeking God through fasting, I recommend that you discover the healthy way to follow your desire to go deeper with God. In that connection, Arthur Wallis, one of my spiritual dads, wrote an excellent little book, *God's Chosen Fast*, which I am sure you will find if you search on line.

More opportunities for prayer opened up as it seemed many of those who had been filled with the Holy Spirit were gathering to seek God for revival. Each Monday evening in a hired room in Wanstead, not too far from Goodmayes, a small group met led by a business man, Fred Smith. In the group was a brother who had been in many of the healing meetings of Smith Wigglesworth and what a privilege to hear some of the amazing things he saw.

However, in spite of all his experiences and having many fine men of God lay hands on him, this brother had never received the Spirit or spoken in tongues. One day he phoned me up and asked me to pray for him and, as you may guess, I felt very inadequate but I quietly sent up a prayer and it seemed the Lord heard.

I said that I could see a table laden with food and set ready for a feast and I told him that the Lord wanted him to pick up his knife and fork and dig in. I then prayed for him and went off to bed. In the early hours the phone rang again. I wondered who on earth would be calling me at this hour of the night. It was my friend, ecstatic, and overflowing with thankfulness that after all these years the Lord had met him and we both retired back to bed happy men.

Working in London as I did, I was blessed to hear from Pastor Ray Shaw that he, Fred Smith and a Bill Grant, who later became a trustee of The Fountain Trust, had started a lunchtime prayer meeting in an upper room in Fleet Street every Thursday. It was a special place to be and the Lord blessed us as we prayed and folk exercised the gifts of the Spirit.

One lunch time, which I will never forget, we were praying as usual and noticed that a stranger had wandered in off the street. He was clearly of Mediterranean origin with olive-skin and dark curly hair. At one point Fred spoke out in tongues and when he stopped, Ray interpreted. When the meeting was over and folk were returning to work, this gentleman was left in his chair shaking his head in unbelief. His question was, 'Where did that man learn such perfect classical Greek?' 'What Fred, speaking Greek?' I asked. 'Yes,' he continued, 'and furthermore, the other man translated it!' I replied to the effect that I knew both men well enough to know that neither of them had that capacity. Before he left in total bewilderment, he said that the interpretation concerned issues in his life which no one in that room could possibly have known about and it was clear to us that the Lord had made a dramatic impact on his life.

Prayer played quite a part of our lives at that time and I used to spend time with another friend, Jim Rattenbury, sitting quietly in St Paul's at lunch time for half-an-hour. Jim frequently attended Westminster Chapel, where the great Doctor Martin Lloyd-Jones drew crowds to hear him preach. He was a man who passionately believed in revival and frequently preached about it, so Jim took me there one Sunday to hear him and I was privileged to meet him in his vestry for a chat – and I was greatly impressed!

Later, after he retired, I heard that the Doctor went around unannounced to visit some of his disciples to hear them preach and see how they were progressing. The story is that he was greatly disappointed to find that many had adopted his style and mannerisms without the passion and spirit of the man himself.

CHAPTER FOUR

OPEN DOORS
AND NEW OPPORTUNITIES

I mentioned earlier about the dangers of the Ouija game and, indeed, would say the same of the occult as a whole. Now, whilst Christine and I were rejoicing in the blessings of the work of Holy Spirit in our lives, we were unaware of the serious effects which remained under the surface as a result of our involvement.

One day we were sitting quietly in the lounge of our flat in Goodmayes chatting and I felt a blanket of fear descend on me like an evil cloud. I felt I was losing my mind and that any minute I would be totally out of control. I looked at Christine and I could see that she too was in trouble. 'Are you feeling what I am feeling?' I asked.

It was a stupid question but I got the answer I needed to hear, 'Yes!' she replied. Christine usually knew what I was thinking, her intuitive gift was strong and developed under the anointing of the Holy Spirit. I immediately jumped up and started speaking in tongues and Christine joined me. Together we cried out to the Lord for deliverance from that fearful presence. I began to plead for the blood of Jesus to cover us (I had heard Pentecostal friends doing this) and a moment came when that dark cloud was cast out of the room and we knew exactly which corner of the room it left.

OPEN DOORS AND NEW OPPORTUNITIES

As a result of our experience of the Baptism of the Holy Spirit and the deliverance we experienced, we found that many Christians were keen to hear our story. It was clear that there was a growing hunger for an authentic experience of Jesus and church which went beyond the lifeless routine which was the norm for many churchgoers.

At that time evangelical Christianity was at an all-time low and very much in defensive mode and, apart from the early visits of Billy Graham and a few old-time Pentecostal evangelists operating in tent meetings, there wasn't a great deal to inspire the saints.

It was into this vacuum that the Holy Spirit began to breath his message of renewal and revival through the many different ministries he was raising up from within and without the denominations. For example, in our area a group of young people from a local Methodist youth group heard what God was doing with us and they began to seek us out to be prayed for to receive the Holy Spirit.

Whilst the invitations rolled in for me to speak at all kinds of gatherings from college and school Christian Unions to youth groups and regular church meetings of all kinds, Christine was busy bringing our growing family into the world and looking after our new Spirit-filled young friends. Thus, without us realising it, a little church was also being born in our home.

Soon there was a group filled with excitement and hope who needed teaching and fellowship, much of which came through Christine as I was still working in London during the week and often out ministering at weekends. During this period, we made many significant connections with others locally and around the UK who impacted our lives and will appear as our story develops.

One such link came in 1959 soon after I had been filled with the Holy Spirit. Mrs Baker, one of the Sunday school teachers where my boys' bible class was held, fell ill and asked me to stand in for her at a local Elim church youth group that evening where she was due to speak. I accepted the offer and turned up to see an enthusiastic bunch of teenagers singing and praising God with gusto and also praying in tongues in rather loud voices.

As I stood up to speak from the book of Ephesians, which was already very special to me, a minibus full of young black West Indians kids piled in to join us. The already-charged atmosphere went up several notches as the 'praise God', 'hallelujahs' and 'amens' accompanied every sentence I uttered. I was overwhelmed and quite sure that full-scale revival had broken out as, when I made the appeal, virtually the whole group came forward for prayer – at last, I thought, my ministry has really taken off!

Afterwards, I was a little disappointed to find that this was a regular occurrence among these lovely people, as they all wanted everything they could get from the Lord. Nevertheless, there on the floor, crying out to God along with all the other bodies, was the young Norman Barnes who was to become a close friend and colleague right up to the time of writing this paragraph. I won't attempt to tell you Norman and his wife Grace's story, as their remarkable journey is well documented in his book, *Destiny Calls – living your dream*, which was published in July 2020 and is currently available. Suffice it to say that I was soon captivated by Norman's enthusiasm and his unwavering belief that God was going to use him in ministry around the world.

At this young age he had a vision, in which he saw himself preaching in a packed shell of a building with over 5000 black people hanging on his every word. He shared this with Charles, the youth leader, who said, 'You believe it and one day it will happen'. However, others were not so sympathetic and felt Norman was a bit of a loud mouth. Well, loud mouth he was! The pastor, a somewhat frail man, tried to quieten Norman down when he prayed in the church meetings but it was to no avail as Norman just didn't hear the poor man. So the pastor resorted to keeping a small bell under the pulpit which he rang when he felt dear Norman should quit. Sadly, that didn't work either for when Norman got going nothing else was in his mind but to finish what he had started.

OPEN DOORS AND NEW OPPORTUNITIES

As time progressed, we both joined in with brother Bernard Tovell who ran Good News, a street-preaching group. Most Saturdays we would end up in London's West End to preach the gospel. One week we were preaching in an alley between a cinema and betting shop. The cinema had recently been updated with a super new quadrophonic sound system. Norman was on the stand and as he shouted out his message a gentleman in an evening suit emerged to ask Norman to quieten down. It appeared that the people in the cinema couldn't hear the film!

After preaching we would invite people back to a coffee bar which was held in the basement of the Congregational church in Orange Street. It was packed to the gunnels with drug addicts, homeless people and ne'er-do-wells who came to hang out, get a coffee and listen to the growing number of Christian music groups who were emerging at the time.

We also travelled around preaching and I was reminded of such an occasion recently when Norman sent me a newspaper clipping which he came across when clearing out a file. We were preaching on the shingle beach in Brighton and this time Bernard was on the stand. There was a group of hippies right there in front of us painting a picture of Jayne Mansfield in blue house paint on a huge sheet of plastic. Jayne, a mega Hollywood star, had just been killed in a car crash.

One of the guys was lighting matches and trying to burn Bernard's clothes. So I took up a position in front of the stand to protect him. Suddenly, I heard God speak clearly to me – not a regular occurrence I can assure you – 'Son, can I have your suit?' Well, it was my only one but without hesitation I said, 'Yes, Lord!' In an instant, one of the hippies picked up the large pot of blue paint and aimed it at Bernard and let go but failed miserably as the pot landed upside down on my head!

Now not only my suit, but every single item I stood up in was drenched in paint, underpants, socks and sunglasses all met the same fate. Someone in the crowd shouted, 'Are you going to call the police?' 'No', I replied, as I was so blessed that I gave God my suit and he literally took it in seconds! So I shouted back, 'I just love him'. Next day in the paper dated the 13th July 1967 the headline was, 'The Christian was pelted with paint but he stood his ground'.

- *Prosper at work* -

Before the event on Brighton beach, I left the small advertising agency I worked at after my time at Peter Robinsons and went for an interview at Field & Crane, a much larger agency in Euston. At this point I was in what I now call, my *Christian period*, no smoke, no drink, no cinema, no TV, no contraceptives, no make-up and not much fun actually.

I knew the Lord was calling Christine and me into ministry but heard him tell me that until I prospered at work and did really well in my job that would not happen. When you think about it going for an interview with a company whose major accounts came into my no, no, category, you wouldn't have given me a snowball in hell's chance of getting the job, but get the job I did and had a successful and happy time there.

At my first team meeting the group who serviced the accounts sat in a circle chatting before the meeting started. One of the guys told a joke the punchline of which was written on a piece of paper. As the paper was opened there were great guffaws of laughter and it was then passed on to the next person and so on. Just before it was given to me, the chair of the meeting said, 'I don't think John needs to see that one', and it passed me by. I never had a problem of any kind from that point on but was always treated with respect!

During the couple of years I spent at Field & Crane, I also enjoyed serving the renewal in different ways and one outstanding opportunity came in 1965. Michael Harper asked me to join a planning group set up to manage an ambitious joint project with Demos Shakarian, the founder of The Full Gospel Businessmen's Fellowship International. The idea was to airlift 200 Christian ministries and businessmen from the US to the UK and then on into Europe, to share their incredible stories of blessing and miracles wherever their travels took them.

Ambitious though it was, it happened, and a sixty-four-page booklet was produced by the FGBFMI which tells the remarkable story of their adventures. Indeed, I hosted a meeting in North London at a huge Baptist church in Forest Gate. What a time it was. We had Jack Brown and Nikki Cruz sharing their testimonies. Nikki's story is told in the book *The Cross and the Switchblade* while *Run Baby Run* – written by Nikki - is well known and these books are still selling today!

On the other hand, Jack Brown was not so well known over here but he told us how he spent 17 years in the New York Penitentiary for murder as I remember it. Then one day God visited him and he poured all his whiskey down the sink and turned his life over to God and here he was with us sharing his moving story. People streamed forward for prayer as they did in gatherings all over the UK. Many people were led to Jesus and others were prayed for to be filled with the Holy Spirit. We were conscious another significant milestone in the Renewal had taken place.

Among the other speakers who graced our shores, were ministries whose lives and stories remain as testimony to what the Lord was doing around the world at that time. There was David du Plessis, the first Pentecostal to reach out to Catholics, who became known as Mr Pentecost; Oral Roberts, I read the story of his healing and conversion on the train going to work one day and I couldn't hold back the tears; Derek Prince, who came to a number of our conferences and his books are still widely read around. Also, Pat Robertson, who still hosts the 700 Club one of the largest Christian TV stations in the United States was part of the American team.

Apart from all that was happening in the Renewal around the nation, our little house group was growing and much of this was down to Christine who made everyone who came feel welcome and at home. Brian Davis, a Pentecostal, and his friend, Howard Barnes, from a Salvation Army family we knew of, were both school teachers working in a local school.

They were full of the Holy Spirit and started a bible class for the boys. The short story is that one term the Holy Spirit fell and almost 200 boys experienced the power of God. Some were delivered from evil spirits, some healed and others convicted of sin. Lads were in tears as they walked from one lesson to the next. The head asked one boy why he was crying and he replied to the effect that it was the Lord at work in his life.

The sad thing is that the term finished and the six weeks of summer holidays lay ahead and when the boys returned to school, it was as if the whole thing had never happened. With hindsight, we came to realise that Brian and Howard should have provided regular times for the boys to get together during the holidays for prayer, activities and encouragement. Looking back, we give thanks for two amazing lads who survived and went on to do great things for God.

John Menlove, just 14 years old and already an accomplished pianist, joined us and became one of our primary worship leaders playing at huge events and facilitating many of our recording projects. Peter Martin ended up serving Norman Barnes in Links International which is another great story in itself, but more about Links later.

Just down the road from where we lived there was a Shaftesbury Mission in need of a pastor and I was asked if I was interested in taking on the role. There was a good building with a flat and a small salary as I remember. However, although I knew I was called to the ministry, I didn't feel that I would make a great pastor, so I mentioned the opportunity to my friend Norman Barnes who was keen to get into his ministry.

Norman said he would think about it and mentioned it to his mum, a woman of prayer. He took her to the building to look around and she was stunned, as this was the very place she had recently seen in a vision and that was all the confirmation Norman needed. So began some wonderfully fruitful years of ministry for Norman and his new wife, Grace. Ministry which not only touched the local area but also sent waves of blessing around the world when Links International was born.

OPEN DOORS AND NEW OPPORTUNITIES

Around this time, I met another lovely man who became a special friend, Andy Milliken. He ran a small advertising outfit dealing mainly with Christian accounts. He was quite a character, quiet, calm and carried a peaceful atmosphere wherever he went. This was quite remarkable, since the major part of his time in the forces during the war was spent as a prisoner of the Japanese. He and his battalion were held in Burma where they were forced to build that infamous railway and the bridge that crossed the River Kwai. He survived but they say one man died for each sleeper that was laid!

As we got to know one another and discovered that we had much in common concerning the Renewal, he asked if I would like to work with him for a time. I accepted as I felt this could be a step towards my desire to devote more of my time to the ministry.

The question was, had I done enough to fulfil what the Lord had said to me about doing really well in my secular employment before taking the next step in that part of my journey? We both felt that I should hand in my notice to Field & Crane and see what their response was when I asked for a reference. I think the letter I received from Geoffrey Lambert the joint managing director said it all.

29th October 1965

J. Noble, Esq.,
c/o Field & Crane Ltd.

Dear John,

I feel that as you are leaving us I ought to express the gratitude of all of us here for the really stupendous work and effort which you have put in on behalf of this Company from the day you joined.

It is difficult to write a letter of this sort without in fact reeling off a string of platitudes, but I would like you to know as you leave us that we are all very sorry to lose you, and we have all enjoyed working with you very much. You have carried out a by no means easy job with extreme efficiency, good humour, tact and patience.

I am sure I speak for everyone here when we sincerely wish you every success in your new venture, and I hope you will come in and see us from time to time. Finally, if there is anything we can do for you at any time in the future, I hope you won't hesitate to get in touch with us.

With very best wishes and many thanks,

Geoffrey Lambert.

As a result, I joined Andy and worked with him for a short time until I started my own business, but more of that later. One of the positive spinoffs from Andy's WWII experience was that he met Mitsuo Fuchida, a Japanese captain in the Imperial Japanese Navy Air Service and a bomber aviator during World War II. Fuchida was best known for leading the first wave of air attacks on Pearl Harbour on 7 December 1941.

After the war ended, the captain became a Christian after reading a gospel tract which had been passed to him. Later he met the author, a missionary working in Japan, who just happened to be the US pilot who led the retaliation raid on Japan. You really couldn't make this up, only our God can bring together the ingredients for such an amazing story! So Andy was able to plug into the captain's evangelistic travels across the United States and Europe to invite him to come to the UK to share his incredible testimony with us.

Over the next two or three years I met, listened to and worked with many of those, apart from Michael Harper, who were noted as fathers of the Renewal. Denis Clark, a South African dance band leader who came to devote himself to Christian ministry in the UK; Campbell McAlpine who, along with Arthur Wallis, came from a Christian Brethren background, served as missionaries in New Zealand. They were baptised in the Holy Spirit before returning to the UK where they worked tirelessly in the Renewal. Then there was my dear friend Cecil Cousens, editor of *Voice of Faith*, a magazine focussing on revival which we devoured every issue.

Cecil was a true minister of grace and faith. I never once heard him share on these basic foundations of our Christian belief without a generous helping of tears as he wept his way through his message. From an Apostolic Church background, he moved to Canada where he was caught up in an outpouring of the Holy Spirit known as the Latter Rain Movement. The movement itself went into error, but in its early years Cecil was deeply touched by the Spirit which shone through everything he said.

I well remember hosting one meeting where his text was from Isaiah 64; 1 (KJV),

> *Oh, that You would rend the heavens! That You would come down! That the mountains might shake at Your presence—.*

I responded with a loud, 'Amen!' but I was soon to regret it. As Cecil, in the nicest possible way, went on to share he turned to me and said, 'Well, I don't know about you, John, but I thought the heavens had already been rent!'

He then went on with obvious enthusiasm to point that when Christ was born the heavens were rent as the heavenly host announced the birth of our Saviour. Again, they were rent as Jesus went down into the waters of the Jordan. There the Spirit descended as a dove and the Father announced that this was his beloved Son. Then again, at the crucifixion when the veil of the temple was split in two and a new way into the heavenly realm was opened up. He brought his message to a close at Pentecost when the Holy Spirit fell on the group gathered in the upper room. Finally, he finished on a high, declaring that we now live under an open heaven for all who care to walk by faith.

Some of those men, and it was mainly men leading at that time although we were among those who worked to challenge that culture as we shall see, took part in a series of meetings I arranged entitled, *The Work of the Holy Spirit in the Church Today*. Surprisingly, I had built a relationship with the pastor of the Ilford Elim Church, surprising as some Pentecostals were suspicious of the Renewal as they felt that those receiving the Spirit should leave their denominations.

He agreed to allow us to use his church building for six Tuesday evening meetings, to give opportunity for testimony and ministry from key people in the Renewal locally and nationally. I was excited but concerned at the same time. My question was, would people turn up in numbers for a midweek meeting? I should not have been concerned, as from the first meeting the building was packed and the atmosphere was electric.

My only regret is that I didn't keep details of all that happened and even my leaflet advertising the meetings and those participating has disappeared from my file. Nevertheless, I can say that they were a huge success. Among the main speakers were Michael Harper; George Forrester, another Anglican vicar immersed in the Renewal; Phil Vogel, at that time the national director of British Youth for Christ; Arthur Wallis and Campbell McAlpine. Alongside were testimonies from people in local churches who had received the Holy Spirit including the deacon of a large Baptist church.

I shall never forget the evening that Campbell came and shared on the importance of holiness in the Renewal. He was a lovely gentle man but he spoke with conviction. Everyone felt his eyes were on them and thus the fear of the Lord fell on the meeting. As he finished his message and closed his bible, I rose to stand alongside him and wondered how he would deal with the response. I was stunned as he turned to me and said, 'Thanks John, I have a train to catch and must be on my way!'

OPEN DOORS AND NEW OPPORTUNITIES

At this point he picked up his bible bag and walked down the central isle of the church and off into the night, leaving me without any idea of what to do. I guess the Lord is most gracious when we are desperate and our only option is to cry out to him for help. I have no recollection of what I said or did. I wish I could tell you what words of wisdom came out of my mouth but, no! All I can say is that the Lord took over as we prayed and folk made their commitment to seek God for humility to handle the blessing which he was pouring out upon us at that time.

These gatherings stirred a great interest and response from across the area. It was clear that a door was opening for me to develop my ministry as invitations to speak and share my testimony came in from all directions. Although I had only worked for Andy Milliken for a short time, he was happy to release me to start my own business. I believed this would provide me with the income we needed to also pursue the ministry which I knew the Lord had called Christine and me to. However, the Lord had other ideas!

CHAPTER FIVE

FULL TIME AND LIVING BY FATH

I hesitated before using this chapter heading because it is my belief that every Christian should be full time and living by faith. Indeed, Paul, in Romans 1:17 (KJV) tells us that, *The just shall live by faith* and some bright spark added, 'not just the preacher!' Of course, they are both right. However, the heading describes the transition that was taking place in our lives as the Lord was teaching us to make the leap from believing that we could decide how to move forward, to trusting him for every step we were about to take.

So I employed a lovely Christian lady to work as my secretary and Christine's brother, Roger, who I introduced to Field & Crane while I was there, came to pound the pavements to work up some business for me. I had the best Wookey Hole handmade paper for my stationery, a great printer and graphic artist lined up and I still had all my media contacts at the ready. Thus, John Noble Advertising was born. What could go wrong?

Actually, things went very well. I already had quite a number of Christian businesses which were signed up for my services and Roger, being friendly and approachable, turned out to be a great sales person. So things were going swimmingly and the future looked bright. Christine was proving to be a great mother and she was also nurturing the young people who were forming the basis of what was one of the first of many House Churches which were springing up around the country. However, we suddenly found ourselves having to come to terms with a word that we have become very familiar with in these uncertain times – recession!

Quoting from the Levy Economics Institute web site, we are reminded that, 'The, so-called, credit crunch of 1966 has long been recognized as the first significant post war financial crisis and one that required the first important intervention by the Federal Reserve Bank'. It goes on to point out that this was, 'in the midst of the robust post war expansion....'

Scripture, in Romans 8: 28 (KJV), assures us that,

'All things work together for good to those who love God'.

However, I can tell you, that at the time it didn't feel like that and it is only in retrospect that we discovered the truth of this wonderful promise.

From our great start we began to book up advertising schedules in various publications on behalf of our clients. As the agent, we were responsible for the payment of these spaces and, as such, we received a commission of between 10% and 20%. I had observed this practice working just fine for a number of years with dozens of clients but we had no experience of credit crunches only robust expansion. So when two of my largest customers went bust it came as a terrible shock and I was devastated. Furthermore, as I was crying out to God and reciting the Lord's prayer, which I was not much in the habit of doing, I heard God speak very clearly. Again this was not a frequent experience for me as it was Christine, who seemed to be the one who had an open line to the Lord.

It was as I got to the line, 'Forgive us our trespasses as we forgive those who trespass against us', that God spoke. You see, I found myself saying, 'Forgive us our debts as we forgive those who are indebted to us', and I never said the prayer that way. It was then that I heard the Lord say, 'Son, you must forgive your customers their debts'.

So, here is God speaking to me which is fantastic but I just didn't want to hear what he was saying! 'But Lord,' I replied, 'I was just about to ring them up to see if I could pile on the pressure to cough up the cash!' But silence, and I couldn't get any peace until I made those calls to tell them what God had told me to do. I have no idea if their response was to think I was mad or whether they fell on their knees to thank the Lord for their good fortune. I know one of them was a Jewish gentleman, so it is possible he did the latter but I will never know.

Of course, I had to tell Christine and then that left us with a dilemma. Should I borrow some money, which might be tough in the middle of a credit crunch. Then I would have to go back to Field & Crane and eat humble pie and ask for my old job back. That would mean ignoring this sense that the Lord was calling us to a greater commitment to His work. The alternative would be to sell our house and trust God completely to provide for us. After prayer, we decided on the latter but had no idea where what we were about to do would take us.

We shared our decision with family and friends. Some thought we had lost our marbles but others, particularly those in the small group that was growing around us, were excited to see what the Lord was about to do.

Obviously, with my business closed down we had no income other than the occasional ministry gifts I received for sharing in groups and churches. However, these were usually quite small and were often described as *petrol money*, as if a preacher didn't need to eat or pay the bills.

Also, I was getting more and more invitations to speak in youth groups and schools and there was no finance available for the speaker in those situations. Furthermore, my understanding of *living by faith* was shaped by stories of men like George Muller. He was a Christian evangelist and the director of the Ashley Down orphanage in Bristol. He was also one of the founder members of the Plymouth Brethren. He trusted God in the work he did with poor children and never spoke about money. If there was no food, he would lay the table in anticipation of the Lord's provision and his story is littered with testimonies of how God turned up.

So while we waited to sell the house, we set off on our journey of faith with no idea of where it would lead us. At the start, Christine had a hugely encouraging and faith building experience. She needed some shopping from Dellin's, so she checked her purse to be sure that she had enough money for her purchases and, indeed, there was a 10/- note neatly folded inside. She popped two or even three kids in the large pram she used to ferry them around, while the others hung on as she made the short walk to Dellin's at top of our road. She grabbed the shopping, collected her change and then remembered that my suit was in the dry cleaners waiting to be picked up.

Christine crossed the road, paused to check her purse again not quite certain she had enough for the suit and, lo and behold, there was still ten shillings but now in coins! 'Ah,' she thought, 'that's amazing, I know I paid in full for my shopping!' She collected my suit and then decided to try for one more thing. The shoes we had left in the cobblers for some time as we were a bit short of cash, were next on her radar. She checked the purse a third time and, sure enough, there was ten shillings ready and waiting and the shoes were back in our possession - job done! When she told me the story, we rejoiced and thanked the Lord together and decided it was a clear sign that God was with us. That particular blessing never happened again, although there were many other occasions when the Lord stepped in with his provision just when it was needed.

My experience was a little different and I was encouraged that, apart from the young people who had no income, a few wage earners were linking up with us. Brian was a good man and a school teacher. He knocked at our door one day and after chatting he reached out as if to shake my hand to say goodbye, not something he was in the habit of doing. When I looked down to my hand there was a crisp £5 note in my palm and my reaction was to say, 'Oh, Brian, thanks, but are you sure about this?' 'No!' he replied taking the note back out of my grasp! Lesson learned – graciously receive what the Lord provides and go on your way rejoicing!

Recently, I was talking to a friend about those early days when we had no regular income and no church or organisation to help us. And I had to say, that whilst there are many occasions when I can recall how the Lord supplied our needs, it seems that most of the time we just got on with life and there was always money or food or whatever we needed right there to hand.

- *The Towers* -

When we finally sold our house and had put our precious possessions into storage, we were ready to move on, but where? Our dear friends, Ken and Maureen Rose, who had linked in with us from the local Methodist church and knew the youngsters who had joined us, kindly opened their home for the group to meet there. So, whilst we had no desire to move away from the area, Ken and Maureen's willingness to take care of our group meant that we were secure in the knowledge that the young people were in good hands.

In the few years prior to us selling our house, I had been greatly encouraged to read the story of an American couple who started a great new missionary work known as Operation Mobilisation (OM). George Verwer, the husband, had a passion to reach the unreached with the Gospel message through literature, and having moved from the United States to London was gathering people to serve his vision here in the UK and around the world. Those who joined him shared his passion and were willing to make whatever sacrifices were necessary to get on with the job. Obviously, as the team grew, they needed accommodation and one such group had been given permission to occupy a large, old derelict house until it was due to be demolished.

Some kind soul heard about our predicament and suggested that we contact George to see if he would be willing for our tribe to move in for a time while we considered our future. To our amazement, he agreed and asked us to be house parents. So we piled our necessary clothing and bedding into the car which Christine's mum had given us after I sold my beautiful Sunbeam Rapier and made the trip to The Towers near Horton Kirby in Kent.

We had heard that OMer's, as they were affectionately called, lived rather frugally on peanut butter and Marmite and slept in greasy sleeping bags! We quickly discovered that this was not a rumour! Initially, we were accompanied by a team from Goodmayes who came to help us clean the place up and drive out the plague of mice before making our beds up with crisp clean white sheets.

This was a revelation to our OM friends, as they were soon to have a creative lesson on homemaking! Christine made it quite clear that serving God does not mean that you don't have to wash or take a shower and there is no merit or divine brownie points awarded for sleeping in a grubby bed! Also, apart from getting her hands on the dirty linen, it wasn't long before she was laying hands on some heads and seeing them filled with them Holy Spirit!

Just down the road from The Towers was The Dartford College of Further Education, now the North Kent College, and by a remarkable, divine coincidence we had already had contact with a group of students from the CU there. Anita, then Helps, later to become Traynar was arranging a weekend retreat for them with our friend Roger Forster, but for some reason that fell through and my name was passed on to them as a possible replacement.

So it happened that a whole bunch of them came over to our home in Goodmayes and piled in for the weekend, sleeping wherever they could find a space. It also happened that the Holy Spirit turned up and they had an amazing time. Little did we realise then that a special link had been made which would impact our lives for years to come. With this in mind, we felt that it was clear the Lord had work for us to do with the students there and soon this same gang were joining us for fellowship on Sundays and popping in whenever they had free time.

Our five kids were so happy there, exploring the large gardens and climbing the towers which gave the house its name. The students loved the children and took time to play with them. I cleaned out the large greenhouse and grew tomatoes and we look back to the months we spent there as a time of blessing for us all. In no way do we see it as a time of testing or deprivation, but one orchestrated for us by our loving heavenly Father and a time which prepared us for all that he had in store for us.

Now, George, OM director, was experiencing some tensions in the movement worldwide. As far as I could understand, some of his workers were, perhaps, a little over-enthusiastic about their desire to see others filled with the Holy Spirit. OM, being made up of a diverse group of Christians with many from a fairly strict evangelical background, found such tensions were interfering with the work. Of course, similar tensions were occurring in denominational churches, Christian Unions, missionary and other organisations around the world. So it was quite understandable that George felt he wanted to avoid any difficulties as far as he could and in his efforts towards this end, he felt he had to ask us to leave The Towers.

To be honest, we were a little upset but accepted his decision. However, I must add here, that some years later George and I found ourselves facing one another at the same conference. After a little good humoured banter between the two of us from the pulpit, we found that there was no residue of ill-feeling and we have been good friends ever since.

In fact, shortly after that George invited me to his Bromley headquarters to lead his weekly prayer meeting. It was there that I learned how he copes with his ginormous work load and the massive amount of correspondence he deals with every day. He's a multitasker! He stood there at the back of the meeting signing the letters his secretary had prepared for him and prayed fervently as he scrawled his way through the pile of mail!

As I pondered how we could respond fairly quickly to George's request, I realised that we didn't have many options and no miraculous answers were forthcoming on this occasion. However, mum Noble came to the rescue! My mother's years in the Salvation Army were spent reaching out to others and nothing was too much trouble. We were always moving over to take in some needy soul to help them through a tough time and ended up with numerous *aunts* and *uncles* who became part of our wider family.

When we shared the problem with mum who lived in Hadleigh, Essex, she immediately responded by saying that we were to move in with her! Now, on the face of it, that sounds like a very generous offer, that is until you realise that she lived in a three bedroomed house and, having lost her second husband, Fred, my aunt Lucy had moved in and had a bed-sit and kitchen in two of the upstairs rooms and the third bedroom was mum's. The situation was further complicated by the fact we had taken on Ray, from TheTowers, as a lodger! So, it wasn't just Christine and me and our five it was Ray as well, which made an invasion of eight and getting everyone into bed in the evening became an art form!

Thankfully, Ray felt he had a call from the Lord to move on to Hong Kong, I am pretty sure it was the Lord but won't blame him if not. Moreover, he found true love there so it turned out well for him and eased the cramped conditions a little for us.

I'm still trying to work out how we managed. I think mum had three kids in her bedroom, and Christine and I had a pull-out sofa and two kids in the lounge with us. Ray must have slept on the floor in the kitchen, no wonder he had the call to Hong Kong!

- A home of our own! -

Our stay with my mum lasted just a few months, during which time I made my first couple of international trips. These were significant as they opened the door for international connections, some of which bear fruit in relationships which continue to this day. However, I will share more about those trips later.

Early on in our move to mum's I was lounging in a deck chair sunning myself in the garden, when I experienced one of few rare occasions in my life when I felt I heard the Lord speak to me directly. I had been meditating on the church as God's new temple and dwelling place which was one of my special loves. The thought of God's people becoming a living temple was the motivation for my ministry. His people united in love and truth by the Holy Spirit, available for him to reveal himself through them in all the glorious character and power of Jesus, was something that was never far from my mind,

Suddenly, whilst meditating on this I heard the Lord say, 'Son, because, like David of old, you have been more concerned for my house than for your own, you will see the house that I will give you today!'

It was true, I was due to see a house later that day in a place called Collier Row, just outside of Romford in Essex and not far from dear Ken and Maureen Rose down the road in Ilford. I had no money and no provable income so there was no possibility of getting a mortgage. You could say that viewing houses under such circumstances was a foolish waste of time, or you could say it was a step of faith, but I did go to see this house with a certain air of expectation.

At that time, Collier Row could be called Bodge City! The whole area was run down and most of the recent work done on houses was DIY of the lowest standard and my visit to the 5 bedroomed semi-detached house I looked at was all the evidence one needed to confirm that. As I entered through the front door, I got the impression that, if you applied another set of cheap polystyrene tiles to the ceiling and covered the floor with another layer of lino, you'd have to bend to walk down the hall.

An effort to build a little cupboard in the alcove under the stairs was made from recycled orange boxes and, over the years, walls had been decorated by simply papering over what was already there, layer on layer. My dear old grandpa, who taught me as a boy the skills of painting and decorating, would have turned in his grave. However, if this was the house my heavenly Father had for us, that was fine by me and grandpa's time would not have been wasted.

I shared with Christine what I had seen and we felt that we should make an offer. We then shared this with our little group and two or three elderly ladies from the Pentecostal church in Ilford where we had previously held meetings. They were women of prayer and whilst they didn't leave their church, they were very supportive and often came to our gatherings. Everyone was excited to think that we might move back into the area and folk prayed and gave sacrificially. Even the ladies joined in giving generously which demonstrated that, beyond prayer, they were also women of faith.

In no time we received enough for the deposit but where on earth were we to get a mortgage? Again, I have no recollection who it was who told me about a lovely Christian brother who worked for The Nationwide Building Society. Apparently, he was a senior figure and responsible for 8 million pounds worth of lending and, wait for it, he understood about living by faith!

I went for an interview with him and he was able to trust the Lord for us and approved a mortgage of the full amount we needed to purchase our dream, or should I say nightmare, house in Collier Row. We were so excited and thankful that the Lord is faithful and always keeps his promises. I am also glad to say that we never failed to make the regular monthly mortgage repayments - not sure if that was down to the managers faith or ours! Most likely it was just down to the Lord's incredible kindness to needy souls like us!

Bible smuggling

During our time in Hadleigh with my mum, I found myself drawn into my first significant international trip. I greatly admired the story of Brother Andrew and his Open Doors organisation. I loved the fact that he refused to accept that any door or *iron curtain*, could keep him from going where God told him to go. I also admired Peter Lyne, a young man from Bristol I was beginning to build a relationship with as we shared a similar vision. As a Baptist he was filled with the Holy Spirit and wanted to follow the Spirit wherever the Spirit led.

He had given his life over to serving God and was praying and asking the Lord what was on the agenda when, one morning, he received a letter from a young student asking him to visit Norway. The young man, Tore Lende, felt it was extremely important for him to visit Norway at this time. However, he had no money to pay his fare and could not guarantee that he would receive any ministry gifts.

However, having received this invitation Pete writes:

> *'I'm ashamed to say, I laughed when I read this. So much so that when I met my prayer partners that evening, I read the letter to them, and we all laughed together. I really didn't take this unusual request seriously. The next morning, I had a huge surprise! (How does the Lord orchestrate these things?) A copy of our newspaper, the Daily Telegraph, landed on our doormat along with the new, weekend colour supplement. This magazine was spread out on my desk, and I was just flicking through the pages when I reached the back cover. The whole of this cover was a magnificent, alpine-like snow scene with the bold words emblazoned across it: Consider Norway for a minute!*
>
> *In moments I was on my knees by my bed with the picture spread out before me as I asked the Lord for forgiveness that I had treated this matter so disdainfully.'*

Pete didn't have a great deal of money but there was enough to buy a one-way ticket to Norway which left him with a few shillings in his pocket. Now, Tore was fluent in English and immediately made a connection with Pete and suggested that he should take him around to meet some of his Christian friends. So it was that doors opened for Pete to share his testimony and speak in various situations for the next couple of weeks, and when he was needed Tore was there to translate. When Pete returned to the UK he had been given enough money to cover all his expenses and buy a one-way ticket home. Pete shared this story with me and said that he wanted to go back to Norway soon.

Meanwhile, I had a vision to follow in the footsteps of Brother Andrew and take bibles into Eastern Europe. So Pete and I agreed to take a trip to Poland in my newly acquired Ford Cortina, having been advised that the saints there were keen to get Russian bibles to distribute to the soldiers who were posted there. We would then motor up through Scandinavia and I would drop Pete off in Oslo for his time in Norway before driving back to Essex, and he would get the ferry back to the UK.

This trip was the first of three that I was to make to Poland and the latter two were not without incident as you will see. This is also where I find myself bitterly disappointed that I didn't keep a journal of my travels, where I went and the people I met. However, on reflection, I reckon it might save my readers from the kind of boring detail that only serves to satisfy my need to ensure that I leave nothing and no one out of the story.

Suffice it to say that we had an amazing time and met some wonderful people. The communist party did not allow the registration of multiple denominations or independent churches so, basically, the Protestants were lumped together and the Catholics, being by far the largest group, were allowed to retain their identity. This meant there was a great deal of co-operation among groups which would not normally work together. Furthermore, the Catholic church retained a huge following as it was the best way for people to express their anti-communist feelings. Thus, we found that Christians from all sides were very open to hear what God was doing elsewhere in the world and we were welcomed everywhere we went. We spoke in homes, church meetings, young people's groups and bible colleges and we had no trouble in finding people who were happy to receive the bibles we brought to pass on to the soldiers. In fact, we heard that some of them were smuggled across borders into Russia itself.

The Poles had a great sense of humour and were also very adept at finding ways around the restrictions placed upon them. For example, in Krakow we met Joseph, a lovely Jewish Christian who managed, not only to survive, but worked publishing Christian books. The authorities were desperate to control the activities of such people, so he was only permitted to print two or three books a year.

Joseph scurried away and returned proudly bearing his most recent production. It was a huge tome of over 500 pages in small print and my first reaction was to think who on earth would want to read this? He then went on to explain that this book contained five other books, each one having had the chapter headings removed and made into a chapter of its own. In this way he was able to get much needed literature out to his many hungry readers who were not at all put off by the size of the volume.

My second visit to Poland I made on my own as the youth groups we had shared in asked if I would go back to their summer music camp. I made the point that I didn't have a great deal to contribute at a music camp as I was not a musician. However, it was not a musician that they required and I learned that the music camp was simply a cover for a young people's bible week which was not permitted at that time. Thus, my journey to the Gdansk youth camp took place and the Lord was present in a very real way as I had the privilege of ministering to these hungry youngsters and praying for them.

Now I have to confess that I have not seen many, what I call, truly remarkable miracles in my life. Nevertheless, during the lengthy trek home from Gdansk to Hadleigh, I had the most amazing experiences which dug me out of what could have been a very nasty hole!

My Ford Cortina came to a halt in a small town in the middle of nowhere with steam pouring out from under the bonnet. My limited knowledge of the inner working of cars led me to realise that the radiator was leaking. I waited for it to cool down and, fortunately, I had enough tools in the boot to begin to take the radiator out but no idea as to what I would do then.

As I lifted the radiator out, I saw that a young lad had been watching. He signalled to me quite clearly to follow him. He led me down a couple of streets to what I could see was a workshop. I stepped inside and there was some kind of mechanic standing there in his overalls with blow lamp in one hand and a soldering iron in the other. 'Hallelujah,' was my immediate reaction. 'It's a miracle, thank you Jesus!' I laid the radiator on his work bench and he picked up a wire brush to clean around the hole from which the water had poured out. I did feel that his cleaning was rather vigorous, but what do I know? After the solder was applied, I paid the man making every effort to convey my appreciation by bowing, shaking his hand at length and shouting my thanks in English with what I thought might be a Polish accent. I then went back to where the car was parked and I put the radiator back and proceeded to fill it up with water again.

Once ready for the off, I took a peep under the car to make sure all was well and to my dismay and shock horror, water was still pouring out on to the ground. At this point I had no idea what to do except panic and then do the very last thing I should have done. Sobbing, I got into the car with tears streaming down my cheeks, started the engine and began to drive, and drive, and drive...

I drove to the checkpoint, showed my passport, and drove out into the *free* world! I went on through Germany and then on to the ferry terminal where I queued to start the last leg of my journey. Elated, I disembarked and motored on to Hadleigh and my beloved Christine and our five fantastic kids. I cannot describe how grateful I was to God that he got me home and I didn't expect anyone, apart from one or two close friends, to believe me, and I wouldn't blame you for doubting either.

However, I know what I saw and that puddle under the car was definitely not a mirage......

My third trip to Poland was to include a visit to Czechoslovakia, as it was called then. My Baptist pastor friend, Barney Coombs, had written a testimony booklet which he had translated into Czech and had produced 5000 copies which he wanted delivered to a contact in Bruno, if I felt able to help. That was a lot of booklets to be sure!

As it happened, Fountain Trust's Geoffrey Gould, had just purchased a brand new Volvo which, when the seats were put down, the floor in the back opened up to reveal a long shallow storage space which would happily hold all the parcels of the 5000 booklets and you wouldn't even know they were there. Of course, such a vehicle had never been seen by most people behind the iron curtain, so there was every chance we would get them through to their destination. We agreed to take the booklets for Barney and he was delighted.

Before we set off, we packed our own cases and filled them with Russian bibles and also a generous supply of clothing for some of the poorer people we were going to meet on our journey through Poland. As we approached the Polish border, I became increasingly uncomfortable about the number of bibles we had stacked away in our belongings. I told Geoffrey how I was feeling and suggested we left some behind for others to take through.

Geoffrey's lightning response was, 'Well, let's just pray about that shall we?' He bowed his head and prayed, 'Dear Lord Jesus please show us what we should do about John's concerns'. After a short time he sat up and assured me that everything would be fine and there was no need to worry about a thing. However, I was not convinced and to my shame, even though I planned the trip and Geoffrey was there at my invitation, because I did not want to cause friction between us, I did not object.

Thus it was that we arrived at the border control and were immediately asked to open our cases. First out of my case was some ladies clothing and the guard eyed me with a sly grin. I looked somewhat sheepish and knowing a little German from my school days muttered, 'Meine schvester' translated, 'my sister'. Whilst he maintained a sceptical smirk, he seemed to accept what I said or perhaps he was not too worried about the lady's clothes.

He then delved deeper into my case and out came a bible. His smirk turned to a frown and he growled, 'biblia!' Then, as he flicked the pages he went on and growled, 'Rosyjski biblia!' Leaving me in no doubt what he meant, he and his colleague went through all our luggage with a fine toothcomb making a rather large pile of the offending literature which they carried away leaving us just sitting there wondering what would happen next.

After what seemed like an age our man returned and sat down and to our great relief said, 'Soon you may go'. We thanked him profusely and now it seemed he wanted to chat. 'Parker fountain pens are very good!' he said. I replied wanting to humour him, 'Yes,' I said, 'they are very popular in England and people love them.' With that he left and again we waited, and waited.

After another lengthy period he came back, 'Soon you may go, Parker pens are very good!' he repeated. At last, the penny dropped. 'Yes, indeed,' I said and turning to Geoffrey I pointed to the Parker pen which was clearly displayed in his top pocket and said, 'Geoffrey, why don't you give the nice man your Parker pen?' which he duly handed over. 'Now you may go,' he told us without so much as a 'Thank you'. We climbed into the Volvo, started the engine up and drove away deeply thankful to God that we had been released with Barney's 5000 booklets just where we had placed them before we left the UK!

We drove on in silence as I mouthed without making a sound that, 'The car may be bugged!' When we felt we were well clear of the border control we stopped and got out of the car. I put my finger to my lips to indicate that we should still remain quiet. After walking 800 yards from the vehicle, I told Geoffrey that I had heard (probably in some spy movie) that the bugs they use could pick up conversations at a great distance.

It took a while but eventually we came to realise that Poles were fairly relaxed about people like us. They didn't like the Russians anyway and it was most likely that our bibles were sold for a handsome profit and so found their way into the hands of the very people they were meant for. There were no further incidents and the rest of our time in Poland went according to plan. We shared the love of Jesus and the power of the Holy Spirit in homes, gatherings and with young people, all eager to have fellowship and hear what was happening in house churches and in the Renewal movement back home.

And so on to the final part of our journey and Czechoslovakia.

We crossed the border without any trouble and found our way to meet with Barney's contact. He was a pastor and a lovely man of God who had suffered for his faith and that light shone out of his eyes. We offloaded our precious cargo which he was delighted to receive. After some refreshment we were ready to leave him and find a guest house while we were in his town.

When we asked where we would find a suitable place to stay. He insisted, 'You will stay here with me in my home!' We knew he had spent time in prison and so we pressed him saying we did not want him to risk more trouble and further imprisonment. We made it very clear that we did not want to cause him any kind of problem and we were happy to stay elsewhere.

At this he threw his arms in the air and shouted, 'My friends, I have been to prison once for seven years and I am ready to go there again! You will stay here in my home with me and my family'. We could not argue with this, of course, we didn't want him to go back to prison but we didn't have the courage to tell him that we were not quite so ready for a time in a Czech jail. We pictured our families waiting for us to get home so we kept our heads down and prayed like mad. During our short stay in Bruno, we heard many stories of courageous Christians, known to the pastor, who suffered serious persecution under the Communist regime. This made us extremely grateful for the level of freedom which we enjoyed back home in the UK which most of us took for granted.

After completing this section of my journeys in Eastern Europe, I found an old address list with all my overseas contacts at the time. Thumbing through it I saw the dozens of Polish addresses I visited. It reminded me, that apart from the many home groups where I ministered and stayed, I also visited churches, bible schools, youth groups and even a Catholic seminary in Krakow where young men were training for the priesthood. I do recall how hungry they were for more of the Holy Spirit How privileged we were to be able to share God's heart for his people with those who lived in such restrictive circumstances.

- *Yugoslavia – kids and all!* -

Our final venture into the realm of bible smuggling involved the whole family. I had received a request for Russian bibles from Peter Kuzmic, a contact in the old Yugoslavia. Christine's mum and dad were keen to get us all to go on holiday with them and when they heard that we were having a long break driving through Europe, they said they would book us into a hotel in the beautiful city of Dubrovnik for a couple of weeks. We jumped at the chance!

So we bought some thick foam, put the back seats of the Cortina down and cut the foam to shape to fit through the whole of the back of the car. Obviously, Christine and I would sit in the front and a large roof rack would hold a tent and all our other luggage. My son, Matthew, said to me recently, that he remembers watching us take the door panels off so that we could fill all the vacant space up with bibles and then the fools who rush in where angels fear to tread, set off on their six-week adventure.

Christine took the complete series of Narnia books to read to the kids for the long boring parts of the journey and that worked a treat. Of course, if we tried such a thing these days we would be banned and receive a hefty fine for breaking all the health and safety rules but hey, that was then.

Amazingly, everything went swimmingly as we travelled through areas of great natural beauty and stunning views until we got to Zagreb where we successfully offloaded the bibles. Then, after good fellowship with our friends, we started the final leg of our outward journey.

Up to this point the roads had been pretty good to excellent and as we made our way towards the coastal road and the seven-hour journey to Dubrovnik, I saw a beautiful new road which gave us a much shorter mileage to our destination. The fact that there was not another vehicle in sight and that there were no road markings was strange but we went full steam ahead until... until that beautiful new road, came to an abrupt end. What stretched before us was a bumpy, unmade route across the mountain.

Now, I am not the kind of person who turns round and goes back, I do not like to admit defeat, so we pressed onwards and upwards. Well, it was a lovely day and the views were spectacular and we stopped by a crystal-clear stream for lunch and in no time the kids had their shoes and socks off and were having great fun splashing about in the water. Now, I do believe in angels but if the old man who suddenly appeared from nowhere was an angel, he could not speak English but he was great at sign language. He pointed his finger at the kids and then at the water and then wiggled it from side to side whilst making a hissing sound. I did not need any further explanation. I shouted to the kids to get out of the water immediately and turned to old man and shook his hand repeatedly to indicate how much I appreciated his intervention. There was no building of any kind to be seen but he trundled off and seemed to disappear as quickly as he showed up.

Even now, after all these years, I shudder to think what would have happened if one of the kids was bitten by a venomous snake in the middle of nowhere and hours away from any kind of help.

So it was that our seven-hour journey became more like ten hours but we did finally get to meet up with Stan and Florrie, Christine's mum and dad, and had a wonderful time and lots of fun in historic Dubrovnik, before making the long trek back home. Thankfully, the return journey went largely without incident. Although it is worth saying that Christine, our intrepid map reader, did manage to direct us into the wrong country at one point. Fortunately, I discovered this when I tried to change some money and heard Italian being spoken not the Swiss I was expecting.

The other scary thing that happened was, as we were making a long descent from a high point in the Alps, I suddenly found that my brake pedal was not having any effect. I quickly changed down in the gears, grabbed the handbrake and managed to slow down enough to glide onto the forecourt of a garage which conveniently appeared on my side of the road. Shaking, I got out of the car and found a mechanic who had obviously had experience of such an event which had happened before.

He explained that the constant use of the brakes as we were coming down the steep windy hills caused the brake fluid to boil and become gas, this rendered the brakes useless! I had never heard of such a thing, but he went on to assure me that if I waited until the fluid cooled down, it would be absolutely fine to carry on. Which, of course, we did but in a much more cautious manner, and I am glad to say that we got back to dear old Blighty all in one piece and very thankful that the angels had done a pretty good job for us!

CHAPTER SIX

CHURCH GROWTH AND OPEN DOORS

We did not get the keys to 24 Wilton Drive, Collier Row, Romford, until November 1969. However, our dear friends, Jan and Richard Menlove, invited us to move into their lovely home with them so that the kids could start the autumn term at their new school. That's real friendship for you but I am sure they were greatly relieved when we were finally able to move across into our new home.

We were all very excited about the prospect of being reunited with our treasured possessions which had been in store for over two years. The big van drew up outside the house and we watched the furniture and the many boxes being unloaded. Christine and I were keeping a special eye open for the children's toy box. You see, we had spent every last penny on the move and didn't have a bean left. Oh, the joy when we saw it being lifted out.

We immediately took it aside and opened it up to search for the all important, money box which we had to raid in order to be able to give the removal men a £5 tip before they drove away, leaving us to unpack the rest of our belongings. It may seem strange to you, but giving that tip to the men as they left brought closure for us on what was a special time of learning to trust through some very challenging days. It also opened an exciting new door of opportunity to develop the vision of simple church which the Lord had given to us.

It was not long before things began to come together. The group we left behind under the watchful eye of Ken and Maureen Rose in Seven Kings, flourished as they opened their home so that friendship, fellowship and meetings could continue. Then the Dartford students, who had maintained their relationship with us, began to join us at weekends. Also, a number of people who had contact with us before we left, and were hungry for something fresh, heard we were up and running and came along and sensed that God was with us.

It soon became clear that getting together for meetings and meals together in one another's homes was not enough for most people. We wanted more and the next thing was to move closer to one another. Christine and I have always kept an open home for those we sensed God was joining to us. Christine loved having a full house and I coped well as long as I had personal space I could retire to. Obviously, with all that was going on we had to face the fact that we needed more space in our little five-bedroom home. We shared our thoughts with others and the group decided to get behind us and share the work and with the help of our builder neighbour, Chas Stanley, who lived opposite, we went ahead and we all pulled together.

One of our number, Mike Kidd, was working in a factory which was being demolished and he found us some reclaimed parquet flooring and six beautiful old gas lamps which we converted for our new lounge. Nick Butterworth built us two super cedar wood tables for the dining room which we still have today. Many others sacrificed time and energy to take on much of the hard graft which had to be done. However, I can't move on without commenting on the incredible commitment of Keith Brown who worked tirelessly helping me with so many of his building skills.

So, our extension to number 24 gave us seven bedrooms and six reception rooms plus a sauna. So, the five bedrooms housed an extra eight people living with us plus our seven, made a total of 15. Many of these went on into ministry or church leadership and are still in touch with us today. Remember, we had just one bathroom at that time and the loo was in the bathroom. So it was a question of first up got the bathroom and then you waited on the nearest stair in a queue for your turn. That was when I learned to lie in bed and let them all get up and go off to work before I rose and usually had to suffer a cold shower unless I was prepared to wait for the water to heat up again.

Ken and Maureen were among the first to move lock, stock and barrel into Wilton Drive but others soon followed and we all kept watch for the next house that came onto the market. Eventually, there were over 200 of us living within around four hundred yards of one another and we learned to share and support one another in so many ways. Not everyone had a car for example, not everyone had a lawn mower but such things were never a problem as no one counted what they had as being their own but gifts the Lord had given them to share with others.

During our whole time in Collier Row, Christine and I maintained an open house. Open in the sense that, if someone needed accommodation, we would pray and share this with the family and those living with us at the time and if everyone, including the kids, were happy we made room for the newcomer. We did this because while we were in Goodmayes we made one or two unwise decisions which taught us to be more discerning.

In 1973 Cathy Witt approached us as her parents had to move out of the area and she had friends in the fellowship and the local school and she wanted to finish her schooling with them. She fitted into the family so well that she never left us and although she was older than our son Matthew, they fell in love. They came to Christine and me to ask what they should do. I think most people would have had a rather negative reaction due to the age difference but we had learned that God is not the God of convention and He moves in strange ways, so we prayed and felt the relationship was right but that they should wait, which they accepted. So it was, that in February 1979, after they had waited patiently Matt and Cathy were married. It was a wonderful wedding! They did the legal bit some days before and then, on the day, we had a great time bringing them before the Lord followed by a sumptuous feast, all prepared by folk in the church. After this we sang and danced into the night. Cathy's parents were not too happy about the situation but they did come and I believe they were overwhelmed by the support people gave them. As time passed they came to really appreciate Matthew and often came to stay with us right up to the time her dad passed away at 93.

Cathy and Matthew have lived with us ever since and have watched over the home family when we have been away. Matthew learned to operate a huge Heidelberg print machine and developed a successful print business until we moved from Romford to Surrey. Then, as we prayed about what to do about the business because there was no way we could move it to Surrey, the Lord answered by fire! Some kids broke into the print shop and set the place alight and it all went up in smoke. We had no insurance, so we thanked the Lord and moved on and, being a jack of all trades, Matthew started a painting and decorating business and, being a perfectionist, he is never without work. A few years back he extended our house to give us seven bedrooms. There are just six houses in our road and they've all employed Matt to do major work on their homes.

Recently, when we were thinking about Christine and her legacy after she passed away, Cathy spent some time working on a list of all the people who lived with us at our home in Collier Row. She gave up after she passed fifty and we know there were some she missed. Christine loved being surrounded by people and I was perfectly happy about that as long as I had my study where I could find some space.

Once the Dartford students finished their courses many of them went to areas where they knew there were groups being established similar to our fellowship. However, some linked in with us including Gill Metcalfe, one of their lecturers, before moving on. Others stayed with us and found love! Anita Helps married Ian Traynar; Lin Vincent hooked up with Steve Milton; Gill Pearson was swept off her feet by Dave Paul and Pat Barton married Dave Bilbrough.

Phil Jones, who was the first male student at the college, married Steph Spencer and spent a year with my friend Jim Holl who led a church in Bromley before moving to Lancashire and planting a link church in Rossendale. Later he moved down the road to Harlow where he planted another church and worked with churches across the area before emigrating with his family to Canada. Furthermore, we are still in touch with them all as, thankfully, so many of our relationships have stood the test of time.

Another divine connection arranged by the Holy Spirit was with a young people's group attached to a large Baptist church in the Romford town centre. Here I have to say that it was not our policy to encourage people to leave their churches. In fact, we pulled a group of denominational leaders together from across the area which we led for years of cooperation in monthly All Saints Nights, a tent mission followed by a great March for Jesus through the town centre in 1976. For the mission we asked Dave Bilbrough to write a song for us and he came up with, *Let There Be Love Shared Among Us*, a wonderful chorus which found its way into many denominational hymn books and is still sung today.

It is true, however, that many people did leave their churches when there was strong opposition to the Renewal and the work of the Holy Spirit. So, back to the Baptist youth group. They were a truly lovely bunch and hugely talented and creative with professional artists, musicians and many who were willing to experiment in dance, drama, poetry, etc. When we first met them, I remember they had a weekly fun evening where they took it in turns to read *Winnie the Pooh* stories to one another. They were so open to God and one of their leaders was a guy called Nick Butterworth, a gifted children's book illustrator. Today, his books will be found on bookshelves all over the world as they have been translated into multiple languages. Nick became a prime mover in the growth and development of the House Church Movement when he linked up with Graham Perrins to produce Fulness Magazine, which subscribers eagerly waited for each edition.

The short story is that the group linked in with us as one of a number of, call them, House Churches, which were springing up throughout the area. This growth brought us to the point where we realised that, whilst these groups were growing and enjoying fellowship and meals together, there was a need for all of us to come together for praise, worship and teaching. Thus, our first such gathering was held in the Cauliflower public house upper room and continued every Sunday evening. We continued to grow with my guardsman friend, John West, from Dagenham joining us.

I well remember one Sunday evening when our worship was in full swing and there was lots of praise and dancing, I popped downstairs to the loo and I overheard the landlord on the phone talking to his wife. 'They're up there again this evening,' he said, 'and they're making more noise than those in the saloon bar and they've not had a drop to drink!'

We also discovered that the son of another local Baptist pastor came to check us out with a list of negative things he had heard about us. It was years later that I learned he found none of the things on his list were true when I met him at that great Christian annual event known as Spring Harvest where he, now the Reverend Ian Coffey, was also a guest speaker!

It seemed that the Baptist churches in the area were keen to discover what was happening in that upper room. On this particular Sunday we decided to give the kids a treat as they all piled in to join with us on Sunday evenings. We got them there early and found an old black and white film of Laurel and Hardy. This ran a little over time and Baptist groups came in with their huge black bibles under their arms just as Hardy was hanging from Laurel's braces out of the window near the top of a skyscraper. They took one look at the screen, did an about turn and were never seen again. However, we had a very special meeting that evening as clearly the Holy Spirit had not been offended by our efforts to have fun with our children.

Our numbers increased further when my Pentecostal friend, John West, living in Dagenham, came along with a small group which had been meeting in his front room. This eventually led to our first church plant into the Railway Arms public house in John's area where the young Dave Bilbrough led the worship with a team of musicians.

Whilst we were still living in Goodmayes, I was approached by a small Shaftesbury Mission which met in a rather nice building in Chadwell Heath to take on the role of Pastor. I didn't feel I was suitable for the job and so I recommended my friend Norman Barnes. Norman took his mum, a deeply spiritual woman, to look round the place and once inside she cried out, 'I saw this exact place in a dream and I am sure you should apply son'. Norman did apply and he was accepted. I was thrilled and often went to support him with the family.

However, when we moved to Dartford, Norman and Grace, who were both from a fairly strict Pentecostal background, had introduced some pretty strict rules about women's apparel in meetings. Hats had to be worn and were available at the door and ladies were requested not to wear trousers. On the other hand, there was a much freer approach in our gatherings and no such demands were made. Sadly, this resulted in a rift growing between us and they would not join with us in any joint gatherings.

Now while we were in Dartford, Anita, one of the students introduced me to Maurice Smith, who had ministered in her home fellowship in Bristol. Maurice was a great guy whose passion was sharing on the grace of God. He had been converted at a Billy Graham Crusade on the 5th of May 1955. Maurice understood that the number 5 in scripture signified grace, thus his testimony is recorded in his book, entitled *5.5.55*! Maurice and I struck up a friendship which ultimately resulted in him moving with his family into Collier Row.

I mention my link with Maurice at this point, because it was he who persuaded Norman to meet with us to pray about our differences. We came together at the Mission and shared frankly about our sadness that we could not meet or work together. All I can say is that the Holy Spirit was present and Norman, most graciously, gave a full apology and we were able to embrace and move forward as Grace did not stand in the way. This was a triumph for good and meant that we had years of fruitful ministry both in fellowship and working in team together in many countries across the world.

- Learning to live with my limitations and play to my strengths -

An important part of my own development was accepting my limitations and discovering my strengths.

Early on in my ministry, I remember being most impressed seeing my friend Roger Forster's wide-margin bible. It was thick with tiny writing in the margins in different coloured inks. So having purchased all the necessary equipment which included the wide-margin bible, inks and pens, I sat down at my desk all ready to go. The only trouble is that I couldn't think what to write. I mumbled some prayer to the Lord like, 'What's going on Lord?' and was surprised to get an immediate reply, 'Son, you've forgotten something!' 'What's that Lord?' say I. 'The brain son, you've forgotten the brain!' says the Lord, and he went on, 'Furthermore, I only want one Roger Forster but I also happen to want one John Noble!' That was a great relief to me and being more at peace, I was able to move on to be myself.

Another great lesson came when, as those who were supposed to *live by faith*, we were often given things, some of which I think came as some people were just trying to get shot of them. Thus, we had been given an old washing machine to help us out with the piles of washing we accumulated. We placed the machine in its place under the working surface and switched it on. It immediately began a noisy, evil dance around the kitchen and I tried, unsuccessfully, to hold it down. I called to Christine to come, *with her superior weight* and sit on it, but that failed and it continued its manic movement and only served to give me a disgruntled wife to add to the problem.

Finally, it breathed its last and proceeded to open its huge eye and poured the contents all over the kitchen floor. As a responsible husband, it obviously fell to me to tame and repair the beast. So it was down the garden to our large shed to find the necessary tools for the repair only to discover, that after emptying the whole contents of the shed on to the lawn, that the all important hammer required to beat the beast into submission was missing. After several phone calls which upset neighbours and left them feeling they had been accused of failing to return said hammer, I found it in the loft where I had left it after I last used it.

Then, returning to my task and taking the machine apart and putting it back together, I found I had bits of machine left over. After crying out in prayer to the Lord for help, which I should have done at the start of the incident, I heard the Lord clearly speaking just two words, 'Yellow pages!' So I found the directory and turned to the page headed, 'Household appliance repairers' and discovered that there were lists of people with the special gift of mending washing machines!

Oh, the joy of this discovery! There and then I vowed never to do any such jobs again. Christine pointed out that it would cost money but I assured her, that as a responsible husband, I could trust God for the money and avoid all the pain of attempting what was impossible for me. That changed my life and saved me hours of unnecessary pain for the rest of my days.

On the matter of my strengths, as time passed, I found that I was able to make relationships which enabled me to bring men and women together of greater gifts than mine. This provided a forum where we could all work together. And in this way our Team Spirit emerged and we began to serve the wider church together. This gift had been overlooked at school where, despite my lack of academic ability, I was chosen by the boys to become form captain. I went on to see that my gift made me a good chairperson, which I can now see was the reason I was elected to take the chair of the Charismatic Leaders Conference for over twenty years.

- *Creativity* -

With so much joy and freedom in our gatherings and fresh revelation about the simplicity of church and our calling to reflect the character of Jesus in our lives together, it is easy to understand why there was such an amazing outbreak of creativity. For example, there was a steady flow of new songs as worship leaders listened to Spirit-inspired ministry and then put what they heard into words and music. It was fascinating to see that while some church leaders were suspicious of our teaching and advised people against us, the songs found their way into the mainstream of church life.

Bob Gillman's *Bind us Together* literally flowed around the world, translated into a multitude of languages even in far-flung corners of the globe. In 1984 at the Catholic World Youth Holy Spirit Renewal Celebration Day, Pope John Paul sang it with around 300,000 gathered in St Peter's Square as they joined hands swaying from side to side in worship. John Kennet's, *Praise Him on the Trumpet, Psaltery and Harp*; Ian Traynar's, *We are Being Built into a Temple*; Dave Bilbrough's, *An Army of Ordinary People*; Dave Bryant's, *Jesus Take Me as I Am* and many, many more were taken from other groups and fellowships. For example, Belfast's Ronnie Wilson's great hymn, *I Hear the Sound of Rustling in the Leaves of the Trees*, all led us to produce the *Hallelujah* song sheets and music books which were widely circulated here in the UK and found their way around the world.

Our first stab at recording these songs was masterminded by our wonderful pianist and worship leader, John Menlove, and a team of technicians who set up a studio in our front room. The result was a series of tapes, *Fruit Salad 1 & 2* and *Fresh Fruit Salad* which, although we were relatively unknown, sold well over 2,000 copies each. It was shortly after this that the lovely Geoff Shearn at Kingsway Music began work with John and, apart from our worship leaders producing their own records, the *Songs of Fellowship* series was born and ran for many years under Geoff's watchful eye.

However, it was not only songs that changed the way we worshipped but also movement, dance, drama and other forms of art which flourished. Christine was a prime mover here as she gathered a group of talented young women and men who were open to the Holy Spirit and willing to experiment. As they talked, prayed and worked together their efforts and those of folk like Nigel Goodwin, whose Arts Centre is still functioning, and later, Riding Lights from York, inspired a generation to use all their talents to glorify God.

Those of my readers who were around at the time may remember the moving performance of *The Prodigal Son* at one of our packed Albert Hall meetings. On the platform the father looks longingly into the distance hoping, praying for his boy to return. Through an entrance at the front of the hall the son appears fearful and hesitant. As soon as the father sees the son, he runs out into the audience grabs the boy in his arms weeping with joy. There were not many dry eyes in the house that night.

Gerald Coates used to ring up Christine to tell her what he was going to speak about before a meeting and the team would come up with something to illustrate his talk. One evening at the Methodist Central Hall in Westminster, he advised her that his talk was to be about the saints breaking out of their shells and working together and the team came up with *Boxes*. This opened with Christine as the narrator singing *You in Your Small Corner*, and the group were all in, what appeared to be, glass boxes, each doing their own thing. Some were playing their instruments to different tunes, one guy was preaching, another praying, one was exercising and another polishing the glass and so on. Christine shouts, 'No, this is not right!' and proceeds to encourage them to break out and to find one another. So that the musicians began playing the same tune and those exercising moved in time and soon a meeting was in full flow. There was lots of laughter and clapping from the audience.

Then one person was shocked to discover a glass wall between the platform and the congregation which they tried to break open but failed. So each one went and grabbed the rest of the team and together we ran forward and blew the barrier down and we all went running down off the platform to hug people watching. Now, the applause was thunderous and Gerald's talk went down a storm.

One of the most inspiring prophetic scripture readings Christine did with the team, was Ezekiel's vision of Dry Bones. I wouldn't attempt to describe this but we managed to find a recording of this piece and we played it at the celebration on Christine's life held at the Leatherhead Theatre in July 2022. You should be able to access this on YouTube.[1] It makes the hairs on the back of your head stand up – it's electric!

She would also encourage artists to paint with colour during worship and individual dancers to move out in spontaneous prophetic dance and ribbon and flag dancers too. From his early days she encouraged the much-loved Andy Au, and he can be seen on the celebration video mentioned above. She gathered a team, which included Andy and our own granddaughter Victoria, to train the 300 dancers to support Noel Richards at his amazing *Champion of the World* praise day at Wembley Stadium in 1997.

I remember one meeting where she was asked to speak on eating disorders and she took a sculptor with her. While she was sharing, he put together a screaming image made with sticks representing anorexia and a large image made from chicken wire plastered with margarine to represent bulimia. At the end she offered to pray for people and they streamed forward many weeping.

I could go on but finally, let me say that she directed mime artist Bill Angel in a TV play and many other performances and, of all things, a Passion Play, put on by one of our churches in Norway. She took her dance teacher friend, Shash Rault with her to help. Neither of them spoke Norwegian but the Norwegians have excellent English. The play was put on for a week locally but it was so successful that they took it to the capital, Oslo, for a week as well!

---

[1] https://youtu.be/E3D4Ld5ch-8.

- *Education* -

Our understanding of how, as God's people, we should influence the community in which we lived was quite simple. We accepted the fact that scripture, and indeed Jesus himself, urged us to be living as salt and light. We took this to mean that, as salt being hidden, our very presence in all aspects of the life of the community in which we were able to engage, should itself have an effect because of the way that we behaved. On the other hand, light is set on a lampstand and should be visible, shining out and confirming our message and displaying our values.

So, in terms of education, having many teachers in the fellowship, as salt we encouraged them to seek posts in the local comprehensive school which was just a mile or so from the area where most of us lived. Of course, it was not long before we had a dozen or so who managed to find employment there. This was a double blessing in that, firstly, it meant that we were in touch with 1200 children, most of whom lived quite close to the fellowship. Secondly, it meant that our own children who were at the school could see familiar faces in the corridors and classrooms.

Then in 1980, as light, we felt it was time to start a school of our own and, thanks to Norman and Grace Barnes, the Chadwell Heath Christian Mission opened their doors to us and Acorn School was born. The fact is, that under our founder Anita's Traynar's leadership, Acorn was the first independent Christian school in this country to launch without using the Accelerated Christian Education (ACE) curriculum. We wanted a school where each child was treated individually and were not lumped together in a one-size-fits-all system. We also wanted them to learn the basic lessons of life which every adult faces but are seldom given a mention in your average state school.

Interestingly, Norman and Grace were so impressed by what they saw that they followed by starting their own Mountain Ash School, when we moved on to premises closer to our community. Thus it was that Daryl Martin, one of our leaders, took on the challenging task of finding suitable premises. He did a fantastic job in locating a hall which had been used by a small independent church which, with skilful negotiating and considerable elbow grease, became the new home of Acorn School with Anita expanding the work.

Later, after the initial success, and the need for more space, Acorn School became Immanuel School and moved to much larger accommodation with plenty of grounds where the children could play. I am delighted to say that, in 2020 with the church then under the leadership of Peter Taylor, the son of a previous leader, Paul, the school celebrated its 40th anniversary at which I was privileged to take part.

Peter and his team have done an amazing job as they have trusted the Lord through the monumental challenges of maintaining a school like this in the current climate. When I arrived at the school after so many years, I was blessed to see gardens in such good order and the various improvements which had been made to the buildings. I also learned that an increased number of black and Asian people are sending their children to the school as they consider a good Christian education for their kids of primary importance at this time.

- *Collier Row Working Men's club* -

When the local Lawns Way Working Men's Club ran out of money and shut down, we saw it as another opportunity to be light and engage with the community on their own ground. The club had been sadly neglected for many years and needed a complete refurbishment. Again, it was Daryl Martin who agreed to take the project on and with his wife, Joan, he put in the finance needed to bring it up to standard. The tenancy agreement with Ind Coope, the local brewer, was signed by Daryl in partnership with Dave Matthews. By this time Dave had joined us with his wife and family from Belfast and was there to represent the fellowship. Everyone gave their wholehearted support and pulled together to keep the costs down.

Indeed, one brother, went on a crash course to learn how to operate licensed premises! Within a few months of hard work, the club was opened much to the delight of the local community who came in their numbers from the start. We met the darts teams, the pigeon racers and discovered many other activities which went on in the area. The church met in the main bar on Sunday mornings, but had to finish by noon so that the club could open for business. In fact, many came early and listened in at the end of the meeting.

Dave and Daryl, supported by Jim our manager, enjoyed a couple of years getting to know the locals and forging friendships. However, eventually they began to see the elephant in the room. Club membership was acquired for an annual fee for which the members got access to cheap beer and spirits. We never did intend to make a profit but then the gaming machines arrived. Sensibly, pubs were restricted to a top prize of around £10, whereas members clubs could have prize money up to £100 which was a lot in those days.

Without properly thinking it through the team introduced a machine with a £50 jackpot to see what would happen. Immediately, takings and profits went through the roof but at a cost. Members stood there, glassy eyed, night after night and poured their hard-earned wages into that machine. After a couple of months, we felt we had to remove it and without this income stream the club would only be viable if the church put money into it. Reluctantly, we took the decision to hand the club over to Jim the manager who, sadly, by then had left the church. The day he took over, he had two machines brought with a £100 limit and he never looked back. In no time at all he became a wealthy man and was able to set up other businesses in the area but at what cost to the men and their families?

The whole experiment was both challenging and exciting and hopefully lessons were learned, particularly with regard to the fact that church and business may not always sit comfortably together. Looking back maybe the project would have been better put together by a business person from within the fellowship having sole ownership and the church standing alongside praying, advising and supporting in other ways.

- Finance -

I mentioned earlier that there was a generous spirit abroad in the group and folk not only shared their homes and goods but they were also generous financially. We did not teach tithing but rather that everything we owned including our time should be available to God. We understood that the Old Testament symbols, for example the temple, the sabbath rest and tithes were signposts pointing to a higher reality. The temple became a spiritual building made of living stones, the sabbath became a life of rest in Jesus and tithing a pointer to laying everything at the Lord's feet.

We did teach regular and spontaneous giving and to be open to the guidance of the Holy Spirit in such matters. There was no compulsion to give, just encouragement for people to be generous, and they were.

For Christine and me, having read about such men of faith as the remarkable George Muller who never spoke about money, we adopted their way of thinking and the Lord never let us down in those early years. However, the time came when, looking back, we see that the Lord wanted to expand our understanding of living by faith, which was not intended just for ministries or leaders but for the church as family.

Together with our children, we had been invited to lead an Anglican church youth weekend at a hostel in the Lake District and we were happy to oblige. It would be a nice break for the kids and dear Anita gladly offered her car so that we could drive up north to complete our mission. We arrived and settled in and received a warm welcome. Then we were presented with our ministry gift, in cash, before the first meeting. This was an answer to prayer as we had very little money with us, so now we could buy ice creams and treats for the children.

We had a great time with that crowd of teenagers and the leaders became good friends. They were using Youth Praise and some of you will remember *Can it be True the Things They say of You*, and *Christ is the Lord of the Smallest Atom* which were sung with great gusto to a slightly out-of-tune guitar. The weekend passed quickly and everyone packed their bags and piled into their minibus and cars and we waved goodbye. We thanked the couple who ran the hostel for their wonderful hospitality and got into Anita's car when disaster struck – the car just wouldn't start.

We had spent the ministry gift and had about enough left to buy petrol for the long journey home – what to do? We went indoors with the couple who knew an excellent mechanic and we explained our plight. I don't believe they were Christians but they absolutely insisted on paying for the vehicle to be repaired, saying that they completely trusted us to return the money to them. We were humbled as such a thing had never happened to us before, what was the Lord up to?

When we got back, the group were gathered round as they were keen to hear how the weekend had been. We shared our sorry story, feeling rather confused as to why the Lord seemed to have let us down but the guys appeared to be quite excited. Then it all came out. The fact is that whilst they admired the way that we trusted the Lord for our finance day by day and never spoke about money, they felt that kind of living was for special leaders and rather beyond the likes of them. They also pointed out that when an individual in a normal, loving family came under pressure it would be talked about and prayed over.

We had to admit that they were absolutely right and we realised that, inadvertently, we had robbed them of the joy of being able to share a corporate experience of living by faith. We saw that it is, indeed, true that, *God works all things together for the good of those who love him and have been called according to his purpose.* And, I have to say, that over the years those words have carried me through far deeper trials than a broken car as you will see later in our journey.

My first bank account was with Lloyds and that was in the days when Bank Managers actually managed banks! It was their job to know their customers and build relationships of trust. When we moved to Collier Row, I made a point of contact with my manager, Mr Choat, to take him out for lunch to explain what we were about. I suggested that some people who were moving into the area may choose to place their accounts with him and he was quite interested and mostly thereafter he took me out to lunch.

As time passed, I developed a positive, almost friendly, type of relationship with Mr Choat as he saw the way in which our people handled themselves. The time came when a small group felt they wanted to help one of our couples to buy their first house but, of course, they needed a deposit. I called Mr Choat to share the plan and ask for his help. The idea was that three of our couples wanted to borrow £2000 each to give the newly marrieds enough for what was, at that time, a generous deposit. As we talked, he made it quite clear that he thought this was a messy way of doing things, 'Let's not worry about that,' he said, 'We'll just make a single loan to your young couple, as I know your people will support them through their purchase'. Imagine such a thing happening in today's climate.

In the early months and years of trusting the Lord for our financial needs we decided not to take out any unnecessary insurance or provision for a pension. Now, I am not suggesting this is for everyone but we clearly felt that, if God could provide for us with five kids and nothing in our early years, then he would be well able to keep us in our latter years. So here I felt it would be helpful to share how this has been fulfilled and has also served to provide income for our ministry in poorer countries. In such places we may receive wonderful, even sacrificial, hospitality but financial giving is out of the question. In the apostle Paul's words, you could call it *tent-making*.

As a youngster I used to collect stamps and was a member of the school stamp club. Travelling home from school one day I foolishly left my album on the bus - never to be seen again. As a result of my loss, I guess I had a latent longing to start collecting again. So as the kids were growing up here was a hobby we could work on together. To be honest I am not sure if this activity was for them or for me and the reality is that as time passed they dropped out and I carried on.

As the collection grew, I inevitably gathered a considerable number of duplicates. Walking through town one day, I noticed that a camera shop had coins for sale in the window and I was struck with a bright idea. I went in, met the owner of the shop and shared my bright idea. I suggested that he might like to take some packets of stamps on a sale or return basis which could bring new customers into his shop. He readily agreed and so began what, ultimately, became a successful philatelic business which continues to the time of writing.

I soon had enough stock to start trading at some of the regular stamp fairs in, and around, the area. The beauty of such a business meant that I didn't need a shop, I thoroughly enjoyed what I was doing and I was also free to do business when it suited me. My customer base grew as I became known and the income enabled us to travel without having to consider the financial implications of being away, sometimes, for weeks at a time.

Now, over the last 10 years I have had to give my time and attention to caring for Christine through the progression of her dementia until she passed away on April 2nd 2022, and I will share more about that in a later chapter. Nevertheless, with the help of my daughters, Sharon and Ruth, I developed a very successful ebay shop which is still producing a reasonable income. This carried us through some seriously challenging times including another move with no home and negotiating the financially lean years of Christine's illness.

So I can say with great gratitude that the Lord more than fulfilled our expectation that he would provide for us in our latter years, as not only are we completely debt free but we have a beautiful home with no mortgage. God is, indeed good, very good.

The sequel to the story of my stamp business is that I gave Christine some money to buy a few things in an auction in order open a Saturday stall in Romford Market. This then led to my son, Matthew, getting into furniture restoration which Christine also sold. She got on so well with the other traders in the market that they apologised when they slipped up and swore within her earshot. They so appreciated her presence in the market that they roped her in to be their spokesperson when problems arose with the local authorities. Furthermore, it was just like her to find creative ways to witness to people who visited her stand. For example, a young Punk guy walking with his girlfriend stopped by to see what she was selling. He with his multi-coloured Mohican hair cut standing upright in the middle of his shaven head. 'What you staring at?' he growled. Like lightning, Christine responded. 'I was just looking at your amazing haircut, it's absolutely fantastic!!' she said, and then continued, 'Did you know that God actually numbers the hairs on your head and he loves you, so you have no need to worry about going bald!' 'Ow did you know that?' he said in amazement and walked on with his girl shaking his head.

Mind you, there were still lessons to be learned about money as I was quite naive. Due to my good relationship with Mr Choat at the bank and, knowing that our house stood as collateral, I felt entirely comfortable to borrow quite large sums. On one occasion I was offered a valuable stamp collection, so I popped into the bank but Mr Choat was out at lunch. The under-manager came out and asked me if he could help. I explained that I needed a loan of £5,000 which he said he was sure that would be fine, and set up the paper work which I signed and went off to do my business.

In due course the loan was repaid, no problems there. However, we also ran our large conferences and gatherings along similar lines and squared up when the event was over, and all was fine for some time. Then, one day, Christine and I were travelling home from a ministry time in the north of England when, suddenly, I was gripped by fear. I told Christine and we pulled over to pray in a layby. After we spent some time praying and asking the Lord what this was all about, I felt I knew what he was saying.

I was absolutely convinced that we were to get out of all debt, apart from our mortgage that is, and we were never to borrow again. We drove home in peace and over the next weeks and months worked until all our overdrafts and credit cards were cleared and, with God's help, we have never returned to that way of living again. Since then, I have often ministered on the subject of debt, including national debt, which at this moment in time is at an all-time high and is in danger of wrecking our nation. It is certainly true as one international banker said, 'I care not who runs a nation, the one who holds the purse strings calls the tune!'

CHAPTER SEVEN

WIDER UK AND US RELATIONSHIPS AND MINISTRY

As the Romford fellowship grew to around 600 meeting in various groups and church plants, inevitably we began to connect with other churches in Essex and beyond. There was a real hunger in many to come together and, in order to facilitate this, we arranged leaders' gatherings and began to minister in these churches. This in turn led to a network developing, which later enabled us to put on larger events and holiday conferences.

At a national level the links with other ministries and networks were also growing which meant that we developed friendships and connections in other parts of the country. I have spoken of my relationships with Arthur Wallis, and Maurice Smith and Peter Lyne. Also in Bristol I met Hugh Thompson who became a good friend. I am not sure who introduced me to Graham Perrins from Cardiff, whose great teaching gift came from his Brethren background, but we were soon visiting one another's fellowships to minister. Among others who we linked up with were George Tarleton, minister of the Congregational Church in Chingford, Gerald Coates from Cobham, Ian McCulloch ex-Brethren from Emsworth, Barney Coombs from Basingstoke Baptist and John MacLauchlan from Yeovil.

In 1972 Arthur Wallis felt led to call together some of these men for a retreat, initially, to discuss bible prophecy. The group of six included

Peter, Graham, Hugh and Bryn Jones and David Mansell all men I knew. As they prayed it became clear that the Lord had a much greater purpose for them and when Bryn Jones prophesied, 'Thrice shall you meet and seven shall be your number', they began to ask themselves who the seventh person should be. Apparently, it was a unanimous decision that I should be invited.

News quickly spread and the group became affectionately known as the Magnificent Seven. This was not a name I liked as it gave the impression that it was, in some way, elevated or special. However, it prevailed and we continued to meet and growing ever closer as we discovered that we had a common understanding of what we believed God was doing.

We had great times sharing and praying together openly and honestly. I was told on several occasions that they loved my honesty as it seemed to provoke us into a deeper level of understanding. My own conviction was that speaking the truth and sharing in love how we feel about one another's strengths and weaknesses is like iron sharpening iron, as the scripture says: *As iron sharpens iron, so one person sharpens another* (Proverbs 27:17) (NIV).

I'm not sure when it was but I remember saying to Arthur that, whilst I saw Bryn as a great gatherer and strategist, I didn't fully trust him as I felt he could be an opportunist. Arthur was shocked and said, 'You can't say that, John!' I went on to point out that I didn't trust myself or my wife, as we are all likely to have blind spots. Which is why we need one another.

As time went on, we believed that the Lord was calling us into *covenant relationships* but on reflection, although I believe that was correct, I don't think that we had fully teased out what that involved for us both personally and in our church relationships. My understanding of covenant as Jesus expressed it, was seen in his commitment to me. However, as we saw in the shepherding and discipleship movements, the emphasis became more about your commitment to one another.

WIDER UK AND US RELATIONSHIPS AND MINISTRY

At the end of our series of meetings we were convinced that others should be drawn in and after prayer and discussion we became fourteen. The additional seven were Gerald Coates, whose Pioneer team I joined much later on, Maurice Smith, who moved in with us in Romford, George Tarleton, who became my very close friend, Barney Coombs, Ian McCulloch, John MacLauchlan and Campbell McAlpine. Again, some bright spark christened the group The Fabulous Fourteen, which surely didn't help our image in the wider church scene.

I was doing some research for this period and came across an article written by a Paul Fahy of Understanding Ministries in 2009 entitled, *The British House Church Movement of the 1970s and its connection with the emergence of the Restoration Movement*. The article was comprehensive but the author had, in some way, gained a jaundiced view of what took place. And, without doing an analysis of the whole work, it was interesting to me to see how people draw conclusions from their own limited understanding of what took place.

Fahy's comment on the fourteen states that, 'In reality the fourteen had ordained themselves, by common consent, to have authority over the church in Britain at that time'. Arrogant we may have been at times, but the mind boggles at the mere mention of such a thing when one thinks of all the great men and women of God who worked across the nation then, many of whom we looked up to for their loving and sacrificial ministries.

Fahy went on to speak about our anti-denominational stance. 'Anti-denominationalism was a very loud message in the early days of Restoration, especially amongst the London Brothers. John Noble actually wrote a book called, *Forgive Us Our Denominations* in 1971. These were seen as creating disunity and were, de facto, sin. However, as leaders waned and fell, as new churches and groups emerged, in time a new, and much harder, denominationalism arose. Restorationism became a series of new denominations within a wider fold of a *restored* charismatic church. At the head of these denominations were apostles, who in reality are archbishops over a series of diocesan bishops leading churches in their agglomeration; thus, New Frontiers is a denomination, Pioneer People is a denomination, Bryn Jones' Bradford church and Harvest Time group was a denomination in the 80s.'

Obviously, Fahy did no depth digging to find out the truth of what he shared. My leaflet, *Forgive us our Denominations* was a cry against denominationalism with the emphasis on the *ism*, and I made the point that the worst kind of *ism* is the, 'I am of Christ' kind which would likely occur among people in our own circles. Not that I particularly feel the need to defend myself but I do think, for the sake of my readers, I need to set the record straight. Since my earliest connection with my Anglican friend Michael Harper, I never ceased working with people in the denominations both nationally and locally who shared similar values.

I shared platforms, attended conferences from earliest times until, in 1984, I was elected chairman of the interdenominational National Charismatic Leaders Conference and remained so for over 20 years. In the same year Christine and I became members of the Spring Harvest team and worked with them for over 15 years. My friendship with Charles Whitehead, who became chairman of the Roman Catholic International Charismatic Renewal Organisation (ICCCRO), led to a long and productive series of *conversations* with the Pontifical Council for the Promotion of Christian Unity on what they came to understand were the New Charismatic Churches (NCC's).

I introduced my colleague, Richard Roberts, to these *conversations*' and, as a result, there is now a 20,000-word paper on the Vatican web site explaining the emergence and growth of the NCC's across the world. You can access this document through this link[1]. The paper was followed up with a second paper on the subject of Networked Churches. This valuable work has opened the door for greater cooperation between charismatic groups and churches around the world. So I hope you will see that far from being anti-denominational I, and others in the

---

1   https://www.christianunity.va/content/unitacristiani/en/dialoghi/sezione-occidentale/pentecostali/conversazioni-con-le-nuove-chiese-carismatiche.html?fbclid=IwAR1B-7CK-m_2TlGBoQh8kzBuDB58lyELMOEJ_BW1DRv39meAYdK-fegWVPZk

New Churches, have endeavoured to encourage unity and cooperation between ourselves and the denominations.

- *The Fort Lauderdale Five* -

Around the same time that we UK leaders began to relate to one another a group in the US also began to meet. They were known as The Fort Lauderdale Five and, having been unhappy about the level of relationships and discipleship in the churches, they started what became known as, The Shepherding Movement. The movement placed a strong emphasis on commitment and covenant relationships. The five were all well known and had established ministries. They were namely Ern Baxter, Derek Prince, Charles Simpson, Bob Mumford and Don Basham.

Dates are a little hazy but I believe we became aware of the five when we met Ern in his London hotel room to chat when he was visiting the city. For many years Ern had been a bible teacher working alongside William Branham, a healing evangelist with a remarkable gift of the word of knowledge. So effective was Branham's ministry, that people almost worshipped him. This led to his sad decline and downfall and Ern pulled back from Branham. We got to hear that Bryn and his team were exploring links with the Fort Lauderdale brothers and so our group commissioned Maurice and me to visit them to see if such a link was appropriate for us.

We were welcomed into the beautiful home of Derek Prince whose wife, Ruth, provided us with wonderful hospitality and I enjoyed a game of tennis with Derek on the court alongside his house. Then we spent time with the *five*, getting to know one another and, necessarily, the conversation turned to the all-important subject of commitment and how our relationships would function They explained that their expectation was that we would submit to their authority.

We responded by agreeing that would be perfectly fine when we were ministering in their networks, we would respect that. However, should they visit us, we would expect a reciprocal arrangement. I further explained that we worked on the basis of mutual submission, so that wherever we went we would expect to serve those we were visiting unless we were asked to stray from biblical teaching or morals. Thus ended our visit as we were unable to agree their terms. We learned later that they went so far as to begin to appoint someone to work with each individual as an overseer.

When visiting my friend Barney Coombs, who had relocated to Vancouver, I asked him about his link with the *five*. He explained that his overseer was a young man in Fort Lauderdale. I smiled as Barney was a man of wide experience and the leader of a successful network of churches in the UK with growing relationships in Canada itself. I said, 'Barney, surely you know that this will never work. Apart from the distance, there is no way that this young man could provide adequate input for you!' He smiled, and it didn't work.

Looking back, we see that this kind of discipleship did untold damage to many who were left disillusioned with leadership and church. Bob Mumford was honest enough to make a public apology saying, 'I was wrong, I repent and apologise', and he asked for forgiveness. Others followed suit and I am glad to say that we were able to enjoy ministry from Derek Prince on several occasions.

- *The great split forward* -

In 1976 the guys from Bristol organised a summer conference in the beautiful grounds of the Monkton Coombe School near Bristol, aptly named the Bath and West Holiday Conference. There was a 1600-seat marquee for the main meetings and seminars in various venues each day. The guest speakers advertised were Bob Mumford and Ern Baxter and The London Brothers were also invited. I arrived a little late having flown in from a visit to Sweden. I have no recollection of hearing Bob Mumford but Ern was very much to the fore.

There was great excitement and the worship was electric with enthusiastic praise and lots of dancing. After the meeting the leaders, including Ern, got together to share how they felt the day's events went. If things went well fine, if it was felt we could have done better we sought to adjust. Ern was not at all happy with this kind of scrutiny as in the US no one would question him in such a way and this rather upset him. Also, in the evening meeting there was one lady whose contribution to the dancing was a little over the top but we didn't feel the need to stop her.

After the week was over and we had all gone home, those who were leading or taking part in the conference were utterly amazed and shocked when we received a letter from Arthur. Ern went on to see Bryn and Arthur to report on his time with us and he expressed the opinion that he felt, as a group, we were influenced by demons! I am sure that most of the recipients replied in their own ways.

In my response, I said that I accepted the possibility that I could be influenced by demons, as my understanding was that if the devil had even a toe hold in my life, he would try to use it to bring me down. Which is true for us all and is a very good reason why we need to hold on to one another to share and pray things like this through together. I also pointed out that the great apostle Peter, for the best intentions, allowed sentiment to prompt his response to Jesus' news about his pending death which our Lord immediately recognised was Satan himself.

From the time that letter was written a divide took place, which my friend Gerald Coates called *The great split forward*. I have met three people whilst writing this book, who told me that they were confronted by members of Bryn and Arthur's team and told that they must choose between John and Bryn. They refused to make that choice and were cut off from their links with anyone in Bryn's network. Indeed, Christine and I had been invited by Terry Virgo to pop down to the Seaford church where he was pastor to talk about women in ministry. This was immediately cancelled.

Looking back with hindsight I can see areas where, had we been able to share in peace together, the course of our lives and ministries could have benefited and changed for the better but that was not to be. I am glad to say that a measure of healing did take place but we were never involved in sharing at the same level again.

Whilst I believe much was lost as a result of what took place at that time, I have to say that many great and good things were accomplished and continue to influence the wider church to this day. For example, much of the teaching on the nature and the unity of church and the importance of strong relationships persists and can be seen in the way there is greater cooperation across the streams, particularly among charismatics.

Great cross-denominational events took place such as Berne 1990 and Brighton 1991 which I will refer to later. Then there was Spring Harvest, New Wine and many other great gatherings and conferences. We saw a new freedom in worship emerge with many gifted worship leaders and song writers being raised up with songs that reflected the emphasis of the ministry on grace as opposed to legalism, the power of the Holy Spirit available to every individual and the immediacy of the Kingdom.

Some of my readers will remember 1974 when Jimmy and Carol Owens' timely musical *Come Together* took the UK by storm. They put on the presentation at the Westminster Central Hall with Pat Boone as the narrator. Groups all over the country were inspired to perform *Come Together* singing, worshipping and praying together demonstrating their hunger for greater unity among Christians. It was a special time and after rehearsals with a choir drawn from our Romford church, we took the musical to 13 centres around the country!

At our final event, as we were preparing to leave, one of our song writers, Bob Gillman, said, 'I've written a new song'. It was getting late and reluctantly we gave him a hearing. He picked up his guitar and began to sing, 'Bind us together, Lord, bind us together, with cords that cannot be broken...'. We were not hugely impressed but we recognised that this was a prophetic cry, a prayer from the heart and...well, the rest is history!

That song went all over the world. Still today, fifty years on, it is stirring hearts as the Spirit yearns and moves through God's people to bring fulfilment to Jesus' prayer in John 17. One of my friends travelling in the Himalayas heard the strains coming from a mud hut and, as I said earlier, Pope John Paul sang it with thousands of pilgrims in St Peter's Square in Rome!

In 1979 and 1980, together with Gerald Coates, we put together a similar musical presentation which took the theme on a step and the *Bind Us Together* tour travelled to cities across the UK, and to Dublin, Norway and Sweden. When we announced that we were going to the Usher Hall in Edinburgh, folk said we would never fill it as the only Christians who had were Billy Graham and Cliff Richard. In fact, we had to turn 500 people away and the atmosphere was electric.

We have many other happy memories of that amazing time but one of the enduring highlights was the meeting in Belfast's Ulster Hall. The hall was packed with Christians from all backgrounds, including a great throng of Catholic nuns in their habits praising Jesus with hands raised in adoration. In the midst of those dark days in the province the Holy Spirit was working and brought his people together in a great demonstration of love and unity. We were so blessed that our friends, David and Mary Matthews of the Belfast Christian Family took the risk to host that wonderful evening.

On reflection, we must have done something right as we were picketed outside the entrance of the hall. On the one hand, the Paisleyites claimed we were undercover Catholics seeking to infiltrate the Protestant churches; on the other hand, fervent Catholic activists accused us of trying to get their people to leave the Catholic Church. Inside the hall we were all just enjoying Jesus and loving one another to bits!

- *More US links* -

Going back to the early 1970's we had contact with Charles and Dotty Schmitt based in Grand Rapids, Minnesota in the US. He and Dotty and Art Katz, a Jewish brother, with his wife Inger also in ministry, located a beautiful property up on the Canadian border known as Steamboat Lake. After prayer, they miraculously acquired the site and under the heading of Camp Dominion they ran a series of conferences.

I believe that it was around 1977 when Maurice Smith and I were first invited to join them to be part of their team for the week. It was a very positive time, although Art had a way of dealing with speakers who he disagreed with. I heard him give one speaker a serious dressing down, explaining that like the Levites who were called to slay their brethren who built the golden calf, he was called to deal with what he considered error. Maurice and I seemed to receive his approval. I pointed out later that I would be very happy to have Art alongside me when walking through a dark alley at night. Everyone saw the funny side of that.

I refer to these camps because I was asking Wayne Drain from Arkansas where it was that he and I first met. His immediate reply was Camp Dominion in 1978 when Graham Perrins and I were taking part. He, Roger Davin from Duluth and guys from their fellowships and people from several other churches in their emerging network were there. Wayne shared his memories with me in a recent email:

It was in 1978 that I met Graham Perrins and you at Camp Dominion near Grand Rapids, Minnesota. Chris Horan, Howie Porter and I had come at the invitation of Roger Davin. I met Charles & Dotty Schmidt there as well. And I thought they were amazing teachers. Art Katz scared me a little bit. We saw that you British guys seemed to value fun and fellowship as much as you did your teaching, it was also obvious that worship and relationships were extremely important.

A few memories of Camp Dominion: Worship was intense and creative. The cabins were rustic with bathrooms that worked now and then. As I was driving into the camp, I met Keith Green as he was driving out. He said, 'Intense group here bro! Tough crowd'. Camp leaders seemed like army sergeants to me. I thought the UK contingent were fun and non-religious. I remember you shocking the Americans at a baptism service when you dove in the pool wearing speedos! I was drawn to you guys right off.

It would be a few months later that a few US leaders involved with Roger Davin would come to UK for the first time. Our first stop was Romford. My team visited Bristol, Cardiff, Cobham and back to Romford. In 1981 June and I spent 3 months with Graham Perrins and Springwood Church in Cardiff. Believe it or not I am meeting with some of those same Springwood Church guys in Wales again after all these years.

Since 1979 I have been to UK 50-60 times through my involvement with Pioneer, Rainbow, Kingsway and Integrity Music. I developed close relationships with you and Christine, Graham Perrins, Gerald Coates, Dave & Rhian Day, Peter Lyne, Noel Richards, Les Moir, Dave Bilbrough, and Paul & Paula Weston. It all started in your and Christine's home and with the Romford Fellowship. Thank you for making room for me and June all those years ago.

Wayne continues visiting the UK and in 2001 he joined Noel Richards and Brian Houston to form the music group The Hudson Taylors, performing in numerous concerts and recording albums together.

Roger Davin also made frequent visits to see us with his talented team. He played trumpet and the group sang barber shop acapella. I believe it was these guys who introduced us to that fun song, *Everybody's gonna be so beautiful in heaven it don't matter if you're ugly down here.* They travelled around sharing in the networks and churches in various areas, including Gerald Coates' Kingdom Life summer conference in Cobham.

People loved his relaxed style of ministry and at times, with his acting skills, he would dress up to perform a monologue of some character from a bible story to make a point. One particularly inspiring talk he gave, which he confessed he received the revelation for whilst sitting on the loo, was entitled *Cell Biology*. As I sit at my computer, I can see that very tape sitting in my son's, *Things I might suddenly need*, basket which means it must have been played recently in his home group. Roger writes:

Our original meeting took place at Camp Dominion I believe 1978. They were days of glorious inspiration and discovery for me. I was coming to be known and recognized, despite my relative youth, as a person with vision and leadership. The connection with you folk ignited and confirmed elements of my passion and vision for what the church of Jesus can, and should, be. You were absolutely refreshing in your integration of faith and life in a non-religious style. High in my estimation was the element of 'friendship' as part of our interconnection as believers.

You visited our church fellowship in Duluth during your trip that first year in the States and invited me to come your way for a visit to you in Collier Row in 1979. It was refreshing and certainly bolstered my unique sense of what the church can be in this world.

I put you in touch with Danny Sposta in Queens, New York as they were part of a small group of churches I was 'looking after' in those years. Dan remains a treasured friend to this day. The church groups were mostly located in various towns and cities in Minnesota, Iowa, Nebraska, in addition to Wayne's fellowship in Russellville, Arkansas. In later years my association with The Vineyard served some good opportunity for growth on my part. I especially benefited from my experience with Servant Evangelism: reaching out to connect with people in creative, unexpected ways.

I continue to be absolutely staggered by God's choice of grace as the vehicle for our redemption and saving experience. His acceptance of us that does not depend on our performance, is transforming as you well know. My memories of those years are precious to me and I continue to be a grateful man. I remain your deep friend in grace,

Roger.

Having made the connection with Roger and Wayne I made several visits to minister with them and the churches they were working with. I must mention one particular trip in 1982 when Christine and I took our 16-year-old son, John, with us. It was quite an occasion for him as we flew into New York, hired a car, and drove all the way to Duluth! We stopped off at churches and groups on the way to share and also took time to take a look at Niagara Falls. In Duluth some of the guys took John off for a trek in the wilderness before we made the return trip home.

Gerald and Dave Bilbrough loved the *Everybody's gonna be so beautiful* song and Dave bought a funny nose and moustache attached to a pair of glasses which he used to wear when he sang the song. Gerald was due to minister in a large Pentecostal church and asked Dave if he would go with him and bring his nose. Gerald hated the way people suddenly become *religious* when they are breaking bread and so he asked Dave to don the nose and sing the song when he gave him a nudge.

The meeting was great until they neared the time for breaking the bread and that *religious* atmosphere began to descend and Dave received the nudge, 'Now!' said Gerald under his breath. So up gets Dave with his nose and starts to sing, at which point the church elders, who were seated all along the front row, stood up in unison and walked out. I don't believe Gerald was invited back to that particular church again.

- *John Wimber and Dale Gentry* -

I became aware of John Wimber when I heard of his visits to David Watson's church in York. His laid-back approach to ministry and praying for the sick, together with the testimonies of those healed, soon travelled around the country. He had contact with Sandy Millar's Holy Trinity church in Kensington and other meetings were arranged for him in London in 1984 at Holborn City Temple and Westminster Central Hall.

PURE CHURCH

It was a well-respected Charismatic Baptist minister, Douglas McBain, who invited me to join the committee which he brought together to put on the Central Hall meetings. They were extremely well attended and I am sure they led to the increased demand for Wimber's ministry in other parts of the country.

Gerald Coates and I had several meals and meetings with John and he came to share in some larger gatherings Gerald put on in Cobham. We both had occasion to stand up for John against some heavy criticism from one or two senior figures in the Renewal Movement. Gerald also mentioned him with fondness in his book, *Intelligent Fire* as he was obviously moved by the acceptance, support and appreciation he had received among us.

I had the privilege of hosting a session at Spring Harvest when John was invited to speak at a main afternoon meeting. Spring Harvest have strict rules for finishing on time as you may be stealing somebody else's space. John was given half-an-hour and he immediately took off his watch and placed it next to his bible. I was relieved and he began his talk with an introduction which, after 25 minutes he was warming to his subject. Obviously, I had to take some action, so I went forward and picked up his watch and said, 'John, what's this?' and with an apologetic look he replied, 'It's my watch!' I said with a smile, 'It's telling me you have 5 minutes left!' He roared with laughter and graciously wrapped up his talk. Of course, he had more time in his evening gathering.

Norman Barnes met Dale Gentry in his travels around the US and loved his dynamic ministry on prayer and revival. So Norman invited him and his wife Jean to minister here in the UK and was keen to introduce them to me and to Gerald Coates. It was immediately clear that the Lord had sent this couple with a prophetic message for us all which was to impact our lives, our churches and networks in a special way. Dale was well received all around and made several visits, including taking time to share in a conference in Madrid that Christine and I arranged for the churches we were serving. However, perhaps his most significant input came when he kicked off the revival and prayer gatherings Gerald and his team arranged at the Marsham Street church in Westminster. These meetings ran for six nights a week, Tuesday to Sunday from June 1997 through to June 1998.

It was an incredible commitment and, although the meetings were not overly crowded, thousands of people from far and wide came through the doors. Many came confessing their sin, throwing books, videos, magazines and other items connected with their situation into a sin bin to be burned. Others were saved, healed and baptised with the Holy Spirit and many more received prayer and prophetic words. For example, Godfrey Birtill, our much-loved worship leader, testifies to fact that his ministry was fired up and entered an entirely new and successful phase as a result of hearing from the Lord at Marsham Street. He also became a great friend of Dale, who always wanted Godfrey to stand alongside him when he visited the UK.

In fact, Christine and I reaped the benefit of Dale and Godfrey working together when we arranged a conference in Madrid in 2004 for the churches we were working with in Pioneer. We drew a small network of these churches together under the banner of Spirit Connect and we felt we should arrange a Cities and Nations conference in the beautiful Fray Luis de Leon centre in Guadarrama just outside the city. We had a programme of seminars led mainly by Bev Webb and her team from the City Life church in Southampton and Godfrey agreed to come and lead worship while Dale ministered in the main sessions.

As you can imagine, it was a special time of stirring worship with Godfrey in great spirits followed by Dale's powerful ministry. The team did a great job in the seminars and there was plenty of time to enjoy the facilities with a lovely pool and space for games. We encouraged folk to think about adopting a nation in their church or at least sponsoring others to go on their behalf. One wonderful outcome of our time was that two of our group met, fell in love, and were later married. My friend, Andrew Cromwell from the UK met Toni Burrowes from Barbados and the rest is history.

However, there is a sequel to the story which is well worth telling. Andrew's father, Ernst, was confirmed and baptised in London by Dietrich Bonhoeffer and, as such, was a friend and had considerable correspondence with him between 1935 and 1936. When Toni discovered this, she recognised the importance of these letters and set to getting them published and, as a result, *Letters to London: Bonhoeffer's previously unpublished correspondence with Ernst Cromwell* was published by SPCK in 2013.

Going back some time before the Marsham Street meetings there came a bolt out of the blue when Gerald and I received a prophetic word from Dale which, incredibly, was confirmed by Paul Cain at a meeting arranged by John Wimber! I am sure my readers have understood that Gerald and I always worked closely since our first meeting. I can't pinpoint exactly when it was, but Dale went out on a limb at one of our joint gatherings and prophesied that the two of us should bring our networks together. Those of us in Team Spirit, our network of churches and ministries, had already received a word to the effect that Team Spirit should die. However, we were not to commit euthanasia or keep it on life support, but allow it to die peacefully and we had no idea what would follow. Now, perhaps Dale's word was shedding light on our future.

Obviously, if that was to happen, we would need to hear from our teams and churches to understand and hear their responses to such a word. Neither of us were of a mind to pressurise those we served into such a radical move without their input. Indeed, if the move was to take place every one would be given the choice as to whether they wished to join us and Gerald's Pioneer or receive our blessing to explore pastures new.

We knew that, in 1990, John Wimber was in the UK with Paul Cain and drawing crowds to their meetings. We were also aware that there was to be a Holiness to the Lord conference at the London Arena with around 5,000 people attending. However, neither Gerald nor I were able to be there but there were a number of our friends in the congregation. John introduced Paul and handed over the session to him as he had some prophetic words to pass on. He took a couple of cards from his pocket and went on to ask, 'Is John Noble here, if so, would he stand up please?' Obviously, there was no response. So he went on, 'Is Gerald Coates here, if so, would he please stand up?' Again, no response and he put the cards back in his pocket and continued to give out various words most of which were received with enthusiasm and much clapping.

Then he went back to the original cards and asked if I had friends in the audience who would stand and again the same for Gerald. When he was satisfied with the response, he went on to prophesy at some length concerning the nature of our relationship and the fact that the Lord wanted us to bring our streams together. Paul's words were soon passed on to us confirming and expanding what the Lord had already spoken to us through Dale. So began a couple of years of sharing, praying and planning the move until Christine and I, together with our son, Mathew and his wife Cathy and their two children, Vicki and Josh, moved across from Romford to Surrey in the summer of 1994.

Only recently, after so many years, Stuart Lindsell, one of the elders of the Cobham Fellowship came to visit me and said that he came across the you tube video of Paul Cain's prophecy. So I was able to hear what he said for myself and, should you want to view it.[2]

There is a sequel to this part of our story. You will remember in an earlier chapter I shared how the Lord provided a house for us after being homeless for a couple of years. Well, we had a similar experience when we moved to be with Gerald in Surrey. The housing market was in turmoil and after giving out mortgages like sweeties the crash meant people couldn't get a loan for love nor money. We were prepared to sell our large extended house with seven bedrooms, a sauna and six reception rooms when one reasonably well-off couple couldn't get a mortgage for the mere £124,000 we were asking for it.

After prayer, we felt it right to let our daughter, Sharon, and her husband take it on with their growing family and then, perhaps, in the future they

---

[2] https://www.youtube.com/watch?v=ojq1fCBj4o0

would be able to pass on some kind of return to us. Thus, we moved to Ashtead, Surrey, with no home and the grand sum of £17,000 which would not buy a lock-up garage in the area. What's more, we believed the Lord was calling us to trust him and put the money we had into a major building fund which the Cobham church was putting together.

The elders of a local Baptist church heard about our plight and as they were without a pastor kindly offered us the church manse to rent until they needed it. We were extremely grateful and made friends with them. As time passed, they heard about Christine's ministry in the supernatural and asked her to pray around in the church. Apparently, there was a nasty atmosphere which prevailed as a result of some past issues which had not been dealt with. They were quite sure this was hindering their plans for the future. Christine was pleased to help and did as they asked. The result was tangible and the atmosphere changed. Within no time at all they had an application for the role of pastor which was accepted and, of course, we had to vacate the manse to make way for the incoming family. However, we knew that God moves in mysterious ways to perform his wonders and, so often, when one door closes another immediately opens. So it was, as a couple from the church we moved to be part of stepped up to offer us a generous portion of their beautiful home to live in just mile or so from where we had been staying.

During this period the housing market continued to struggle and after a year in the church manse and a year or so with our church friends, they felt it was time for us to move on. Thankfully, house prices in the area were at an all-time low and, although we had no cash to buy, we sensed a rise in faith and began to look around to see what was available. Quite quickly we found a fairly new build, a detached house, in a private road which Christine was sure was to be ours. I thought, far-be-it for me to disagree, so I left her to do the negotiating.

Remember, this is Surrey, one of the most prestigious areas in the country. The house had four bedrooms and the garage had been made into an extra room and a detached double garage had been built next to the house. The elderly couple were leaving all the curtains, carpets and fittings. Christine went in with a low offer of £192.000 which I thought wouldn't have a snowball's chance in hell but it was accepted! All that remained was a little question of a mortgage and deposit.

Christine's dad, not known for his great generosity, gave us a gift of an amazing £10,000! The church came back to give us the amount we had put into the building fund and we then discovered that, as a result of the road widening of the M25, we were due another £10,000 after we moved in. I can't think how we managed it but the Halifax tipped up with an interest-only mortgage and we were all set to go! Jehovah Jireh had worked his mysterious ways once again. Furthermore, it wasn't too long before Matthew rolled up his sleeves and built an extension giving us seven bedrooms, an extra bathroom and space to get back to having a few more people sharing their lives with us.

- *More Significant US Connections* -

I don't feel able to leave this chapter without mentioning a number of significant relationships which developed out of our earlier visits to the US and other conferences around the world. Obviously, the link with Roger Davin, Wayne Drain and the Gentry's led to return visits to spend time with them.

I already mentioned that we toured churches linked with Roger, particularly in the North-West, and Wayne down in Arkansas. Wayne and June were always most hospitable and we spent time with them whenever we could. One year we took our friends and worship leaders Sue Rinaldi and Caroline Bonnet with us to share first, with Dale and Jean in Houston, at Pastor Jack Nichol's church. Then on to Wayne and June, where many of their folk, as students, had been converted in the '60's in the Jesus Revolution. What fun we had with them.

Also in Texas, Christine and I went to Austin where our UK friends doctors Tony and Felicity Dale had moved. They previously led the

Tower Hamlets Christian Fellowship in East London. Now they run a community medical insurance company and have made a huge contribution to the growing house church movement in the States through conferences and the magazine *House2House*.

Derek Prince, who hosted Maurice Smith and me on the visit to Fort Lauderdale, together with others from the group of *five*, apologised for their part in what became the controlling discipleship movement. After we heard this, we invited him and has wife Ruth to speak at our Spring Bank Holiday Celebration one year which we held in Brentwood, Essex. This local conference started with a few hundred in attendance and quickly grew to over 2000. Derek kindly accepted and we were so blessed with his great teaching ministry and the way he tirelessly prayed for the sick.

At some point in my travel, I connected with Jamie Buckingham well known as a ghost writer for Nick Cruz's, *Run Baby Run* and John and Elizabeth Sherrill's, *They Speak with Other Tongues*. He was a very funny man and a great storyteller with many books to his credit, for example, *Where Eagles Soar* and *Risky Living*. We hit it off and he and his wife Jackie and their family became great friends. He came and ministered among us in the UK and I often ministered in his Melbourne, Florida church. He generously let Christine and me use his ocean-front condo in Melbourne Beach and, as a result, the area became a favourite place for Noble family holidays. We even married our son John and his lovely wife Tina there one year.

However, I must share one other amazing testimony from our visits to the States. It was at the 1991 Brighton International Conference which I worked on with Michel Harper, Father Tom Forrest and Lutheran Larry Christenson, which I will talk about later, that I met Miguel Escobar. He came from the huge Jotabeche Pentecostal Methodist church in Chile and was one of their healing evangelists. We also became friends after that conference and kept in touch.

Christine was suffering with a great deal of pain with her hip which was clearly in need of replacing. Miguel was in London and heard about our situation and he called us up. He suggested that we should go to his healing meeting and he would pray for Christine and then, surprisingly, he went on to say that if she didn't get healed, he knew a top doctor in the US who would do the op for her as he had for Miguel's wife in the past.

We duly went to the meeting, Miguel prayed and Christine was not healed. True to his word he contacted the doctor who was, indeed, a highly-qualified man whose expertise was much sought after. When he heard about Christine's condition and her ministry, he spoke to us and said he would see what he could do for her. After a short time, he came back to us and said he was willing to perform the surgery but there was a matter of the hospital costs, the anaesthetist and the prosthesis to consider.

Again, he contacted us to say it was good news, the hospital had waived their costs and the anaesthetist was happy to help on this occasion. All that remained was the prosthesis, which he assured us was the top of the range titanium job. When we asked how long we could expect it to last, he assured us that they would dig Christine up to reuse it! Furthermore, the supplier said he would give it free of charge if Christine agreed he could watch the op as he'd never seen the procedure before. She replied to the effect that he could sell tickets if that would help. So everything was in place, we just had to find the cost of flights and accommodation while Christine recovered.

I was going to fly in from South Africa where I was sharing ministry with Gerald and Noel Richards in Pretoria at the Hatfield Baptist Church. This all meant that there was a fair amount of cost involved in travel and accommodation. You can imagine our surprise when a youngish man from the church tipped up at our house before we left with a cheque for £5000 to cover all other expenses – we were blown away! As it happened when Dr Tom and his wife Nancy picked Christine up from the airport they immediately took to Christine and said that, in fact, they would like us to stay with them. They then confessed that they were a little cautious, as they didn't know who we were and had found in the past that some Christians had proved to be a little difficult to live with.

The operation was a huge success and Tom and Nancy became firm friends. They visited us in the UK and one year Nancy even joined one of our teams travelling to Thailand to work with our friends with refugees from Burma and in the villages of northern Thailand. The Dave and Carole Summers other incredible thing is that Christine's surgery took place in November and the following January Christine took a team of nurses from Norway to teach basic health care to village women in south-central India. The villages were quite remote and, of course, no toilets. Not having made a full recovery Christine was unable to crouch to go to the loo. So Paul Raj, their host, had the bright idea of cutting a hole in a red plastic chair which was then carried on the head of an Indian lady who followed Christine wherever she went.

Chapter Eight

EVENTS AND CONFRENCES, CONFERENCES, CONFERENCES...

In 1971 many of us in the Renewal took part in The Nationwide Festival of Light led by our very good friend Peter Hill who received an amazing response to his idea to highlight the growing emphasis on pornography in society. He gathered a number of celebrities who shared his concern including Malcolm Muggeridge, Mary Whitehouse, Lord Longford, Bishop Trevor Huddleston and Cliff Richard. Mary Whitehouse was considered a prude by some at the time but, interestingly, she was in the news recently under the headline, *Was Mary Whitehouse right?* as it seems pornography has a stronger grip than ever on many today.

Other public figures supported the event such as David Kossoff, Dora Bryan and even Prince Charles sent a message wishing the day, 'Every good wish for its success'. And, indeed, it was a great success as around 30,000 people gathered peacefully in Trafalgar Square and worshipped, prayed and listened to the talks. While the Festival was taking place the first gay pride march, not known by that name at the time, marched across Trafalgar Square behind us. It was quite small but noisy and accompanied by numbers of police. As I remember it, one single policeman was allocated to the Festival.

At the end the crowd walked through the streets to Hyde Park, singing as they went. At 4 pm in the park they were joined by others who were unable to get into Trafalgar Square. Among those performing there were Cliff Richard, Dana and Graham Kendrick, and the reverend Jean Darnall led the rally. The main speaker was the Hollywood street evangelist Arthur Blessitt, famous for having travelled all over the world carrying a 12-foot wooden cross wherever he went.

With all that was going on in the Renewal here in the UK and beyond there was a growing sense of need among leaders, and those caught up in the movement, for fellowship. This hunger created a readiness to seek out relationships with Christians in other streams who were experiencing the blessing of the Holy Spirit. This, in turn, led to an increasing unity among leaders and saints from other backgrounds.

I remember my friend Clive Calver speaking at Spring Harvest one year and saying that he saw the divisions among the Christians at the time tended to be either horizontal or vertical. Horizontal unity, as those who shared the blessings of Renewal were finding fellowship across the streams, whilst those within the denominations, who felt threatened by what was happening, clung to their roots – vertical unity. Thus, the desire for conferences and gatherings where teaching, testimonies, prayer and worship together was encouraged.

- The National Charismatic Leaders Conference -

In the late '70's Michael Harper began to call leaders of the Charismatic Movement together to meet at the Whirlow Grange centre in Sheffield. The initial gatherings were quite small, about a dozen or so, but it grew quite quickly and was the forerunner of what became The National Charismatic Leaders Conference. From the start it brought together a cross-section of leaders from most of the denominations and the fellowship was good and there was a genuine sense of unity.

Michael chaired the conference until 1983 when he experienced opposition from some members as he was going ahead with plans for a much wider gathering without consulting with the group. Not something I felt he needed to do as we all arranged events as we felt led. However, he resigned and the conference decided to hold a vote to elect a new chairman. Now I had gone out of my way over the years to work at friendship wherever there was an openness to explore relationships, but I was completely shocked and overwhelmed when the group elected me to lead the group.

It was a fascinating experience for me as the group grew to almost 100 and consisted of a truly diverse body of leaders with some quite strongly opinionated characters among us. At times it was a bit like having a tiger by the tail as we did not shy away from tackling controversial issues.

For one or two it was quite a stretch when we opened the conference up to some of the growing number of women in leadership. I remember one brother, who shall be nameless, who opened his bible up when one of the women ministered and refused to look up. Nevertheless, we survived and enjoyed some wonderful times of worship and fellowship, and friendships were made which led to working relationships which extended far beyond the yearly meetings.

So I had the privilege of chairing the conference from 1984 through to 2006 when I handed over to a co-chair of my colleagues, Charles Whitehead, respected leader within the Catholic Renewal and Hugh Osgood, founder of Churches in Communities International. I am glad to say that the conference continues to be held annually at the High Leigh centre in Hoddesdon.

- *Spring Harvest* -

The great Spring Harvest Annual Conference was started by Clive Calver and Peter Meadows in 1979. I had a relationship with both men in different contexts. Clive, with his mission team, In the Name of Jesus, which included Graham Kendrick, and Pete, a musician who played in our coffee bar outreach in the basement of the Orange Street church near Trafalgar Square. The first conferences were in Prestatyn in North Wales, but it grew over the years to three separate weeks over a number of different locations with around 90,000 in attendance at its peak.

Christine and I were invited in 1982 and took part in the team for over 15 years. What a joy and a privilege that was with so many new friends made and wonderful experiences of the Holy spirit at work. I clearly remember at one of the early conferences, when thousands gathered in the big top evening meeting and began to sing in tongues. The sound was eerily heavenly and seemed supernatural. Many were convinced that it was beyond anything that we could have produced and the angels must have joined in.

As part of the team, we took part in an extensive programme of seminars and were part of the platform party in the main evening meetings. I took my trumpet and, as such, was the first person to play an instrument on stage apart from Graham Kendrick with his guitar, a drummer and a keyboard. I am not sure how much that was appreciated as the next year they had a full band and my trumpet went back in its case.

Christine was allowed to prophesy but had to write what she saw down and pass it on to me to read. It must have been a blessing, as the following year she was allowed to prophesy herself and the third year she was the first woman to preach on the main stage! Obviously, her release opened up the way for many more women to take a full part in all the events from that time.

We have many memories of our days at Spring Harvest and could fill a book with our recollections, but one thing we loved and regularly took part in was an after meeting to pray for people who wished to be Baptised in the Holy Spirit. That meeting was a highlight and such a joy to see people released and go back to their churches to take the blessing home with them. However, there is another occasion that stands out in my mind that I must share.

I believe we were at the Minehead site and we had taken part in a great week where most people had been thoroughly blessed. We had a fun-packed time with lots of laughter and a few tears as folk got their lives sorted out. It was the final meeting of the week with around 5000 people in the Big Top and, traditionally, it was a time for breaking bread. Sadly, as is often the case when we come to break bread, the atmosphere can become rather serious and can have a *religious* feel which is quite different to other days.

The stewards tended to creep around slightly leaning forward as if they didn't want to draw attention to themselves. Suddenly there was a loud screaming and when folk lifted their eyes to look around, there was a man standing in the middle of the tent hanging on to a guide rope. Clive Calver, who was leading the meeting, went white as a sheet and immediately signalled to Christine and Gerald to get down from the platform to go and confront the man. Afterwards, Gerald admitted that he held back and let Christine go first because he didn't have a clue what to do.

Christine arrived on the scene and shouted at the man, 'What is your name?' The man replied with a scream, 'I am Beelzebub!' Christine immediately responded, 'Don't be so stupid, you are not nearly important enough to be Beelzebub – get out in Jesus' name!' The man stopped screaming and collapsed into his chair and the meeting continued. I asked permission to pray and asked the Lord to calm people's fears and allow the peace of God to fill the place. However, there were a lot of people, particularly youngsters, who wanted prayer before they made their journeys home.

- Greenbelt -

With all the tapes, records, literature and creativity which was emerging from our network and other centres of renewal, I started a business to make all this available. I called it The Rainbow Company and we regularly mailed out brochures to our increasing fan base. There were, of course, many Christian bookshops and outlets to sell these products but mostly they were pretty uninviting places to visit. In fact, my book, *The Battle of the Sexes*, was stocked in a few of these shops and someone told me they went into one and asked if they had a copy to purchase. The answer was a mumbled, 'Yes', and the person serving reached under the counter and quickly placed the book in a brown paper bag to make sure that no one else could see it.

Apart from the books and records, etc, we encouraged our creative people to make things like pottery, cards, a tape storage rack and so on. We also bought lots of fun things, for example, rainbow laces, braces and jewellery which brightened the shop up when we went out on the road. We bought a T-shirt printing machine, a badge-making machine and a baseball cap printing machine. We had a series of transfers made with scripture verses, pictures and Christian themes and then a whole lot of humorous slogans which went down a storm. For example, *Baptists are wet all over*, *There's a Methodist in my madness* and *A sprinkling of Anglicans never did anyone any harm*. Christine and the team could hardly keep up with the queues.

Apart from our own meetings and events, we were regulars at the annual Greenbelt conference which ran over some days. One year we found a battery-operated flashing headband, which quickly sold out and so I drove back to the suppliers for another batch. This was the year that Cliff Richard was singing in the late-night onstage performance, and unbeknown to us the kids put the word out that all those with the headbands should keep them off until Cliff walked on the stage and then all switch them on at the same time. The atmosphere, to coin a phrase, was *electric* as, in the darkness of the night, in excess of a 1,000 flashing lights went on in the crowd to welcoming cheers for Cliff!

When I was serving in our tent one day, a well-known speaker came into the shop and asked who the manager was and I stepped forward. He wanted to know if I realised that the Rainbow was the sign of the gay movement. I mischievously said, 'Oh is it really? I thought it was a symbol of God's promise that he would never destroy the earth by flood again'. He assured me that he was right, so I told him we were getting the Rainbow back for the One who gave it to us in the first place.

- Festival -

In 1981 Gerald and I began to develop a relationship with Dave Tomlinson as he pulled away from his involvement with Bryn Jones' Harvest Time network of churches. Dave led a church in Middlesbrough and worked together with his friend Philip Mohabir, who pioneered church planting in Guyana and Guyanaian communities around the world. They led the Teamwork network.

We spent days together sharing our understanding of how God was leading us at that time in relation to the function of apostolic ministry, the role of women in leadership and questions around law and grace among other things. We also ministered in one another's churches and leadership teams. In 1983 we took our wives and went to Florence for a break which was great fun as we enjoyed being together. Then, later that year, we hosted the first of our summer Festivals at the Staffordshire County Showground.

We brought in our good friend Peter Fenwick, who had a significant work in Sheffield and the surrounding area, to stand with us and Festival continued for five years and grew to around 5,000 in attendance. We invited a wide range of ministries and worship leaders, including Don Double, Ishmael, Nick Cuthbert, Bill Angel, Peter Lyne, Donn Thomas from the USA, Graham Cray, Ian and Rosemary Andrews and even Jonathan Porritt of Friends of the Earth came one year.

We also had lots of fun as we enjoyed relaxing in the evenings with chat shows and other entertainment. On one evening the four of us, Dave, Gerald, Peter and I decided to dress up and do a presentation of the *Alternative Version* of Genesis chapter one which had been published in Punch Magazine. It featured a frustrated Adam who could not understand if he was the first person created, where all the bits of broken blue and white pottery came from which he kept digging up in the garden. He also enquired of the Lord why he had designed the earthworm to empty its bowels on the surface of his beautiful lawn. When he awoke after Eve had been created, he immediately asked her what the nasty lumps on her chest were.

Gerald was the narrator, Dave played God, Pete was Adam and I was the Devil. I wore a rather horrid mask and we had folks in fits of laughter. At the end Gerald turned to me and asked why I was wearing the stupid mask and ripped it off and underneath my face was made up to the same design. People were glad to see that we enjoyed life and did not take our roles as leaders too seriously as many other ministries seemed to live on some higher plane.

- *Spring Bank Holiday Celebration* -

As the run of summer Festivals were coming to an end in 1987, my team – Team Spirit - felt we needed another opportunity to bring people from the network together for fellowship, teaching and worship. So began our Spring Bank Holiday Celebration in Brentwood, Essex which ran from 1986 to 1995. The first couple of years we were in the grounds of Pilgrim Hall, a local Christian conference centre. However, we rapidly outgrew the site there and moved to the Brentwood Centre which could hold 2,000 in the main hall and had plenty of room for camping and marquees for children's work and seminars.

Again, we were blessed to have some amazing speakers to minister to us amidst a full programme of seminars and with the Zippa Gang great team to run the children's programme. Jamie Buckingham come to share at our first event with his wealth of stories full of insight and humour. Then we had Johnny Barr, one of God's characters we loved, and Floyd McClung, author of the much-loved book, *The Father Heart of God*, in 1987. Derek and Ruth Prince came to be with us again in 1988, followed by Kriengsak Chereonwangsak, founder of the Hope network of churches in Thailand.

We loved having a prophetic couple from the US, Charles and Paula Slagle, who also travelled around some of our churches to share. The Heartbeat band was a great hit as was the amazing Jackie Pullinger, known for her rescue work among drug addicts in Hong Kong and her best-selling book, *Chasing the Dragon*. Terry Virgo, long-time friend and leader of the New Frontiers Team, came to share ministry on grace, Martin Scott from Gerald Coates' Pioneer Team stirred and encouraged us and Joseph Kobo with his team from the Transkei in South Africa, testified concerning the growth there among the tribal peoples in the rural homeland.

- *Berne 1990 and Brighton 1991* -

In 1983, Michael Harper, Lutheran Larry Christenson and Catholic Father Tom Forrest met together after the All Africa conference in Kenya which they had been attending for a chat and a cup of tea. They all had a passion for world evangelisation and out of this meeting, which became known as the famous cup of tea meeting, they were affectionately labelled, the gang of three. The International Charismatic Consultation on World Evangelism (ICCOWE) was born. It was their desire to bring Charismatic and Pentecostal leaders together from all denominations and every part of the world to hear the stories of revival and get their thoughts on how better they could serve one another and even work together.

However, before the Brighton 1991 conference which was the result of their planning, a European conference took place in Berne, Switzerland in 1990. This was planned following some years of meetings between denominational and Catholic Charismatics and, of course, Michael was involved as, indeed, was I and we were both a part of a committee which put the whole thing together. Martin Beuhlmann, leader of a successful charismatic church in Berne, who later became the National Director of Vineyard Germany, ably co-ordinated the conference with a team from his church.

This was an amazing event as it was only months after the Berlin wall came down in 1989 and was, therefore, the first time that Christians from Eastern Europe were able to attend such a gathering. This inevitably meant that there was a real atmosphere of excitement and joy in that we were able to come together and there were some incredible stories from behind the Iron Curtain as you can imagine. Our own Andy Au, creative in dance, was there with his flags and banners and he led a huge March of Witness through the centre of Berne. Some months back, I read Jeanne Harper's book on Michael's 48 years of ministry, *Visited by God*, and whilst there is a great deal about the Brighton conference, I was sad that I couldn't find a mention of the Berne meetings.

Nevertheless, Martin Beuhlmann came to my rescue:

> *'Jesus - Hope for Europe' in Berne 1990 was the third European Ecumenical Event after Strasbourg 1982 and Acts 86 in Birmingham. The European Charismatic Council (ECC) decided to follow the invitation of the Swiss constituency to do this conference in summer of that year. It included a 'March for Jesus' with Graham Kendrick leading worship and Andy Au dancing at the front of up to 10,000 participants. Together, we walked from the conference centre to the Parliament building. This was widely reported by the Swiss press and television.*
>
> *Of the conferences 5,500 participants, 1,850 found a private home to accommodate them. There were 500 participants from Poland, 300 from Romania, 150 from Bulgaria, 150 from the German Democratic Republic, 500 from France, 300 from Spain, 500 from Italy and others from the rest of Europe. It was an amazing celebration of the Church in its variety. The much-loved Cardinal Raniero Cantalamessa was one of the speakers, along with Michael Harper and many others.*

EVENTS AND CONFERENCES, CONFERENCES, CONFERENCES...

The planning followed some years of meetings between Denominational and Catholic Charismatics and, of course, Michael was involved, as was I and John Noble. At the time I was leading the successful charismatic community, Basileia Berne, before taking on the leadership of the Vineyard Movement in Germany, Austria and Switzerland. It was, indeed, an amazing event after the Berlin wall came down prior to the conference as the socialist governments fell in 1989 and 1990. So the conference became a celebration of freedom and community between the nations.

Olaf Franke from Germany remembers:

On Tuesday morning I was tired and not suitably dressed as I was camping nearby and Peter Dippl caught me at the entrance and said, you must translate! I was shocked but happy as we were not impressed with the somewhat slow translation of the fiery Father Tom Forrest. So, I ended up next to the pulpit to translate the MCs of the day, Charles and Sue Whitehead. That was the first time I met them and we have remained friends ever since.

I recall the wonderful atmosphere of unity and worship and the speakers David Berly on social justice and serving the poor and homeless and Kalevi Lehtinen on evangelism. Also, last but not least, I had to translate your dear Christine as she shared a vision of how Jesus dived into our worship and thoroughly enjoyed it!

My dear friends Charles and Sue Whitehead share their recollections:

Charles:
As I was a member of the Planning Committee for the conference we met regularly and were hosted by Martin Buehlmann who administered the whole event. As we drew near to the date, we were well below the numbers we had planned for and unbalanced in our mix of attendees. Then, suddenly, the Berlin wall came down and we found hundreds started to come, mostly by bus, from the Eastern European countries, none of whom had booked in.

The local Berne Christians responded amazingly, inspired by the Lord they opened their homes to take in these unexpected guests who had hardly any money and could not pay for their accommodation or, in some cases even their food. I remember that packed lunches were supplied to everyone, and the Eastern Europeans collected all our disposable plastic packaging, washed it, and saved it to take home with them. They could not believe we were throwing it away!

The thrilling result of these dear people being able to come was that we ended up with exactly the numbers we had planned for, but more to the point was that we were 50/50 Catholic and Protestant Churches, 50/50 male and female, 50/50 East and West, 50/50 young and older participants. So the Lord provided at the very last minute the numbers and the mixes we had prayed and hoped for! It goes without saying that the result of all this was an amazingly wonderful conference with a tangible sense of the Holy Spirit at work in our midst.

Sue:
On the final night an appeal came from the stage, by the Eastern European delegates, that we in the West should not rush into the East now the wall was down to 'help' them. They needed to grow as themselves and not be 'westernised'! Sadly, I don't believe that was honoured!

I do remember feeling that the faith of our East European friends was much stronger, probably due to the persecution they had experienced. As the final evening closed, we had all been given light sticks, the Eastern delegates were asked to light theirs first and then reach out to ignite ours from the West.

Travelling back to our accommodation it was a joy to see the 'light' going out into the world - very symbolic! Oh, and I should mention that the local Berne council had given us free transport all week! It was a brilliant conference and clearly in the Lord's will. I do miss those times of gathering in His strength.

In preparation for the Brighton conference there were two other international gatherings. The first was held in the beautiful, Christian-owned, Garden Hotel, Singapore in February 1988 and then in Jerusalem in May 1989, with the intent of drawing in key international leaders for encouragement and planning. I couldn't find mention in Michael Harper's writings of the Singapore meetings and I am afraid that I remember very little about the time myself. However, I do recall that I met the powerful, charismatic Anglican Canon, James Wong and ministered in his church. In return he came to share with us in the UK and also introduced me to the lovely Bishop of Singapore, Moses Tay.

The Jerusalem meetings went through ups and downs which put the conference itself in jeopardy. Jeanne recorded that 'The committee was torn and Michael wept'. She went on, 'Tears are powerful and in the reality of facing *no*, the Lord's will was seen and obeyed'. I met and fellowshipped with many wonderful people. For example, Dr Paul Raj from India, who became a firm friend and with whom I formed a strong relationship and will share more about this special connection later.

I also remember having breakfast with William Kumuyi from Nigeria. Chatting as you do, I asked him how large his main church was in the capitol Lagos? 'One hundred thousand,' was the reply. I quickly moved on to avoid him asking about our *little* group in Romford. He was a very gentle man but had a powerful ministry and graciously came to visit us in the UK on a number of occasions.

I think it is worth reporting that sometimes there is a price to pay when we seek to reach out across the denominational divides. We were delighted to see two prominent leaders of the Elim Pentecostal Church at the conference. The General Superintendent, Eldin Corsie, a lovely, kind and sensitive man and Wynne Lewis, the popular leader of the Kensington Temple church in London.

The year after the Jerusalem gathering, I was at the Elim Church annual conference and I don't recall how or why I happened to be there but I found myself in a rather special meeting. Apparently, I believe it was a student doing some research who had gained access to the records of the conference attendance and discovered that Eldin Corsie was with us there. Now, the Northern Irish Elim group at that time were very cautious about relating to Catholics and they had a strong influence in the church. As a result, sadly, Eldin was forced to resign as Superintendent and there was now to be a vote for someone to replace him. I was utterly amazed to watch the proceedings and see that Reverend Wynne Lewis won that vote and succeeded Eldin in the role, the conference being blissfully unaware that he was also there in Jerusalem.

As we went on to plan the 1991 conference, someone discovered that on June 25, 1865, Hudson Taylor knelt on a beach in Brighton and cried out to God asking him to supply skilled, willing workers to bring the gospel to the inland provinces of China. So it was felt entirely appropriate that our world evangelisation conference should be held in this location.

Jeanne Harper in *Visited by God* writes:

> *At the conference: It was different! 'The plan that I will give you will be so different that it will sound impossible, but possible for the ones who trust My words and act on them'. That was a word of prophecy given at the Prayer Vigil at Jerusalem.*
>
> *The conference drew together world leaders from 115 countries. About 1500 were Anglican/Protestant, 800 Roman Catholic, 730 Pentecostal/non-Denominational and 10 Orthodox. There was a good representation from Africa (370), Asia (320), Latin America (50), North America (480), Oceania (180), with the remainder from Europe and the UK – 3100 in all.*
>
> *Throughout the conference the themes 'Evangelise the world' and 'Do it together' came again and again. For many, a highlight was the talk by Raneiro Cantalamessa when he spoke on Charismatic unity and institutional unity, and affirmed both. 'The Charismatic Renewal', he said, 'is a current of grace [...] a prophetic force [...] a sign of the times [...] the only existing reality that is genuinely inter-denominational'.*
>
> *Archbishop George Carey and Cardinal Basil Hume both addressed the conference. Some other important contributions came from Third World leaders like William Kumuyi, Gresford*

> Chitemo, Kriengsak Chereonwangsak, John Toguatu, Miguel
> Escobar and Omar Cabrera. Large crowds gathered to hear them
> speak of the massive growth of their churches, and the simple
> Biblical principles on which they are based.
>
> Nigel Ring headed up the administration team – an enormous task
> with 60 speakers, 12 languages, 30 workshops, 3 different Holy
> Communion services, all the arrangements for venues, and the
> eating facilities for 3100 delegates, plus the 1500 at the parallel
> conference at the Brighton Dome.
>
> This last offered the British the same ministry from the same
> speakers, yet there was little enthusiasm for promoting it among
> UK Charismatic leaders. But I remember the strong presence of the
> Lord amongst the 1500 who did come to the Dome. John Noble,
> the House Church leader who missed the Leaders' Conference in
> order to lead the Dome meetings, said he wouldn't have missed it
> for the world!'

My friend and colleague, Peter Butt, who shared in our Team Spirit team, handled the administration for the Dome meetings and writes:

> The evening gatherings in the Dome were an overflow for the local
> believers to attend and experience something of the blessings of the
> conference. We received key speakers from the main conference
> each evening which you led and hosted. I believe Dave Fellingham
> and his band provided the worship and I collected the speakers to
> ensure their arrival at the Dome. Among them were Jack Hayford
> from the USA, Omar Cabrera from Argentina, an Anglican Bishop
> from Nairobi and Miguel Escobar from Chile. I think Father
> Cantalamessa, the Popes preacher, was also with us.
>
> Dr George Carey, the Archbishop of Canterbury, addressed the
> conference with great dignity and enthusiasm and was warmly
> received by the delegates – if not by members of the press who
> were rather outspoken in their criticism of his involvement with
> 'Fundamentalist Christianity'!
>
> There was an impressive – a glittering – array of about 60
> speakers. Among them were well-known leaders such as Jack

Hayford, Tom Forrest, Michael Harper, Larry Christenson, Vinson Synan, Kriengsak Chareonwangsak and Terry Virgo, prominent House Church Leader. Less renowned, but no less effective, were many of the other speakers – such as Nigeria's William Kumuyi, Chile's Miguel Escobar, Argentina's Omar Cabrera, Papua New Guinea's John Toguata, Nigeria's James Ukaegbu, Singapore's James Wong, Hong Kong's David Wang and Australia's Dan Armstrong.

There was much to thank God for during and after the conference and many new relationships were formed which bore fruit in the years after. I referred earlier to my friendship with Miguel Escobar and later I will give an account of a special link with Dr Paul Raj from India which led to multiple visits to the tribal people of south-west central India, situated along the banks of the Godavari River.

- Other international gatherings with Michael Harper -

There were other international conferences organised by Michael in which we took part, in Malaysia in 1994 and Penang in 2000 on evangelism and the work of the Holy Spirit. Also, in Malta in 2004 there was a significant gathering to engage with the important matter of the 'suffering church worldwide'. Reports on these and other European conferences can be found on the International Charismatic Consultation (ICC) web site, formally the International Charismatic Consultation on World Evangelism (ICCOWE).

- *Albert Hall*
and Westminster Central Hall meetings -

Those of us in ministry in the London area were enjoying working together and were excited to see growth in our fellowships. We also found that other groups in the capital and beyond were keen to connect with us and share our vision for a dynamic church of the future. It, therefore, seemed that the obvious next step was to provide meetings where we could gather for praise, worship and teaching, and what better place for that, in the very heart of the town, than the, beautifully intimate, Royal Albert Hall?

Undeterred by the huge cost of hiring this building, we found a date and booked our first meeting on the 6th January 1975. We did no expensive advertising and Nick Butterworth, our brilliant resident artist, produced a simple handwritten announcement to say, 'Gerald, John, Nick, Maurice and George invite you and your friends to join us and Praise God Together at the Royal Albert Hall' with the date, time etc. and, believe it or not, over 5000 people packed the house! We kept a fairly open platform to enable those of us taking part the opportunity to interrupt one another if we were so inspired, and also to allow room for the operation of the gifts of the Holy Spirit.

One of the highlights of that first Royal Albert Hall meeting was an interview with the indomitable Malcolm Muggeridge which Peter Hill, George Tarleton and I did:

PH
Looking at the present state of the world do you think that it can ever be changed?

MM
I don't think it could. But, of course, men can be changed and every Christian must believe that we can be reborn – that is the message that our Lord had. It's the most important single fact about our existence.

One of the great fallacies of our time is to imagine that men can change things. A very simple illustration of what I mean is the incessant use of the word problem. If you are old, as I am, you have an ageing problem. If you are a boozer, they say you have a drink problem. The mis-use of the word is that it assumes that every single situation in which we find ourselves has an answer in men. It hasn't. In fact, precisely what is wrong with the world is not an energy crisis, or an inflation crisis, or any of these things. What is wrong with the world is one very simple thing – men are trying to live without God, and they can't!

JN

I don't want you to make any predictions, but do you feel that we are approaching a major crisis within the next few months, or the next couple of years?

MM

I have absolutely no doubt about it. It is a crisis of what is called Western civilisation. Western civilisation is collapsing. The situation as I see it is rather as it was when the Roman Empire, which seemed so enormously strong, which was so fantastically rich, the centre of everything, collapsed.

I think of Augustine, in Carthage, when a messenger told him 'Rome has been burned'. To Augustine this meant the end of everything he believed in. And then he reacted as a Christian – as we must react – and said to his flock: 'Men build cities and build civilisations and men destroy cities and civilisations, but the word of God, the truth, has been revealed to human beings and especially to us – that cannot be destroyed.'

There were another couple of meetings there and in one of these Christine and her dance drama team performed a touching enactment of the story of the prodigal son to a song. Many were visibly moved when the father, looking out from the edge of the stage saw his son returning through a door at the other end of the hall. Immediately, the father ran down to grab the boy and pull him up into a joyous dance before returning home to further celebrations.

On another occasion those of us leading the meeting felt we wanted to address the whole issue of Christian marriage. So the dancers arranged a simple dance which could quickly be picked up by couples who were then invited to take part. Quickly, the arena was full of couples dancing, and at the end there was an opportunity to put things right if there had been any issues in the relationship and to rededicate themselves to one another. After this, stewards went around offering copies of my newly-published book, *The Battle of the Sexes*. This proved to be a blessing for many at the time as there were few Christian books addressing the more delicate matters in marriage.

I referred to the last meeting of the Bind us Together tour performed at the Hall in 1981 but our final meeting there was in January 1982 entitled Glorious Triumph. This was a New Year celebration to proclaim God's victory, with the evangelist Eric Delve, Graham Kendrick, Dave Bilbrough, the band Giantkiller, Expression, our Romford choir conducted by Pat Bilbrough, and Gerald Coates. It was a great and exciting end to our series at the Royal Albert Hall. However, on reflection, I wonder if our success, accomplished with such comparative ease, contributed to what I see now was a subtle change of emphasis. I feel, in retrospect, without realising it, that perhaps we leaned more towards preaching what I call the gospel of the church, rather than the simple message of Jesus' gospel. I don't know but with hindsight I consider it may have been one of things that was a cause of some of the problems we faced later in our journey.

- *Westminster Central Hall* -

Over a period of time, out of a series of God-given connections, we developed a relationship with our Catholic Charismatic friends. A key link in this chain of events was Charles Whitehead, who came to lead ICCRO, the International Catholic Charismatic Renewal Office and, as such, he was highly influential in encouraging the growth of Catholic Renewal worldwide.

I first met Charles at a leadership conference Gerald and I had planned in the 1970's. He was seeking the Holy Spirit's direction for his life and like many at the time felt he was at the crossroads. Should he link with one of the new emerging networks or stay in and work within the denominational structures? He told us later how grateful he was as, apparently, we made it very clear that we believed, for him, it was the latter as we both felt the Lord had placed him there to fulfil a role.

Looking back it was strange that at the time, doctrinally, we were further apart from the Catholic position but felt closer to them relationally than to other denominational groups, some of which regarded us with suspicion. I think the truth was that the Catholics did not see us as a threat and we did not feel threatened by them. So here was an atmosphere in which we could thrive and influence and bless one another.

Against this background of trust, we began working together and Westminster Central Hall meetings were an important part of that. Charles reminded me that a Catholic brother, called Richard, helped organise the meetings and timed every speaker on his stopwatch. Neither of us could remember his surname. However, we do recall Myles Dempsey, a lovely man and a fully committed charismatic Christian, was also part of the organising team.

Sue, Charles' wife, reminded us that at their first meeting they sat at the back, at the second Charles took up the offering, and at the third meeting he was one of the hosts and comperes! The couple won our hearts and became a vital force in bringing together the group of New Church leaders and Catholic charismatics from the UK and the US in talks in Rome which became known as The Gathering in the Holy Spirit (GHS). These talks prepared the way for the small contingent from among the New Church leaders who began meeting with the Pontifical Council for the Promotion of Christian Unity to create a greater understanding between one or two groups.

I digress. So back to the Westminster Central Hall, where the much-loved Dom Benedict Heron OSB, one of the pioneers of the

Catholic Renewal and a lovely man, was a staunch supporter of our meetings, and a key speaker was Cardinal Leon Josef Suenens from Belgium. He was one of the major organisers of the Second Vatican Council and very committed to the Baptism in the Spirit and to the work for Christian unity. His efforts to ensure that the Baptism of the Holy Spirit and His gifts were the province of every believer became enshrined in Catholic teaching.

This vital truth meant, that when there was an outpouring of the Holy Spirit on a small group of students at an American university retreat weekend, the event could be endorsed as a genuine moment of grace. This retreat, known as The Duquesne weekend, unleashed the Charismatic Renewal in the Roman Catholic Church in the late 1960s which continues to this day. Other speakers included Colin Urquhart, John Wright the renowned Anglican evangelist, and our own David Matthews. I particularly remember Dave's talk as he was sharing his understanding of what it meant to be the church. Now, remember that this was a capacity crowd of 2000, split fairly equally between Catholics and mainly New Church Christians. As Dave concluded his message the whole congregation rose to their feet to applaud what they considered to be a simple and accurate portrayal of what the Church of Jesus Christ was intended to be.

It was an exciting time for us all to be together in this way with heartfelt prayer, exuberant worship and dance, singing in the Spirit and a flow of spiritual gifts. Christine's dance and drama group were always welcome and often brought moments of joy and laughter but sometimes those special, holy moments, when we are conscious that the Lord was present among us.

- The Gathering in the Holy Spirit -

Having referred to the GHS meetings which opened door for the *conversations* with the PCPCU and ultimately led to the paper on the

New Churches published on the Vatican web site, I must make mention of the European Charismatic Consultation which preceded all this. Evangelist Kim Kollins, a Catholic lay worker with a passion for prayer for Christian unity, was co-chair of the ECC which brought together Catholic and non-denominational charismatic leaders for prayer and dialogue.

Her efforts were such a blessing that a link developed with the ICC, the International Charismatic Consultation, which Charles Whitehead was chairing, and leaders from North America came to join us. Thus in 2002 the group became known as the Gathering in the Holy Spirit, described as an informal encounter between non-denominational and Roman Catholic leaders sponsored by the Centro Pro Unione and its director Father Jim Puglisi. These meetings continue to be held regularly and have been a great source of blessing to all who attend. Father Raniero Cantalamessa, preacher to the Papal Household, frequently came to address us in such humility, we came to love and appreciate him and his teachings.

As the *conversations* continued, we dropped the non-denominational label in favour of New Charismatic Churches (NCC's) which more aptly described what was being recognised as a growing worldwide movement. Also, as we explored the movement in all its forms and in many places, we discovered that there was already a great deal of co-operation and working together going on across the streams particularly in mercy and mission projects. You can find out more about the GHS meetings by visiting the consultation website. [1]

An interesting example of how meeting and fellowshipping together can change our understanding and our relationships, is seen in the journey of Pastor Ulf Eckman and his wife Birgitta. He joined us as Pastor of the Word of Life church in Upsala, Sweden and leader of a network of churches throughout the world. We knew he was interested in exploring the Catholic Church and he encouraged groups of his pastors to visit Rome to experience something of the Catholic Renewal.

---

[1] https://iccowe.com

He played a significant role in our GHS meetings and, from being a little cautious about his *faith* teaching, I warmed to him and Birgitta as we spent time together.

In 2014 Ulf announced his intention to leave his Livet's Ord church in order to join the Roman Catholic Church as he found himself growing ever closer to Catholic doctrine. The decision to leave his church was mainly amicable and I know that Charles Whitehead, who had ministered in Livet's Ord previously, was welcomed back to share again after Ulf had departed.

- *Kingdom Life* -

Gerald and his team put on a series of local summer conferences based in his home town of Cobham in Surrey between 1979 and 1982 which Christine and I were pleased to support. They were well attended and among the key speakers were Pastor Jim Hammond from a large charismatic church in Vancouver which we visited together; Dave and Dale Garret from New Zealand, well-known for their Scripture in Song ministry; our friend Roger Davin and, of course, Cliff Richard, who did a slot to the delight of many of the young people. My 14-year-old son John went forward for prayer that day!

However, our abiding memory of those weeks was not the incredible ministry or amazing worship, but the mad dash to get our daughter-in-law, Cathy, who was pregnant with our first grandchild back to Romford before the baby was born in the back of our car! As it was a Monday evening the roads were pretty clear and I dread to think how short a time that journey took as we hammered through London at break-neck speed. The Lord was obviously with us, for as we raced down the Embankment there was a guy in front of us going quite fast but too slow for me as I tried to pass him without success. I soon saw the reason for his presence as the police pulled him over to give him a ticket while the angel of the Lord kept us from being stopped!

Needless to say, we made it and the beautiful Victoria Louise arrived weighing in at 7lb 14 ounces. Cathy reminded me that Christine turned up the next day with the largest bunch of flowers she had ever seen. Apparently, Christine explained that she bought every single pink flower there was in the shop!

- *The Scottish Bible weeks 1987 - 1991* -

My friend and team member, Jim Holl and I had developed good links with a group of churches in Scotland. John Hawker, who led a church in West Kilbride at the time, came up with the idea of a summer camp for the area which Jim and I supported. The first two of these took place on the stunningly beautiful Isle of Arran, just off the west coast of Scotland. They were relaxed times with lots of family fun and ministry but not packed programmes, so plenty of space to enjoy yourselves. I believe it was the second week when the glorious Scottish rain poured down and the whole camp was washed out. We all ended up in a large hall which the locals kindly opened up for us, and the rest of the next day was spent drying out tents and clothes – the fun of camping!

From there we moved to Kelburn where we found a great site where we made ourselves at home. As I remember Jim, Christine and I shared and supplied most of the ministry with some of the locals and one or two invited speakers while Jim's wife Sylvia spoke on marriage and family life in the seminars.

However, the star event one week was the visit of the lovely American Pentecostal evangelist, Jean Darnell, who seemed to adopt the UK and worked here to serve the Renewal. She was well known for a vision which she had in 1967, which has in part been fulfilled, but people remember it and still refer to it today as a vision of revival in Great Britain.

Jean saw the British Isles were covered in a green haze with lots of pinpoints of light piercing through which turned out to be fires breaking out all over the nations, from Scotland in the north, to Land's End in the south. As these God-lit fires joined together they burned brighter and she saw rivers of fire flowing from Scotland to Ireland, Wales into England and some crossed the Channel into Europe. The fires were people, intensely hungry, longing to see a powerful *Acts of the Apostles* church released across the land.

You can imagine the blessing that Jean brought to our camp that week as she shared her heart and prayed, spending quality time with people. We had five good years until we felt the week had run its course, with many other events taking place around the country which could provide all the ingredients which go to make a great Christian family holiday week.

- Vision in Action -

I met Tony Pullin and his wife Muriel when visiting the Patchway Fellowship in Bristol, which Hugh Thompson had started in his own home. When Hugh left Bristol, he asked me to continue to visit the fellowship. During that time, I came to appreciate Tony's tender heart and his great teaching gift, and he went on to play a foundational role (with others) in what became the Bristol Christian Fellowship. When Tony handed over the leadership of the church to Dave Day, he continued to serve on the team but later returned to full-time employment which, after a couple of years, led him to Carlisle. However, it was clear to me that he still carried a call to ministry on his life, which I am sure he was fully aware of, so we kept in touch.

Tony reminded me that whilst he was in Carlisle, David Matthews prophesied that God was going to give him his own vineyard. That actually happened when the company Tony was working for promoted him to a national position, which meant he had to move to the Nottingham area in 1988. I encouraged Tony to move to join the Ravenshead Christian Fellowship where I was working with Steve and

Cathy Coup, which he did. Soon freed from employment, he developed from there a fruitful ministry serving a growing number of churches across the Midlands. In 1998 he and Muriel moved farther south to Stratford on Avon and were based in Stratford Christian Fellowship, later to be known as Heartlands.

Our good friends Steve and Cathy had a passion for mission and followed a call to the Welsh-based mission, World Horizons, led by Rowland Evans and have been working there ever since. Graham Bell, the brother of Stuart Bell leader of the Ground Level network, and his wife Molly took over the leadership of the Ravenshead church when Steve and Cathy left.

When Christine and I moved to be with Gerald Coates in Pioneer, Tony encouraged the Midlands churches to link with the Pioneer network. In 1998 Tony organised a Midlands Conference for those churches at Hothorpe Hall, Northamptonshire, where Stuart Bell was invited to minister. The conference was a great success and everyone was blessed and keen to have a follow-up get-together. So in 1999 a larger group came together for a weekend with the much-loved Jeff Lucas, who was part of Pioneer at that time.

Jeff's storytelling and humour touched our hearts and, I am sure, played a part in ensuring these conferences became a regular feature for the Midland churches. Thus, the weekend in 2000 moved to the larger Hayes Conference Centre in Swanwick. In 2001 Tony shared his heart to bring this growing network together under the banner of Vision in Action, focussing on translating exciting, fresh vision into relevant action.

This first Vision in Action conference included ministry from Jeff Lucas, Steve Lowton from Leeds and David Mniki from the Transkei in South Africa. Dave and Pat Bilbrough and Godfrey Birtill led our worship and this wonderful weekend was the forerunner of the annual conferences which continued until 2015. Tony worked hard to bring in ministries which encouraged and inspired the churches and when, in

2006, he passed on the leadership to Phil Collins, leader of Chawn Hill Church, the youth and children's work was expanded.

I won't attempt to summarise all the conferences, which became known by the acronym VIA, adding the meaning of A Way Through, from the Latin *via* - a way. They were a great success, but the 2004 gathering was special, with Guy Chevreau and David Ruis coming from the Toronto Vineyard, where the revival was on going. Then in 2006 Jeff Lucas brought Dary Northrop and his wife from the Timberline Church in Colorado, where Jeff shares in the ministry team.

CHAPTER NINE

WARTS AND ALL AND MOVING ON

I didn't want our story to ignore some of the low points of our lives by focussing on all the wonderfully positive things we experienced. Of course, neither do I wish to dwell on the negative as I am incredibly grateful for so much of God's blessing which has accompanied us along the way. However, I have been disappointed when I have read some accounts of ministries which paint such a glowing picture of life in the Spirit which is seldom the reality for most people and certainly was not the case in our journey.

Since moving to Collier Row, Romford, in 1969 we had experienced 15 years of consistent blessing and great fellowship. We saw church growth across the whole area and enjoyed the tremendous release all kinds of gifts and creativity. We were developing friendships locally, across the UK and beyond. Our kids enjoyed the excellent school Anita and her team had built and everything in the garden seemed rosy. However, we all know that there is an enemy who loves to lurk in the garden waiting for an opportunity to sow his seeds of discontent.

My experience of the breakdown of relationships in a church, or among a group of friends, usually takes place when we don't deal with personal issues as they arise. In other words, we don't keep short accounts, so that when things come to a head, we end up dealing with multiple concerns as people unload in an atmosphere of hurt and confusion. In that kind of situation, it is near impossible to bring resolution and restore calm which is especially true when leaders are involved and I was undoubtedly part of the problem.

There is no way I could explain all the dynamics of what happened, except to hold up my hand and accept my weaknesses which must have contributed to the collapse of many, what I believe, were genuine friendships from which I have never fully recovered. I suppose this experience played a part in my threatening to write a book entitled, *How to Agree to Disagree Agreeably*, which I admit I have never managed to write yet.

So, what can I say about my part in all this and some of what I hope I have learned? Firstly, my friend and colleague, Nick Butterworth, who was also my partner in the Rainbow Company business on a 49% to my 51% basis, came to see me. He wanted to say that he was withdrawing from our arrangement which was a massive blow to me as his artistic ability was a major reason for the success of the business.

I couldn't give a full account of his reasons for taking this action but, on reflection, I can see that his desire to maintain the high standards and quality of our product base against my expansionist ways must have caused him great conflict. Also, I must confess that I had run up some debt which I took full responsibility for and ultimately resolved, but again that must have been a problem. There may well have been other issues for Nick that I am not aware of but I still hold him in great regard and have benefited greatly from his amazing gift and learned a lot from his approach to life. So I was deeply saddened when Nick and others chose to move away.

Since writing about this I recently received an email from Nick saying that he would like to come and see me. I was delighted but had no idea what was in his mind. It was a real joy to see him and I was not disappointed as we spent a couple of hours reminiscing. Before he arrived, I had been wondering how he had been in his walk with Jesus.

However, without me having to ask, he shared how one of his great joys was being out walking his dog in the woods while singing and praying in tongues. After our time came to an end I wrote to thank him for the visit. I shared how I felt that our time together was rather like what I expected our first chat in heaven would have been, but thankfully before we ever arrived.

Then to Maurice Smith, another key person in my life and so often my travel companion as we ministered around the UK and internationally. He was much loved as a story teller and an extraordinary sharer of the grace of God. Even after all these years I seldom complete a talk without referring to one of his stories or something he said. However, he used to get under real pressure at times when he stood up to minister, and would even take his false teeth out in his handkerchief to pop in his pocket as they made him feel sick. Also, the truth is, he was quite fearful of being in a car when someone else was driving, so I often handed the keys for him to drive and he truly was grateful.

I know he loved me and valued our friendship. On one occasion we were in a fellowship meeting and he asked me to pick him up which I did. He was very light and I sat him on my shoulder, from his perch he went on affirm our friendship, telling the people that if it wasn't for me, he wouldn't be where he was as I had, at times, carried him through. I felt very humbled as we had great times and lots of fun together.

Again, looking back I see there were a couple of things which caused him problems. At one point the school was struggling financially and I made an appeal to the group for a special offering. The reality is, that schools such as ours seldom work with a surplus without support. The group were incredibly generous in their giving and I simply asked everyone to pray and ask the Lord what they should give. I had no intention of putting pressure on people but trusted that what came in would see the school through a difficult period.

Sadly, Maurice was unsure what to do and came to me to see what Christine and I were giving. With hindsight, I can see that I was wrong to share our intention and I should have made it completely clear that whatever he and Eileen, his wife, decided would be fine by me. So when I told him what we were planning, even though I did say that he should make his own decision, he received that as a real pressure.

On top of this, Maurice had been greatly influenced by Norman Grubb, a lovely man of God who married the daughter of the great missionary C. T. Studd. He, himself, followed in his father-in-law's footsteps and became a missionary, and on his return to the UK wrote many books and was greatly sought after as a speaker. With his love for the doctrine of the grace of God, Maurice latched on to Grubb's teaching on *Christ in me* emphasising the truth that Christ, in all his reality, dwells in me. Which is so true and is underlined by the scripture that tells us the saints became known as *Christians* or *little Christs*.

The sad thing is, that it is not a great leap to stretch this truth to make wrong assumptions about our ability to sin. So whilst we rejoice in the fact that Christ is, indeed, in me it does not, therefore, mean that I am unable to fail or to fall into sin. The fact is, that we remain vulnerable to the devil's attacks and pride can become a snare that leads us away from the continued enjoyment of the Lord's abundant supply of grace. It seems, for some in the fellowship, this became their route out of relationships and was a slippery slope away from Jesus himself. Maurice moved away, as did Nick and many others which left us with a great sadness and missing many dear friends of long-standing.

Maurice did contact me after some years and sent me a copy of his last little book entitled, *The Art of Happily Going Nowhere*. I see it is still available on Amazon with the apt description:

> *After a lifetime spent on the road, a tireless speaker on spirituality and personal development, Maurice Smith finally made the greatest discovery of his life. He learned the art of happily going nowhere. In this short, direct, beautiful book, a natural storyteller brings ancient spiritual wisdom alive with a simple message: ' Relax. Be still and know.'*

It's a while since I read the book which I couldn't find among my other volumes for some reason. However, the impression I was left with after reading it, is that Maurice found peace by meditating on his inner self. This seemed to me to be a form of Buddhism, but I must say it was not the Maurice I knew who often told the story of how he discovered the loving Father God whose great hobby was collecting failures! On the other hand, Nick went on to pursue his career as a children's artist and is now possibly one of the most loved and successful in his field. His adorable books have been translated into many languages and have found their way into the hearts of children all over the world.

Among the lessons learned, there was one thing that has stood me in good stead over the years. It has caused many people to smile as I recount the story of how I came to appreciate what can happen as we misread one another's facial expressions, and how we assume that people correctly read ours. At the time all this upsetting business was going on one young lady, who I knew well and had the privilege of marrying her and her man, came to me and complained about the pressure I put on her and called me 'authoritarian!'

I well remember smiling and saying to her that she was one of the people that I had absolutely no chance of persuading to do anything against her will. She was a very strong-willed woman, a bit like my beloved Christine in that respect. I am sure that there were others who felt like her and I may well have been guilty of giving that impression but it was, and is, abhorrent to me to think that anyone would do something I suggested out of fear or false loyalty.

Again, thinking back, I quite often had people come up to me after a meeting and say to me things like, I could tell you were not happy about this or that, when it was not the case at all. I also became aware that, at times in every-day life, I was surprised at the reactions I received. For example, when I was pushing my trolley through customs an official would often beckon to me to pull over and open my case, whereas if Christine took the trolley we always sailed through unscathed. I was with Gerald once and he was backing into a parking space which meant that, technically, he was driving down a one-way street the wrong way. I smiled at the policeman who had stopped us and he immediately asked me what I was laughing at? I did try to persuade him that I was not laughing at all as I thought it was a serious offence, but he was not convinced.

Perhaps one of the most the most challenging situations I faced produced all the evidence I needed to realise that I was not always the best person to resolve some of the difficulties I found myself in! At the time I was making regular trips to the USA and it would have been very helpful to have a multiple entry visa. I went to the American Embassy in Grosvenor Square to make my application. I completed all the necessary forms and went to the counter with my passport. The nice lady behind the glass window looked the papers over and asked me what evidence I had of my intention to return to the UK? I explained that I had a return ticket and a wife and five children to come home to. She immediately retorted to the effect that a wife and five children might well be a reason to stay in the US!

Well, I won't bore you with the incredible lengths I went to getting letters from the elders of our church, other Christian leaders, legal advisors but all to no avail until, finally, I believe I heard the Lord speak! I felt I heard him tell me to tear up all the letters, get a new passport and send Christine to the Embassy which I did. Christine took her knitting and her smile and quietly waited to be called to get the passport.

It was a long wait and I just had to pop in to see how she was getting on, but she quietly told me to go away as I was giving off bad vibes! I could not complain about that as after three hours or so she emerged triumphant, waving my passport with the beautiful multiple entry visa stamp intact!

It was in situations like this where I learned that Christine and I were a great team when we relied on one another's gifts, and the truth was that she had a God-given smile that could soften a heart, open a door or make a way for the Holy Spirit to work. I did not have that kind of smile and came to realise when it was best for me to take a back seat and be there to support her and give her covering so that she felt secure in the operation of her gifts.

When people got to know me, they seemed to trust me so that I was able to provide an environment where gifted people could come together and function as a team. So over the years I came to accept the reality that my demeanour and the way I respond to events could, at times, muddy the waters and work against my intentions. Whilst I am more aware of this as I grow older and seek to pull back and perhaps apologise, I know I can still fall into the same trap. I see this as another reason why we need one another as we learn to yield and receive help from those we love and trust. All this underlines and confirms the need for plurality in relationships and the importance of working together in team, which is clearly the way the early church was structured with different ministries working in harmony together.

- *Moving on* -

When we came together in the Romford Fellowship after the loss of so many friends who we not only loved, but also worked closely with in the development of our growing network here in the UK and in other parts of the world, I found myself asking where do we go from here, Lord? Often in such circumstances things I have said in past ministry to others come back to challenge me. I distinctly remember asking the same question when encouraging folk whose lives or work had been shattered. What do we do now, Lord? Well, I would say, we surrender to Jesus and ask for his strength to pick up the pieces and, by His grace, we move on. I found those words coming back to me like an echo and I knew I had to take my own medicine.

As best as I was able, I drew folk together who stuck with us and encouraged them to join me in taking up what remained, and then endeavour to continue the work the Lord had given us to do. I am glad to say that still today there is a group in Collier Row now led by Peter Taylor, the son of one of the leaders who continued with me at that time, and Anita's school celebrated its 40th anniversary in 2020.

Apart from the work in the Romford area, we had a team of ministries who served the fifty or so churches which linked with us here in the UK and also visited the other countries where we had growing responsibilities. In Team Spirit, as it was called, we had an understanding that there were three categories of those we were working with: groups or churches we sought to bless but we had no other responsibility; those we had developed a friendship with where there was a mutual need to maintain and nurture the relationship; and then those we were building with which required regular contact, advice and involvement. *Blessing, friendship* and *building* helped us to ensure that we were not failing those in our sphere of ministry.

Looking at the brochure we produced at the time to explain what we were about, I recognise that, as a reaction to the loss that I felt, my gift of inclusivity went into over-drive. The result being that what is a strength became a weakness as I brought several very good friends into the team who were greatly gifted in ministry but who didn't fully embrace our ethos. This meant that we lost something of the cutting edge we had, not a major disaster but not the best way to move forward.

I think it is worth mentioning the new structure of the Team and those involved as they were all great people many of whom, if they have not gone home to glory, I am still in relationship with after all these years.

There was, what we called, an advisory group of three guys who were working closely with me and were recognised as senior ministries. Norman Barnes, Founder of Links International which I will refer to later; David Matthews, who joined us from Northern Ireland where he established The Belfast Christian Fellowship, a radical community bringing together Catholics and Protestants during the *troubles*; and Phil Vogel, who together with his wife Hilary, were faithful in encouraging Christine and me as we launched into our ministry from the beginning. He was a director of British Youth for Christ and worked with David Pawson at the Millmead Centre before taking on the leadership of Guildford Community Church. The Team itself was made up of further nineteen men and women in ministry with seven *partners* with limited time they could give.

Obviously, Christine contributed in many ways but ensured that creativity was at the heart of what we were about. Andy Au, having planted a church in Brighton, offered training in movement in worship and supported projects in south-east Asia. Anita Traynar, now Martin, pioneered our school and worked as an educationalist, whilst Ian Traynar led worship and ran Lifesong worship training courses. Wes Sutton, also a worship leader, headed up the youth work at Spring Harvest for five years. Terry Brewer and Bren Robson, were both part of Guildford Community Church leadership. Terry had experience of a multi-cultural inner-city church and also working with young people. Whilst Bren had a real concern for releasing women in ministry and social justice.

Dave Summers established Malvern Christian Fellowship, and having trained with New Tribes Mission moved to Thailand with his wife Carole and daughter Rebecca to work among tribal people and the poor. Vin Wiffen, Peter Doherty from Essex, Dennis Marshall from Stevenage and Derek Poole from Northern Ireland, were all church leaders who brought gifts of administration, teaching and evangelism, which were available to support churches and encourage leaders. Stuart Murray, founder and co-leader of Tower Hamlets Christian Fellowship, was an author and church strategist with experience in education. David Mills, after having worked with the Church of Pentecost in Ghana as principal of the Bible College, returned to lead the Highthorn Church in Yorkshire. He was available to share from his remarkable experience of living and working in an African church in a measure of revival. Grace Barnes, Norman's wife, had worked with him in Ghana and travelled extensively encouraging women in ministry.

Peter Butt joined us from an Assemblies of God background and served me tirelessly in administration, but was also a great bible teacher and developed a year-long leadership training programme. Chris Hill, from an Anglican background moved into Pilgrim's Hall in Brentwood where we held area-wide meetings and conferences which was also a bible teaching and counselling centre, He had a special interest in the Holy Land and led tours there each year. I mentioned Phil Jones from the Dartford College who joined us after he had established the church in Rossendale, Lancs. As a church leader he was prophetic, worked with young people and was a song writer.

Finally, Jim Holl and Ian Farr, both men I am in touch with regularly at the time of writing. Jim came from a Baptist background and together with his wife, Sylvia, planted a church in Bromley, Kent and worked with us and our links in India, Norway and South Africa. Ian, on the other hand, spent some years in India with OM until he and his family had their visas revoked. He came back to the UK into church leadership but continued to serve and develop his links in India and later in South Africa where he is living now.

The seven partners were men who, at the time, were unable to give themselves to full-time ministry. Rod Boreham was converted in my bible class when he was 14 and worked with Christine in her drama group. He was also serving the Team in writing, teaching and administration. John Hawker was the church leader in Scotland who started the Scottish Bible Weeks which I mentioned in my previous chapter. Peter Martin converted in a revival movement in his school served in general administration and with Links International working for Norman Barnes. John Norton led the Church in Chadwell Heath and established Mountain Ash school and was a trustee for Link International for some time.

Alan Pavey, a successful business man, encouraged new church plants in south-west England and the London area. He was a trustee of the Pilgrim Hall Centre and masterminded our first Spring Bank Holiday weekend. Tony Pullin played a foundational role in the Bristol Christian Fellowship, was an inspirational bible teacher and ended up leading the Via Network of churches in Pioneer. Ken Rose and his wife, Maureen, you will have read earlier played a vital role in the start of our work in

Romford and continued to serve us in the development of the Team and in many other ways.

I realise that sharing this information about the Team as we moved forward was quite a lot for some of my readers to get their heads round, but I felt it was important for the record. Also, some of you will remember input that you received from different members of the team. Obviously, it is just a snapshot of where we were at the time and some things changed and others developed as we journeyed on to the early 1990's when we received the prophecies which brought Team Spirit and Pioneer together.

- Significant international connections -

Over the years the Lord led me, Christine and the team to meet many key people in our travels, people who opened doors to us all over the world to our mutual benefit. It would be impossible to cover all of these but there were several areas which I do feel I need to refer to which were important in the context of our journey.

CHAPTER TEN

SCANDINAVIA

I never did visit Finland but I did often meet, and have fellowship with, Kalevi Lehtinen, son of an Olympic 5000-metre champion, who was an international evangelist with Campus Crusade. He played a great part in bringing together other European evangelistic organisations to encourage co-operation across the continent and was an inspiration in the various groups I was involved in with Michael Harper and the charismatic Catholics.

I did, however, visit Denmark spending time mainly with youth groups, and one occasion I will never forget was when I was in Copenhagen with an evangelistic team. They had been out on the streets and found a bunch of Turkish immigrants who they dragged into the coffee bar for refreshments and a preach. I was asked to share my testimony but there was a problem, the immigrants couldn't speak Danish. Just one of their number knew a little German so they found one Danish guy who knew some German but he didn't speak much English.

I began to share my story with, 'When I was a young man...', pause for translation into Danish and then from Danish into German. At this point, the Turk who was supposed to understand the German wandered off to collect a friend who he brought to the front with a big smile on his face. After a long period of confused deliberation, it was discovered that my, 'When I was a young man...' had been received as, 'Bring me a young man', and the meeting dissolved into fits of hilarious laughter. I never did get to share my testimony with these Turkish immigrants but they certainly seemed to enjoy themselves. Not one of my finest hours and, sadly, I didn't get the Spirit's gift of tongues and interpretation to solve the problem.

I spent many happy days in Sweden and made friends wherever I went as they were most hospitable! As I said earlier, my first visit was passing through with Peter Lyne on my way to drop Pete off in Norway. It was in Arlingsas, a small town just outside of Gothenberg, where we stopped off and I met the Tubin family, and Rune Tubin opened the door for me to return, and introduced me to many of his friends. Thus, I visited a group in Boras on several occasions and also spent time in Orebro, at the Orebro Mission, and in a home church led by an ex-Salvation Army officer who had been Baptised in the Holy Spirit.

In Stockholm I made contact with one of the leaders of the Filadelfia Church who invited me to share in other home church groups around the city. It was also in Stockholm in 1979 that Gerald Coates and I took the Bind Us Together team to put on a presentation hosted by Ylva Eggehorn, the famous Swedish Christian poet and hymn-writer. My friend, Bosse Nyberg, translated for us and kindly offered my book, *The Battle of the Sexes*, for sale. Apparently, there is no Swedish word equivalent to *sexes*, so he described it as the battle of that which is between the legs, which caused a few wry smiles!

I returned to Sweden many times and enjoyed sharing in all kinds of emerging renewal groups in various parts of the country. I travelled from Ystad and Malmo in the south up north as far as Alfter, a tiny village where a Christian doctor and his family lived. He ran a health spa where the rich and famous from around the world came to receive his advice and therapy. I was there one winter with a small team which included my colleague, George Tarleton, when we were given the sauna treatment. After sitting in the heat and steam for some time we had to run out into the cold and jump into the lake's icy waters, before rolling in the snow. I must say I felt very invigorated once we dried off and sat down for our meal!

Whilst I enjoyed our visits to Sweden and meeting so many lovely Christians there, I never made the kind of long-term relationships which resulted through our links in Norway. Perhaps it was due to the bond that came about between our two countries during the war. Wherever we travelled there seemed to be a strong desire to build together and learn from one another. The Lord truly opened a door for us into that beautiful country which enabled us to be part of an amazing movement of the Holy Spirit which developed and grew over many years. The strength and endurance of our friendships is evidenced by the fact that, fifty years on, two couples came to contribute at our celebration of Christine's life in Leatherhead in June 2022.

I have to say that I find it incredibly difficult to give an account of what took place through the times we spent travelling around the home churches and charismatic groups in Norway. Apart from my and Christine's input, many of the team made strong connections as well. Dave Matthews, Nick Butterworth, Jim Holl, Dave Bilbrough and Ian Traynar all spent quality time with friends, many of whom travelled to be with us at leaders' gatherings and conferences in the UK. However, my long-time friend Hans Kristian Strand, kindly took the time to write this report of the growth of the house church movement from his perspective as someone deeply involved from the start. I thought it would be good to share this and then add some of my experiences along the way.

- House churches in Norway -
by Hans Kristian Strand

How this movement started and developed in the 1970's to the 1980's.

The charismatic movement arrived for a few Norwegian Christians the last couple of years of the 1960's. However, early in the 1970's a

PURE CHURCH

fresh new wave of people getting involved in what the Holy Spirit was doing increased rapidly. At that time, it was mostly young people who responded and received the charismatic experience as certain cities and towns became centres for what was happening.

In Oslo, in 1971/2, a priest in the Norwegian Seaman's Church, Hans Jakob Frøen and his son Eivind who, around that time established Youth with a Mission in Norway, were key in teaching on the anointing of the Holy Spirit. They had been in contact with Michael Harper in England, Brother Andrew from Holland, and Dennis Bennet from the USA. Even David Wilkerson of 'The Cross and the Switchblade' fame came over and had an open-air meeting in a market place in Oslo.

They all came to speak in conferences, especially in Oslo, as hundreds, maybe thousands, of people experienced the Baptism in the Holy Spirit in those meetings. Also in Oslo there was a group of 'Jesus People' called 'Guds Fred' or 'God's Peace', within the Lutheran church which operated in a similar way to the house churches. They had daily fellowship in a big apartment and arranged 'Gospel Nights' in one of the biggest churches in Oslo. The American Lutheran priest Don Brendtro and our own, Jørgen Aas, were leading that together with the brothers Øyvind and Gregers Lundh. In fact, Gregers and his wife Magnild are now a part of our house church in Gjøvik today.

Around Lake Mjøsa, in the towns of Gjøvik and Hamar, there was a strong youth movement and a release of the Spirit among hundreds of young people. One of the reasons why those two towns were affected in such a way was because there were leaders who were really dedicated in sharing and praying for the Spirit to fall upon people. Olav Slåtten in Gjøvik and Arnold Børud in Hamar were among them.

Skien and Porsgrunn, a couple of hours south-west of Oslo had a similar experience, as did Molde and the surrounding areas on the west coast. In fact, the organisation 'Ung Visjon' or 'Young Vision' started there. In all these places there were established teams going out to evangelise in the summer with subsequent conferences with speakers from England

and the USA. Also, quite a few travelled to England to join the summer charismatic conferences taking place there.

With reference to the emergence of house churches here in Norway, for my part it all started back in 1974. My wife, Marit, and her friend Barbro, who married Trygve Brekke from Stavanger, were student nurses together and through Barbro we heard about Tore Lende on the south-west coast, close to Stavanger. Tore wanted to gather about 30 people in a small place along one of the fjords close by where Hugh Thompson and Peter Lyne from England were invited to take part. I was still studying at the university of Oslo and had part-time work as church assistant in the Lutheran church where Marit and I lived. It was a small miracle that enabled me to attend.

The plane waited ten extra minutes for me at the airport in Oslo, and the ferry from Stavanger left the harbour at the precise moment I placed my feet on the boat. I had never met any of those who were there before but felt very much at home, and I still have all the notes from that conference 7th – 10th of March 1974. What is more, the Lutheran church paid for everything. The atmosphere, the singing and dancing and, of course, the new way of preaching just changed my way of believing in God, my own little paradigm shift took place there in March -74.

Tore Lende went on to be an important support and driving force, having had a revelation about what church is really all about. He visited us regularly and already at that point he had written a pamphlet called 'Given to Each Other' which meant a great deal to many people. Back in Oslo we began to meet with Barbro, Tor and Liv Thorild Undheim, as well as Åsulf Kvammen, as we were all still students there. The two boys brought their guitars, and new songs from Åsulf almost every week made these small gatherings very special happenings. What a joy it was to sing those new songs about exactly how we felt about God, our Father, and about being the living body of Christ together. We also regularly received new songs from England which were an encouragement.

PURE CHURCH

That summer and autumn of 1974 became one big revelation for all those of us meeting together, but we had so much more than just meetings. We used every opportunity to gather for meals, walks and for football or tennis, in other words just being together as friends! We took holidays and weekend trips together all year round and in that safe setting so many things came up. We were just married, the first kids had just arrived, we were on our way from studying into work and our friendship made it easier to open up on any and every subject. We did not feel we were religious people who had to confess our sins all the time, trying hard to be good people. Very quickly we found out that this ordinary and simple life as a Christian is, actually, the best way of living and soon more people wanted to join us, friends of friends who were discovering Jesus in a new and fresh way.

The link to England was important for us. Tore had been in contact with Peter Lyne in 1972 and invited him to Bryne and also to our small group in Oslo. So it was that John Noble and Peter Lyne came driving by car to Oslo late in November 1973 where they met Tor, Liv Thorild and Åsulf. Liv Thorild said she still remembers John sharing from Psalm 133 and the real meaning behind having 'a holy fellowship'. Then John came back again in 1974 with Marice Smith and I well remember how it dawned to me that GRACE is the centre of the gospel. Also, the book of Ephesians really came alive when John opened it up to our small group.

In 1976 Hugh Thompson and David Tomlinson came over for a weekend conference in Oslo. Tore Lende, of course, took part but also pastor Erling Thu from the west coast was with us. Later, Bryn Jones also paid us a visit, but he went mostly to Bergen for the special contact he made with Noralv Askeland. In Bergen they were not really interested in the thinking about house churches. I believe Bryn and Noralf wanted big churches from the beginning, churches with more influence, more visibility and with a very clear leadership structure. As time went on, Bryn's brother Keri was recognised as the apostle to the 'Christian Fellowship' in Bergen.

Graham Perrins, also from the UK, came over and developed a special relationship with Tore and the larger group in Sandnes and Bryne, just south of Stavanger. They had grown as a house church with many creative women in their twenties and early thirties with many musicians, singers and dancers! In August 1976 quite a few of us Norwegians went to join our English friends at the Bath and West conference. We were all camping in our modest tents together and enjoying good fellowship with a group from Sweden.

That summer was one of the driest in history, but we all felt we could drink freshly from the river of life we found there. The lively worship and dancing was something very new for most Scandinavians in those days. However, I did notice that there seemed to be some tension between the American speaker, Ern Baxter, and the English ministries. I clearly saw that there was a difference in the way they spoke about leadership and grace. Later, I found out that there was a split between those who put on the conference and those who supported Bryn Jones and his team.

In the late 1970's a new group of people from Askim and Skiptvedt, one hour south-east of Oslo, wanted contact with those of us in Oslo. They had a strong emphasis on living and working together and even shared a lot of their finances together. Lars and Eirin Bjerke were leading that house church of about 30-40 people and they were good builders and very creative. Lars was recognised as a clever potter and his product sold very well. They were soon fascinated by what they heard from England and it was not long before John Noble was invited to the group. So, in the summer of 1979, they arranged a conference in their big house with between 60 and 70 attending and John and Nick Butterworth came to share in the ministry.

Almost every year from 1976 to the end of the decade, some of us Norwegians crossed the North Sea to join leaders' conferences in Pilgrim Hall, Sussex. This was important for us and a big encouragement. It was at these gatherings we got to know and appreciate David Matthews, who began to visit Norway and our small house churches and he especially loved it when he could fish for trout in the rivers here. He built a strong friendship with Henri and Swan Olsen in Haugesund which lasted many years.

PURE CHURCH

Late in the winter of 1979 a large company of people came over to Oslo to bring a presentation of 'Bind us Together'. The house church in Oslo rented the meeting hall in the Munch Museum where the world-famous Norwegian artist, Edvard Munch's painting, 'The Scream', is housed. Around 350 people showed up, a big group for us at that time with no well-known names on the poster. Musicians, singers, dancers and speakers in a Christian show was something very new to Norwegians. John Noble and Gerald Coates were the narrators and the whole evening was a real blessing. The team were accommodated in the homes of our people in the church and it was all great fun.

The next day John, Ian Traynar, a worship leader, and myself went by car to Lillehammer to join a growing house group there. After a great evening we drove back in the middle of the night with a great deal of snow and ice on the road. Such conditions were unheard of for our guests as back home their roads would have been closed.

Good literature was also something we appreciated and receiving our first copy of 'Fulness' magazine was a revelation in itself. For us it had the wow factor! Inspiring articles about a new way of understanding church life and living as ordinary human beings with Jesus as our friend; knowing we have a good heavenly Father who enables us to live in unity because He sent the Holy Spirit to dwell within each one, was releasing. Artists Nick Butterworth and Mick Inkpen created living pictures of the values expressed in the articles with sensitivity and humour, so that the design work hit a chord within that made us want to devour every page of the magazine.

With permission we produced a similar magazine in Norway and released it in the summer of 1981. We borrowed the drawings from Nick B and wrote articles inspired from what we had experienced during those years. We called it 'Steiner' meaning 'Stones' with the thought that we are living stones and being built into God's temple. It was well received, but we did not have enough resources to continue circulating our magazine and so it had a limited life.

I also subscribed to 'Restoration' magazine from the brethren in the north of England. It was good and there were similarities to Fulness, but it was more traditional in content and design. We also appreciated the series of small booklets from the UK which were very inspiring for some of us in Norway - 'The Church in the House', by George Tarleton, 'Forgive us our Denominations' and 'First Apostles, Last Apostles' by John Noble. Nick Butterworth wrote 'Sunday and the Rest', then 'Not Under Law' and 'Free from Sin' were by Hugh Thompson and Gerald Coates. From these helpful booklets we understood the importance of church life and unity in the church and how the grace of God makes it all possible.

The view we have of God and what really happened on the cross is mirrored in the way we build church and conduct our relationships. John and Christine Noble's book 'Battle of the Sexes' was a great contribution to understanding family relationships, as husband, wife and kids are an essential building block of society. In Norway we thought that 'Forgive us our Denominations' was so important that it was translated into Norwegian in 1977 and all these years later people still ask for that small book.

In the summer of 1980, we arranged a rather big conference with the UK speakers, John Noble and David Matthews, in Valle, a town right in the centre of Norway by the foot of Hardangervidda. People were inspired, and many were baptised in the river there. As the Prince of Wales Charles and Diana were married in August 1981, John and Christine Noble, David Matthews and Dave Bilbrough all came over to Kristiansand, joining us with about 200 people there. One of the days John and Dave Bilbrough took a flight to Molde on the west coast to take part in a conference with the group 'Young Vision'. It was an inspiring time. The young people responded to Dave and John had them up and dancing in a great conga line around the hall.

Later that month Marit and I, with our two small kids at that time, were invited to spend the autumn in Collier Row with John and Christine Noble and their family. We stayed till the end of November. It was a good, but busy time for everybody in their big house as it was the launching of Team Spirit, a group of ministries coming together to care and support churches in the UK and other parts of the world. Also, they were recording music and song cassettes along with song sheets for both UK and Norway. In order to complete the work, John Menlove was busy recording for weeks in one of the rooms on the ground floor.

John and Christine were travelling around in the UK and a lot of people were moving in and out in the Romford and Collier Row areas. We saw, first hand, all the good things of being a part of such a close-knit fellowship, and we also saw some of the challenges and pain involved in developing some of the house churches into a harmonious group moving together in the same direction. We moved back to Norway and our home in Gjøvik before Christmas, inspired and motivated to take the house-church model further. So, around a couple of times a year the first 7 to 8 years in the 1980's we arranged leaders' meetings. All the time new people were invited to join, but it was mostly leaders from Pentecostal and other charismatic churches who came to those gatherings and some positive relationships were made.

There was a popular slogan at the time that 'Big is beautiful' which, in some situations, may be true. Certainly, we should all remain pragmatic and where things are really working, we should be willing to see if our small relational groups might connect into a larger expression of church. However, many leaders from England and from our own country were keen for their churches to grow in size and influence, and identity became an important issue and, for some, it was more important than relationships. So they started to put the emphasis on having a name for the church.

They used the argument that you cannot just keep caring for a child without a name, to simply say that we are Christians is not enough. They made the point that the world around us becomes confused about these new groups of house churches without a building and with no name or publicity about their meetings. Alongside that discussion, some were influenced by the thought of having a stronger leadership with a pastor to head up the team was necessary. Thus, many were rather quickly into something different from where we started and they were beginning to introduce more structure into the house churches.

Of course, that was a natural thought as we grew in numbers but there were other possibilities. Some took the opportunity to continue with the idea that each house church of, say, 10-12 people was independent and free to carry on as they felt led but kept open to other groups in town or the surrounding area. However, others moved on to become churches with one main leader and some actually called their leader 'pastor'. Musicians were brought together as a worship team, larger halls were usually rented, chairs were placed in rows and the Sunday service was the main thing.

In Gjovik we continued with our home groups every fortnight, but the focus turned to the Sunday meeting and much of what we had added seemed to have taken us full circle! It was not long before we experienced church splits over leadership, doctrine and which source of 'apostolic' input was right. So why did this happen when we started so well? How was it that we ended up as so many other denominations, and why didn't the house-church movement take off as we had hoped?

As I said earlier, Marit and I are still fellowshipping in a small house church in Gjovik and relate to, and work with, other Christians in the area wherever we can. I travel in ministry to poorer areas of the world with my cousin, Haavald Slatten, who runs a successful charitable business which enables us to take clothing and aid wherever we go. I am still very much in touch with John Noble and Haavald translated his book, 'The Shaking', written in 2002 in the UK into Norwegian and it was published here by YWAM in 2004.

I say this, because I know that in his book John closes with an epilogue in which he refers to a vision he had after the book was finished. In the vision he saw, not only the great institutions of this world shaken and collapsing, but also the church itself was shaken. I know too, that he made it clear that the shaking occurred so that, as scripture tells us, 'only that which could not be shaken would remain'!

PURE CHURCH

In talking to John about 'that which cannot be shaken', he would say that the unshakeable bedrock of the church is relationships. First, a relationship with Jesus who justifies us before the Father and then our relationship with one another as we are baptised into the one Body of Christ, the church. Jesus' great prayer for his church in John 17 was that we should be 'one as he and the Father are one so that the world may know that he has sent us'. In Ephesians chapter 4, he points out that we are called to 'maintain the unity of the Spirit in the bond of peace until we come to the unity of faith'.

Thus, we start from a unity in the Holy Spirit and walk together and work together towards a unity of faith and understanding. He would also say that God's goal is not bigger and better churches but rather transformed communities, so that means the church is God's agent to establish the kingdom of heaven on earth. So it is our responsibility to discover those who the Lord is joining us to and then in love and tolerance see how we can affirm and co-operate with others along the way.

John's openness to find the Lord at work in other Christians has taken him and his wife, Christine, into many areas of the world where they and their teams have been able to support and encourage those working on the ground for Jesus in tough situations. Some of these journeys are mentioned in other chapters of this book. For my part I am grateful to God for a friendship that has endured the test of time and John has often expressed his appreciation of our love and support for him and his family. Thank you, Jesus, for your greatest of gifts - friendship!

Great job Hans! Thank you and a few more memories from me...

There is no way I can do justice to the many visits I, and the team, made to beautiful Norway. Beautiful in the incredible scenery displayed in every season of the year, and beautiful in the way we were received and loved by so many friends everywhere we went! I must thank God for the impact these people made on our lives and I like to feel that we were able to bless and encourage the hungry saints we met and worked with there.

Hans mentioned the Lutheran priest Hans Jakob Froen who led the Seamen's Mission and his son Eivind who established YWAM in Norway. I met the saintly Hans Jakob and learned about the great work he was doing to introduce people to the work of the Holy Spirit. Baptised in the Holy Spirit in 1938 the Lord spoke to him about his future ministry but it was only in 1971 that he formed the successful Agape movement to promote the work of the Spirit.

Reidar Paulsen, pastor of the Bergen Frikirke, was another priest I met on several occasions. He also worked tirelessly to advance the work of the Holy Spirit through gatherings, literature and encouraging young people. He was always ready to engage with others from other streams who shared his vision for the Church. He interviewed me for one of his publications and we shared good fellowship together.

Indeed, I made many friends in the Bergen and the surrounding area as there were a growing number of House Churches emerging there. Kare Kristing and his wife Astrid were among the first we stayed with and Kare's family and his brother's family were members of a group called the Free Friends. They asked me to share my testimony with the group. However, the Free Friends were not greatly impressed and I did not find them to be very free or friendly either, and it was not long before Kare and his brother were asked to leave and soon there was a thriving church in Kare's home.

Hans mentioned this group in his account as being led by Noralv Askeland. However, in its early days it was Kare who led the group and they invited input from the Bryn Jones Harvest Time team. It was the team's policy to install someone of their choosing to lead a church they were working with and Kare had to step aside for Noralv. I think Kare really struggled with that and left the church and developed other relationships in the area and beyond.

PURE CHURCH

I think it was Hans who introduced me to Kjell Haltorp, a Pentecostal pastor from Arundal. I visited his church to speak and from there we developed a friendship. Kjell is a real evangelist and readily accepted an invitation to join us on a trip to rural India, and what fun it was to have him with us. He was never slow to speak to anyone we met along the way from whatever background and immediately sought to introduce them to Jesus. In the villages he seemed quite at home away from the luxuries of Norway and happily slept in the open air on a charpoy bed made of string across a wooden frame. Being a tall man, his feet hung over the end of the bed but he never complained.

In writing about Kjell, I searched his name to see if he was still around as I had not been in touch for some years. Immediately, I came across a news item to the effect that at 83 years of age he had just been arrested as he arrived in Istanbul, Turkey in preparation to preach the Gospel there. I must say that, at first, I was surprised that he was still travelling in mission, but then I realised that it was what I should have expected from a man who, I am sure, will keep doing what he does until the Lord calls him up higher!

Looking back to my earliest travels in Norway, Tore Lende was often one who opened doors and stood alongside me to interpret when I was speaking. Now, I have had many wonderful people all over the world to interpret for me and in that respect I have been very fortunate. However, I have to say that Tore travelled the whole spectrum of emotions with me when he was translating; if I laughed, he laughed; if I cried, he cried; if I shouted, he shouted; if I whispered, he whispered and he was not just acting, he was right in there with me every step of the way.

Asulf Kvammen, who was a student with Hans and his friends in Oslo, came from Tore's church in Stavanger where there was a great group of musicians and singers. When he went back home after finishing his studies, apart from his work as a vet, he gave himself to worship and was soon writing songs which found their way into the heart of the renewal across Norway and beyond. I used to call him the Graham Kendrick of Norway.

In Oslo after Hans, Asulf and others went home when their courses ended, Tor and Liv Thorhild continued make their home available for fellowship and a strong and talented group of young people came together. I had the joy and privilege of visiting them on many occasions and watched them grow in spirit and influence. I am proud to say that after half a century has passed, we are still in touch and they took part, with Hans, in our celebration of Christine's life in June 2022 in the theatre in Leatherhead.

I am reluctant to move on from my memories of Norway as I wanted to say a personal, 'thank you', to every church and all the people who made us so welcome. People who shared their lives and homes with us and showered us with love, friendship and practical support. In the face of feeling overwhelmed by your kindness and generosity, I can only say the I am comforted by the thought that we have eternity to sit down together in the presence of Jesus and 'chew the cud', as we say, to our heart's content. Bless you in His dear name!

Chapter Eleven

INDIA AND SRI LANKA

As I shared earlier Ian Farr and his family spent some years in India with OM before he lost his residential visa. After he returned to the UK he continued to visit and support his many contacts there and it was Ian who first introduced me to this wonderful country with its brilliant colours, fragrant and heady aromas and amazing people. They say you either love India or hate it and I loved the place. And one of the first trips I made was with Ian and we visited at least three locations where I found special people devoted to working with children and the poor and needy.

In the stunning beauty of the foothills of the Himalayas nestles the town of Mussoorie not far from Dehradun. After what seemed a perilous car journey along mountain roads we arrived at the home of Ken, or Yip as I knew him then, and Frieda who, in 1974, began their work among needy and orphaned children, taking them into their home and fostering. From those humble beginnings grew a Shishya, a community which has continued to develop the work and remains a testimony to their faith until today, fifty years on.

Ken tells a story which, to me, illustrates the depth of their trust and journey with Jesus. Ken spent time walking a lonely path with a nomadic tribe in the mountains. One night he slept on the floor of a small hut, with only enough room to stretch out his long frame with his head tucked between a bag of rice and a bag of flour. Throughout the night, mice jumped over his head from bag to bag. In the morning, Ken found his host reading an ancient bible who explained that the book was given to him 30 years before. All that time he had been praying that someone would come who could tell the village about it. So Ken was amazed to find that he became the answer to a 30-year-old prayer and was most happy to share the Good News, news that they belonged to the God of immeasurable love who had answered their prayers.

Moving on to Delhi I met Freddie and Kiran Martin, or I should say Dr Kiran, as it was her qualification as a medical doctor and her Christian faith that led her into the slums of that great city. It was there that saw the start of Asha, a most profound and incredible work, now over 35 years old. Rather than trying to tell the story as I heard it from her originally, I felt it was far better to take the words straight from the Asha web site:

In 1988, Dr Martin heard about a cholera outbreak in a south Delhi slum. She was inspired to use her talents to help the poor and marginalised, so she went to the slum, set up a borrowed table under a tree and began working to save lives. As Dr Martin learned more about the hardships and deprivation faced by the people there, she started to devise ways to address their problems. After some time, and with growing cooperation from the grateful community and the Indian government, she acquired like-minded helpers and began to form Asha Society.

Now, 31 years later, Dr Martin is an influential figure in the field of slum development and Asha's programmes are benefiting more than 900,000 people in around 100 slum colonies of Delhi. Dr Martin's early model of urban health has developed to meet the changing needs of slum communities and achieves consistently impressive results. The slum housing model that Dr Martin developed in the 1990s has been widely praised and accompanied innovative work in women's empowerment and primary and secondary education. That was followed by a highly successful financial inclusion scheme devised in partnership with the Ministry of Finance, Government of India, and most recently, Dr Martin's groundbreaking work to improve slum children's access to higher education has seen an astonishing result.

In 2002, Dr Martin's achievements were recognised by the Indian Government when she was awarded the Padma Shri, one of India's highest civilian awards, by Mr K R Narayanan, the President of India. Dr Martin has worked with senior government officials to increase financial inclusion for slum dwellers, and they have also taken a keen interest in the progress of Asha's higher education initiative.... In addition to Asha's work being awarded Best Practice by UN-Habitat, it has also been praised, studied and replicated by organisations in many countries.

High praise indeed but fully deserving as this, in essence, all came about by the dedication, faith and ingenuity of one incredible lady! I was privileged to meet her again on other trips with Ian but as another insight into this entirely unpredictable country, full of surprises and the unexpected, I share what happened when we were a little late leaving for our flight.

It was Diwali, the Festival of Lights, a very special day in the Hindu calendar for Indians. Millions of rupees are spent on fireworks and even every beggar seems to find money for such things. We went onto the balcony of the house to watch proceedings and the crowd began firing rockets at us! We quickly retreated into the house! Freddie then drove us, together with Jim and Sylvia Holl who were in the team, in his 4 x 4 to catch our plane and as we sped through the city all along the way people were throwing fire crackers at us. They landed on the roof and exploded under the vehicle. I was amazed that we made it to the airport, and was not at all surprised the next day to read of all the fires and accidents that occurred every year as a result of, what is truly, a *festival of lights* in more ways than one!

My next port of call with Ian was Madras, now re-named Chennai. It was here that I was to meet Jochen and Johshy Tewes, a wonderful couple who became our great friends as both Christine and I visited them on several occasions. It was not just their friendship that we valued but their vital faith and ability to get to the heart of so many needs among the youth of India.

Jochen travelled to a number of countries with Inter-Mission, the German charity he worked for, to see where they might expand their work and India won his heart. In 1974 he registered the Mission, met and married Johshy and, with her experience of working with orphans, they began their ministry to train underprivileged young people. Since that time the work has mushroomed to multiple locations with schools, apprenticeships, computer studies and much more for both boys and girls, with thousands equipped and now working in the market place.

Once when we visited them Johshy took us to see a new arm of the Mission which she had developed to empower women using micro-enterprise. We saw some of these ladies, over 10,000 of them, whose lives were changed, giving their testimonies and sharing their stories. Some of them are now running successful businesses which employ others and so the work continues to multiply and has a life of its own. I know they both have great satisfaction in seeing many of those who have been through the system giving themselves back to advance the work.

Through Jochen and Johshy's hosting us and ferrying us around we visited many churches and groups around the city and were often helped by Shelton, a fine young man who also translated for us and generally looked after us. It seemed nothing was too much trouble for him and Grace his lovely wife.

I must also mention one special church in Chennai where we were welcomed, blessed and made many friends – the Power House Church led by a beautiful couple, Jayakaren and Kavita. They were energetic, full of the Holy Spirit and the worship was awesome. However, they were not just a happy bunch but were deeply involved in many aspects of the community. We saw them respond to flood victims and reach out to other needs in the community. Christine and I were thrilled to be able to share with a group of artists, who also used their skills to connect with neglected groups to share Jesus.

PURE CHURCH

When we were with them, they held their meetings in a shopping complex which meant they were accessible and people were easily able to connect with them. I know Jochen and Johshy loved this group and their daughter, Zippora and Timmy, her husband and their family joined them and Zippora was part of the worship team.

It was on our way south to visit Pastor Paulose on the Hindu island of Rameswaram that we visited one or two other churches Ian was in touch with and went on to spend some time with Father Berchmans. As his title suggests he started his ministry as a Catholic priest in 1978 but he carried a longing to do something more creative to enrich the simple people he encountered. Apparently, he experienced a spiritual transformation in 1983 in a meeting organised by DGS Dhinakaran, another well-known Tamil evangelist. After which he began organising evangelistic meetings.

He also began composing and releasing Christian worship songs which were mainly bible verses. These were well received by Tamil Christians and drew others into the meeting to hear the Gospel and receive prayer for healing. In fact, many were healed and word spread and the crowds grew. In the course of repeating the songs over and over as they worshipped people were memorising the scripture passages. As result of the blessing about 5 acres of land was donated to Berchmans by the villagers of Kalaya Kovil near Madurai.

Later he established his 'Jebathottam Trust' in the area, which now hosts an auditorium with a seating capacity of 2000. There is a 24-hour prayer chamber and board and lodging facilities and a shelter for helpless women. *Jebathottam* is a Tamil word meaning Prayer Garden. I see online that the Father composed around 120 songs which have made a deep and lasting impact on the Tamil-speaking area.

So on to Rameswaram and Paulose, where in his early days he faced many trials and considerable persecution as the island is basically a shrine with a major Hindu temple at the centre. Every year thousands make their pilgrimage there and the priests were not happy with what they saw as competition. However, Paulose and his family prevailed and over the years they have built a large complex with a school and community projects and they have trained many evangelists to send out into other parts of India.

Sadly, Paulose passed away some time ago and now his sons, aptly named Israel and Billy Graham, lead the work. I thoroughly enjoyed visiting Rameswaram as, apart from the Paulose family and seeing their great work, I was able to indulge my passion for bird watching. There is an abundance of beautiful birds to discover in the undergrowth, on the trees and all along on its wonderful sandy shores.

It was on a later trip that we visited the Golden Triangle as it is called and Christine was with us. So, whilst we did meet with churches where Ian had contacts, we were also able to do the tourist thing and visit the Taj Mahal, the Amber Fort and enjoy the mystery, the beauty and the hustle and bustle of that busy tourist destination.

- Paul Raj and rural south-west central India -

As I said earlier, I met Dr Paul Raj at the 1989 Jerusalem conference and we immediately made a God-connection as he shared the story of his conversion. Paul was brought up in a high-caste Brahmin family and went to Hyderabad university where he studied as a Doctor of Philosophy. While he was at the university, he became ill with Elephantiasis and a Christian friend urged him to travel to a healing meeting for prayer. Paul was not at all interested but his friend persisted and bought him a ticket to travel to the meeting and Paul felt obliged to go.

The short story is that Paul went forward for prayer and was immediately healed. He then went on to be baptised and as a result of this, he was disowned by his family. Nevertheless, Paul felt God's call on his life and went to visit the renowned Indian Missionary E. Stanley Jones for advice. Jones, a friend of Mahatma Gandhi, was the founder of the Christian Ashram Movement which had spread to many parts of the country. He was also the author of *Christ of the Indian Road*, which sold over one million copies. When Paul shared his story and his belief that God was calling him, Jones pointed to a map of India around the Godavari River area. He went on to explain that this was an area which he had always wanted to visit but now that he was too old, he felt that this was where the Lord was calling Paul to work.

Paul accepted the challenge and made preparations to travel by boat into an area which could not be reached by road. Apart from all the usual provisions he would need for such a trip he bought himself a battery-operated loud-hailer. This tall Brahmin man, all dressed in white, disembarked from the boat and began to set up his equipment aware that he was being watched from behind trees and bushes. These people seldom had any unusual visitors and were, therefore, very cautious. Once everything was in order Paul took the microphone and blew into it to check that it was working. As he had not checked the volume, which was on maximum, the sound was deafening. Immediately scores of these tiny people, many wearing nothing but a thong, ran off in all directions - not the start Paul had hoped for!

He went on to tell me that it took two years for him to learn the dialect and then to earn the trust of these lovely people to the point where he could begin to minister to them. At the time of our first visit there were over 300 village churches where the people met to worship, pray and receive teaching. What a joy it was to begin to visit some of these groups, but to do so we often had to travel by boat or trek across the fields in single file, singing as we walked. As we neared a church, the villagers would come out to meet us shouting 'hallelujah' and join in the singing. When we arrived, they would bring out the charpoys for us to relax and enjoy the chai, that is tea boiled with milk and sugar over an open fire. Then they would massage our tired legs and the women would whisk Christine away to shower her, fascinated to discover if her skin was white all over!

Paul was not a great fan of Gandhi as he said that, whilst he criticised the apartheid in South Africa, he did nothing to dismantle the caste system which kept the poor trapped in poverty. He said that Gandhi's reasoning was, you can't give an elephant ant food or an ant elephant food, so the system remained intact. He was also critical of the missionaries and churches who worked into a caste with no requirement to come out of the system. In his churches he would not baptise anyone, rich or poor, who would not renounce their caste, which was a challenge, as every caste, apparently, had some privileges. He also insisted that all his converts had to share in the washing of one another's feet, a custom established in every one of his churches.

This area, around the river, was extremely volatile as, apart from the animists, who worshipped nature and had their holy trees and holy places, and the Hindus, who were also aggressive, there were the Naxalite communists who hated the Christians as well. Indeed, on one visit after we left a village where we had spent time and had meetings, we journeyed on to our next port of call. As we relaxed after arriving, we saw that messengers ran in to tell Paul that the home we stayed in at the previous village had been burnt to the ground immediately after we left. Paul also made it clear that in the early days many new converts were attacked and others murdered after they were baptised. However, these occurrences did not stop the growth of the churches.

In 1999 when Christine took a team of women to do health care in the villages, Paul shared with her that Australian missionary Graham Stuart Staines along with his two sons, were burnt to death in their vehicle by members of a Hindu Nationalist group named Bajrang Dal not far from where they were. Christine decided not to tell the team the news until they were safely out of the area for their peace of mind. After some time we learned that Staines' wife returned with her daughter to continue working in the area, such was her dedication to her calling.

Another serious problem was that, as more and more trees were cut down to make way for cash crops, flooding in the region grew worse year on year. With the loss of the trees, when the monsoons came, the surface soil was washed into the river which became silted up so that the annual flood covered an ever-widening expanse and homes, even villages, were washed away.

Paul had a great concern to see his people educated as this was one way they could escape the poverty trap. Workers in the fields received minimal wages and worked incredibly long hours. So opening schools and other places of education was a priority and when we introduced our friend, Pam Mackenzie, from the Pioneer People church in Cobham, to Paul it was clearly a God-inspired hit. For the next few years Pam did a stalwart job for Paul and across the wider region writing papers and researching a variety of subjects including language development. From one of my many reports I wrote:

> *It was our first visit for some time since Pam had developed the links. She is now helping schools with training and curriculum work, looking at water projects and pursuing contacts to enable literacy progress to move forward for these wonderful tribal people. Our cases were weighed down with books, games and resources for use in the village schools. Pam and Cate Collins, from the Pioneer Farnham church, were there to meet us having been there for a couple of weeks. It was amazing to see the huge strides made in developing the English Medium School in Bhadrachalam and astounding to see the entirely new technical college with its 1000 students.*

Of course, there is a story behind the opening of the technical college which I must share. My friend Daryl Martin and his then wife, Joan, who has, sadly, since passed away, had adopted a family of girls with Asian heritage. When they received an inheritance, they felt they wanted to make a gift to some kind of project which reflected the girls Asian background and they asked me for my advice. I told them about Paul and his incredible ministry and shared the fact that he placed 100% of all the gifts and resources he received into furthering his work among the tribes.

Unlike many other third-world leaders I had observed, who first ensured they had property for themselves and their families, Paul lived in a simple room in the Lutheran church building where his busy team conducted all their activities. So I said to Daryl and Joan that I felt Paul really needed a place of his own where he could live in peace and see all the people who came to meet him on a regular basis.

They readily agreed and we made the preparations for a trip together to share their concern and pass on a substantial gift. Paul was delighted when we arrived and they told him about their intentions. Immediately he loaded us into the church minibus and took us to see a plot of land he had already found in an ideal location. After a great visit and seeing many of the new projects Paul had lined up, we returned home satisfied that we had accomplished what we started out to do, but that is far from the end of the story. On my next visit, I enquired of Paul how the home building was coming along, so he called his driver and off we went to take a look. To my utter surprise and amazement what I saw was a completed first stage of the technical college I talked about earlier!

Paul has long-since passed away, but while writing this section of my story I went on line to see if what he started back then was still ongoing. This is one of many write ups I found which shows the good intentions and tremendous ability of the man to make things happen:

The Dr Paul Raj Engineering College, Bhadrachalam was established by the late Rev Dr Satish Paul Raj in 1997 in the Temple Town of Bhadrachalam to impart Technical Education to the students in the agency area and thus contribute for the development of the down-trodden. His philanthropy and missionary zeal made his vision complete in the establishment of an engineering institute with excellent infastructural facilities and was the very first engineering college in the private sector in Khammam district of Andhra Pradesh.

Paul was not only a big-picture man, raising great projects like the engineering college, but he exercised wisdom in the complicated cultural issues which confronted him on a daily basis. We were walking across the fields on our way to visit a village church with a group of young people when he called a boy over and scolded him giving him a smack across his head. I waited until we were on our own before asking about the incident which had rather taken me by surprise. He explained that the boy had sidled up to one of the girls which was strictly forbidden. He said that he had to be seen to punish the lad in public otherwise he might have had a knife in his back later.

He also had to deal with the matter of underage marriage which was often practised among some of the village people. He always sought to verify the age of a young bride which was often not a simple matter under the circumstances. Then there was the problem of the man who came to the Lord with three wives, what was he to do? If he retained one wife and turned the other two away they would be consigned to poverty with no one to care for them. Paul instructed the man to keep the current wife with him and provide a home and support for the other two women, which was an acceptable solution to everyone.

Christine and I thoroughly enjoyed our relationship with these poor but relatively happy people who would share their last meal with you. Christine took pictures of her family to show the women and on one visit she took a Polaroid camera. The women were amazed and delighted to see the photos emerging from the camera so quickly. In another village she paid for everyone to have a full meal which, under normal circumstances, the women would have to cook and serve the men and children first before having what was left themselves. Christine insisted that the order be reversed and the church elders had to serve the women and children first and then they were allowed to sit down themselves.

I was often called upon to baptise people in a lake or pond. The candidates would come in one by one and Paul would call out their new Christian name which was usually the first name that came into his head. Once, as a dear woman was about to go under the water, he shouted, 'Maggie Thatcher!' I stopped and insisted that he needed to think again, as I remember it was this lady who was called 'Christie'. For some reason Paul could not pronounce Christine's name any other way. Even our welcome banners would have John and Christie Noble emblazoned across them. When I finally got out of the water, I discovered that the little fish which had been nibbling my legs were in fact leeches!

We also visited an extremely remote area where the men were still hunting with bows and arrows. One old man, who was completely naked apart from his thong, was said to be over 90 years old was carrying his weapon. When he saw me he got very excited and pointed to my pony tail and then to his head. It was clear that he was proud to be able to show me that he had a pony tail too. The reality was that in some of these places they had never seen a white person before.

In one village Paul explained that after breakfast he wanted Christine to pray for a woman who was struggling with a breech birth, and he was not sure how long she could survive. We immediately said that we should go there and then and we took our travelling companion, a teacher, John Hallet from Ravenshead with us. Christine went straight in to the primitive mud hut whilst John and I prayed in tongues outside. In no time we heard the cries of a baby coming from the hut and a little old man came running out and returned grinning with a rusty razor blade and some thread. Apparently, when Christine laid her hands on the woman, the baby stood up, turned round and popped out. The razor blade was used to cut the cord and the thread to tie it off. John and I could hardly believe what we saw.

Apart from our many trips to be with Paul, he frequently came to the UK. Looking through my file I see that he visited many of our churches where they loved hearing his stories and readily responded to his needs. As a result, we were able to take considerable financial support to the work over the years. However, as well as Pam Mackenzie's help with education and the Norwegian nurses' team with health and midwifery care, some other people were able to contribute specialist skills.

For example, my Norwegian friends, Gunnar and Ingrid Delhi, had a profoundly deaf son and worked with the deaf community in Oslo. They met Paul and went on to raise £25,000 from their government in order to begin research working with the deaf in Paul's area. Early on, Pam and Mike Forestier-Walker from Pioneer People and John Hallet from Ravenshead church went to train teachers in the English Medium school. They trained 19 teachers, 9 staff and a further 10 teachers committed to the village school programme. They also left a lengthy report to help with future planning. Paul and Mary Dennison from Hayling Island connected with Paul and linked him with the technical college where Paul worked. This led to a long and happy exchange between them and Paul Raj. I could go on but I think you can see that this God-inspired relationship proved to be very fruitful, both in terms of what we were able to give but also in the blessing and joy we received in return from our Indian friends!

- *Sri Lanka* -

If you ever needed evidence of a woman operating in an apostolic role, then look no further than Jenny Sunnadurai, supported by her colleague Karen Dey, working in Sri Lanka and beyond. Over the years Jenny and Karen have risked life and limb to reach the Tamil people with the gospel in the war-torn areas of the country. Not only did they take the good news but also finance for food, medicines and practical help. As a result of their tireless work, they have seen many come to Christ on the island and also among the Tamil refugees who ended up in other parts of the world.

Some years ago, Christine and I visited the Parlaam project in Wattala just outside of the capital Colombo. The project began in 1995 when Jenny had a desire to begin to assist those she found in need of the simple necessities of life - like food, education and health care. Her mission to provide relief and social services began and soon a school was established, followed by a children's hostel, medical assistance, and a vocational training centre. We were greatly impressed.

As a result of our initial involvement with Jenny and Karen we learnt that they began to plant Tamil churches wherever they found refugees who fled from the atrocities of war. The first churches were nurtured in Switzerland in French and German-speaking areas. There followed plants in France, Canada and back in Sri Lanka with even a group which they inputted in New Zealand. We were thrilled to be invited to serve these churches in several conferences and learned to love their willingness to embrace the gospel in its simplicity and present a creative approach to worship. What a joy it was to see a group of young classical dancers express their beautiful culture at one of our great Pioneer conferences.

Karen recently wrote:

Jenny & I continue to travel across these nations to visit our churches, to train up leaders and to keep the revival fires burning. Having handed on the responsibility of leading the project work to our faithful team leaders, we carry on the work of giving apostolic input to our churches along with other fellowships apart from our own. We continue to see wave after wave of revivals that leads to more churches planted and lives changed in the nations. God has been so faithful and good to us as we constantly see His hand of intervention in the good times and the hard times. He always goes before us to make a way where there seems to be no way.

Our other visit to Sri Lanka was with Laura Ruth, a young lady who Christine built a strong and lasting relationship with. Laura would say that, whilst they were certainly friends, she felt that Christine's advice and input in helping her through some very tough times, meant that her position was more akin to her being a disciple. When Christine met Laura, she was involved in the Welsh missionary movement, World Horizons, as she was passionate about sharing the gospel overseas. However, Laura battled with serious mental health problems which threatened her ability to carry out such work.

The short story is that with Christine's help she found the strength to achieve all that was in her heart despite the disease that plagued her all through her journey. She fought her way through all kinds of ups and downs, even having been sectioned for some time, to eventually become a mental health worker herself, as well as continuing with her mission ambitions and a successful time as chaplain to a large Llanelli store. Recently, I had the privilege of helping her publish her book, *Wildfire – Mission and Madness*, which gives us a full and honest account of all she went through and also what she learned as a psychiatric social worker. It is fully endorsed by other professionals and will be of great help to sufferers and carers alike with plenty of practical advice.

In her missions work she made several trips to Sri Lanka, including a visit after the tsunami of December 2004 which claimed over 30,000 lives. On this occasion she took aid and went to give practical and building help to survivors. The trip we made with her was to support her and give encouragement to the local Christians she had contact with in Galle Fort by planting a church in Hikkaduwa.

She had already raised funds for the women in the local prison, many of whom had babies or young children incarcerated with them. It was a mixed prison and the men and the women had no toilets. Laura contacted the authorities and received permission to build a toilet block and nursery for the women which made a huge difference to these needy souls. We spent time visiting the prison and meeting local Christians, many of whom had stories of physical persecution from Buddhist monks who felt threatened by their presence.

Whilst writing this chapter I had a message from the incorrigible Laura to tell me that she was soon off on a 40-day trip to Nepal and, typically, she tells me she is 'praying for the leading of Holy Spirit during this time and to hear the voice of Jesus in this adventure with him'. Take heart from the example of this amazing young lady and know that if she has been able to overcome such huge challenges, then many of us can also succeed if we are determined to launch out when we feel God has spoken.

CHAPTER TWELVE

AFRICA

This vast continent featured quite regularly in our overseas schedules and a wonderful place it is, with so many countries but more important is the complex diversity of the multitude of tribal groups. Several countries we visited just once or twice and other places more frequently. That being the case I will give South Africa a separate section as we visited this incredible nation on many occasions and made many lasting friendships there.

- Ghana -

My first experience of Africa was a trip to the West African country of Ghana, which sits between the two French colonies of Ivory Coast and Togo. However, before I share my memories of that visit, I must first pay tribute to team mate Norman Barnes. You may remember that I shared Norman's belief that he would preach to a congregation of 5000 Africans as a result of the vision he had as a young man. As time passed and Norman did the open-air work preaching with the Good News Team, he went on to accept the role of pastor of the Shaftesbury Mission in Chadwell Heath. It was not too long after this we began to work more together with others in a wider ministry.

During this time, we would meet to discuss what was happening and share the opportunities which were opening for us and pray as to how we should respond. At a couple of our meetings Norman shared that he had received an invitation from a Christian in Ghana to visit with a view to ministering there. We all felt it would be incredibly risky to go without having some knowledge of the person and what he was going into, so we advised him to write for more information, which he willingly did.

I think it was the third time Norman approached us as he had received another letter stating that the brother had planted three churches. Whilst we were still cautious, we felt that it was right to prayerfully move forward and after Norman received £1200 in unsolicited gifts, he booked the flights and planned the trip. The full amazing story of what happened is recorded in Norman's excellent book, *Destiny Calls*. Believe me when I say the trip was not without some serious challenges before Norman linked up with David Mills, a contact which someone in the UK gave him if he was in trouble.

Norman honoured his commitment to complete his visit with Nicholas, the extremely poor brother who had invited him, and then went on to spend time with the Mills family. David was a white missionary working with the Church of Pentecost, probably the largest network of churches in the country and it was here that Norman's dream to speak to 5000 took place and he wept as the Lord fulfilled the promise given to him as a boy.

From this experience and subsequent visits to Ghana, the charity Links International was born as a channel through which Norman could encourage and support all manner of projects. I was privileged to chair the charity on behalf of Norman for several years and well remember the joy of seeing the day when the total amount given passed the £1 million pounds mark. Years later and still today Links continues to grow, having been handed on under Norman's watchful eye, and it is impossible to evaluate all that has been accomplished through Norman's dogged obedience to the vision God gave him.

So it was, after Norman's visit in early 1979, Dave Bilbrough and I accompanied Norman on a further trip in 1982 and it was, indeed, an eventful time. We stayed with David Mills and his family and David ferried us around to visit various churches and ministries around the country. We were greatly impressed by the exuberance and dancing in the worship and the generous and cheerful way the people gave. There was a currency crisis at the time and the cedi was worth very little but people danced and queued up to make their offerings and David urged us to receive the gifts as they would have been offended had we refused.

Dave Bilbrough writes:

> *For me the trip was hugely influential. I had visited Europe and the United States in ministry trips before but this was my first time in Africa. I was immediately impacted by the vibrancy and commitment to worship, the landscape and the warmth and generosity of the believers. The whole trip certainly opened my eyes and, I am sure, prepared me to see a wider perspective concerning worship in the worldwide church.*
>
> *We met the king of Ghana, visited one of the slave forts on the Cape Coast and at home base engaged with the Mills' talking African Grey parrot! Our trip was extended due to a military coup during the Jerry Rawlings era, which delayed our return. Then from the intense heat of Ghana we arrived back in London to be greeted by snow! The impact of that trip remains with me as strongly as ever. The joyful abandonment, colour and vibrancy of the Ghanaian church made me realise that we have so much to learn.*

All the leaders wore suits in the burning heat and we were obliged to follow the custom. However, when I stood up to preach, I started by saying that we British brought many things into your country, some good and others not so good. I then went on to say that it was the British who gave you the suits which your leaders wear. So, I said, 'As someone from the country that gave you the suits, I feel at liberty to take my jacket off and maybe start a new custom!' They all laughed as I went on to roll my sleeves up before carrying on to share. We had a great time wherever we went and Dave was well loved everywhere.

However, due to the currency crisis, as Dave said, it happened that there was another military coup and all flights into and from Ghana were stopped. Jerry Rawlings directed operations from his aircraft above as he flew around to see where the trouble spots were. At the airport people were desperately trying to get flights out of the country, and as the currency was so devalued, they were trying to pay with suitcases full of cedis, it was quite chaotic. Our families had seen the news in the papers at home and were worried for our safety but we were able to contact them by phone to assure them we were fine. Of course, they were hugely relieved when they welcomed us back into the London snow!

- *Niger* -

In January 2003 Ian Farr and I made a trip to what had been a French colony, Niger. Surprisingly, the contact came through Paulose in Rameswaram, India who must have had some contact but felt unable to visit himself. We stayed in the capital, Niamey, and the country, which is one of the poorest in the world, is mainly Muslim with Christians numbering a mere 65,000. It was quite clear that the saints there suffered discrimination and, in some cases, quite severe persecution and it remains so to this day.

Ian reminded me that their kind hospitality meant that they left us with a large jar of deep-fried locusts in our room which we felt obliged to leave for their personal consumption. He also remembered that we had a meeting in a *historic church* with leaders from other denominations attending. My notes, which I found in an old file marked Africa, seemed to indicate that it was in this meeting I preached on Psalm 133 and John 17:23 which was a call for the leaders to stand together in those difficult and trying times.

Other than that, we spent time in two local churches who welcomed us and gave us plenty of space to share our hearts with them. It was in one of these churches, according to my notes, that we met a man whose father had been killed by the police. He testified to the fact that the Lord had given him the strength to forgive the policeman for what he had done. I also have one photograph from our trip given to me by a team of Brazilian missionaries who were committed to working with the Christians there. What a fine happy group they were and were typical of the Brazilians I met on my travels in other parts of the world.

- *Nigeria* -

Our first visit to Nigeria was a bit of an eye opener. Having travelled extensively throughout the world we thought we had seen it all but Nigeria was a new experience. Our first trip was with our friend, Frances Bolton, a Nigerian barrister working in London. She aspired to bless and encourage her people back home and arranged meetings for us with her friends in Onitsha situated along the banks of the River Niger.

Arriving at Lagos airport was a little like visiting a war zone! Apart from the thronging crowd, people were shouting and screaming and even waving their fists at customs officials. It was chaotic and quite scary. After we managed to get through customs, we had to try to find the people who came to collect us which, by some miracle, we did. They guided us out of the building to the car park and we were followed by some men one of whom literally tried to get the wallet out of my pocket. I dreaded to think what it would have been like if we had been on our own.

The drive to our lodgings was equally traumatic as we were stopped seven times by police who were obviously looking for a bribe. When the guys who collected us refused to cough up, our cases were dragged out of the boot and searched but, somehow, we were allowed to continue. Was it our bibles which they found which did the trick or prayer? We will never know.

The next day the long drive to Onitsha was a lottery. Road works on the fine dual carriageway suddenly directed us into a single carriageway with no signs. This meant that we were soon facing speeding traffic coming in the opposite direction. It was only after we arrived that we were told that one should never stop on the road, as the likelihood of being hijacked and our luggage taken was a real possibility. My prayer life was certainly rejuvenated on that journey. Phew, thank you Jesus! It seems He wanted us to get to our destination.

Frances had various groups lined up for us to meet and share with but the highlight was to be a huge outdoor crusade which had been planned. As it happened, they were quite disappointed as only around 5000 turned up. Such meetings in Nigeria often attract hundreds of thousands even up to one million on occasions. A rather flimsy platform had been erected and after various delays things got under way with a time of worship.

After a while, what I can only describe as a small cavalcade of Mercedes drove up and out climbed Bishop Benson Idahosa. He was followed by his white minder and an entourage of others all dressed in fine silk African dress. I didn't get the impression that they had been invited but they all proceeded to climb on to the platform which promptly collapsed. The only people who remained in their seats were Christine and me and the worship leader.

After some hasty repairs, the bishop proceeded to take up an offering which he graciously accepted and the entourage left as it had come. Later in the meeting a second offering was taken and we heard afterwards that the brother who was taking it to be counted was held up at gun point. Thankfully the gun failed to fire and the offering was safely counted and banked. In my ministry I was at pains to explain that I didn't have a Mercedes and that riches are not a sign of spirituality. I am not sure how that went down but we did get to speak to a group of poorer pastors from rural areas.

As we fellowshipped with this group it was clear that they were not impressed by the *big ministries* who never visited the poorer areas - I wonder why? We had a lovely time with these men who were keen to hear what we had to say and during the time Christine had a vision which caused great excitement. In view of the content it is worthy of sharing here:

I saw Africa and then the vision zoomed in on Nigeria as a green and lovely place. As I watched there welled up from the centre a bubbling thick oily, sticky and polluting liquid which ran across the land. Wherever it went it polluted, dirtied and destroyed.

Then I saw a fountain spring out of the ground. It went high in the air and this was clear, beautiful water. Where the light caught it, you could see all the colours of the rainbow. As this fountain dropped to the ground it formed little streams and rivulets which began to cleanse the stinking fluid but then something terrible began to happen. The clear water blended with the polluted water and you couldn't tell the difference and the situation was worse than before.

Then God spoke into my heart the words of Isaiah 43:18-19 (NIV), 'Forget the former things; do not dwell on the past. See, I am doing a new thing! Now it springs up; do you not perceive it? I am making a way in the wilderness and streams in the wasteland'.

As I looked again, I saw something wonderful happening. All over the country there were small springs welling up, the same beautiful water but this time it did not get polluted. Slowly, where the springs were bubbling it became green and lush again. As I watched many of these patches of green joined together and the life of God returned.

These village leaders were thrilled and asked Christine if they could circulate the vision widely among their people which, of course, she gladly agreed. Their understanding was that the discovery of large deposits of oil in the country had the effect of corrupting even the church. In 1971 there was revival in the outpouring of the Holy Spirit largely through the Charismatic Movement which was like a fountain of life and blessing. Sadly, they felt that this mixed with the prosperity teaching which followed and ruined what the Lord had accomplished.

However, they also took heart that God was going to do a new thing through many of the poorer rural groups who were hungering for more of the real presence of Jesus.

Our other trip to Nigeria came about as a result of my friendship with Jamie and Pam Handscombe. Supplyline was a charity founded by my friend Arthur Wallis and his wife Eileen to provide help for some of their poorer international contacts. Eventually the charity was handed on to Dave Tomlinson's Team Work, and after some time Jamie took on the directorship. He, along with Bryan Pullinger and others in the team, developed the charity with a particular emphasis on the city of Jos in Nigeria.

Jos town is the capital of Plateau State, on the Jos Plateau of central Nigeria. The religion there is primarily Muslim which means the minority Christian church suffers regular persecution. Pastor Thompson Nwosu, leader of the Redeemed People's Mission, with his wife Glenda, run a thriving work there and Jamie invited us to visit with him in 2008. Jamie writes:

Supplyline personnel had been working with Thompson Nwosu and the people of the Redeemed People's Mission since 1988 and we had the privilege of inviting John and Christine Noble to pay a visit to Jos, in Northern Nigeria, in 2008. This city was where the Christian denomination led by Thompson was based and where they had established two schools, various medical outreaches and a hub for dozens of church groups in the mainly Muslim north.

For me, as director of Supplyline, it was a great opportunity to benefit from the experience and expertise that John and Christine were able to bring to a work, avoiding importing English cultural restrictions and being sensitive to what God was saying and doing with the people there. They spent time in the secondary and primary schools, taught in the church situations, sometimes with nearly 1000 people present and had input into leadership groups ... as well as a bit of ornithology thrown in during the rest times! Not least, this visit laid the foundation for the kind of relationships without which no work of God can progress.

AFRICA

- Zambia -

I made just a single trip to Zambia in 1993. As with so much of our international travel, not having kept records, the old memory banks don't provide the information needed to give a fair report. However, I believe it was Dave Day's team in the Bristol Christian Fellowship who put me in touch with a group of churches around Chingola in the Copper Belt region. Apart from sharing in the churches I was invited to speak at one of their larger inter-church conferences.

I reckon this is worth mentioning because I shared the platform with Bishop Ngwiza Mnkandla from Zimbabwe. Ngwiza is the leader of Faith Ministries International, a network of churches in Africa and the UK. He was responsible for the resuscitation of the Evangelical Fellowship of Zimbabwe which he chaired for many years. He also had a relationship with Barney Coombs and the Salt and Light network of churches.

I was greatly impressed by his willingness to be frank and honest about his fellow African brothers in a way which a white man like me could not do. In his talk he shared how, while he was with Barney in the UK, they were out having a walk when he saw Barney bend down and pick up a scrap of paper from the side of the road. When he questioned Barney as to why he did this, Barney explained that he liked to see his town looking tidy. He then began to challenge the group about the heaps of rubbish which piled up in every street and which was generally ignored by all.

But he didn't stop there but drove the point home:

'Give an African a car and he will run it into the ground and then leave it in the yard until the chickens come roost in the back!' I was shocked, but there was more: 'When a tree falls across our path in the woods, what do we do? We walk round it instead of cutting a way through, and so our journey becomes longer and longer.'

There were nervous ripples of laughter as folk identified with what he was saying and, far from marginalising the group, he had touched a nerve. He had gained their attention and was able to go on to share how our lives as Christians should not only manifest the spiritual side of our faith, but also demonstrate the practical results of believing in God's order for the world in which we live. There was quite a response and I came away from that trip with a fresh realisation of how important it is for us to work together across the cultures as our ministry will become so much more effective.

- Tanzania -

I believe that it was in 1998 that Karen Lowe, leader of Antioch Church in Llanelli at the time, invited Christine to join a team to visit Tanzania to minister to the Maasai people in the Serengeti. Christine's friend Laura Ruth was not part of the team but remembers the ladies reporting on their time:

Hi John,

> *I do remember Christine going to Tanzania with Karen and the all-female team that travelled with her. When they returned, I heard the reports and, apparently, they had an amazing time with some fun tales of how Christine was struggling to understand the strong Llanelli accent of some women on the team who were all sleeping in a tent. One lady announced that she had found an earring in her shoe. Dear Christine thought she said she had found urine in her shoe; that caused much laughter! I also remember that a bad situation occurred in respect of an attempted sexual assault on one of the women by a Tanzanian man. Christine stepped in to strongly rebuke the man concerned and resolved the issue.*

I also heard that Christine spoke to a group of Maasai men and women gathered in a large hut which the Maasai people live in known as Manyatta huts. They are often circular and made of mud, sticks, grass, cow dung and cow's urine with a long pole in the centre to support the roof. When Christine stood up to speak, she grabbed the pole and drew her right foot up and tucked it into a pose very like that which the men adopt when standing with their long rungu sticks. She immediately had their attention and they listened to every word of her talk intently. When she finished many came forward to receive prayer. This was typical of the way Christine connected with people far removed from her culture and I have watched her in similar situations in other parts of the world.

The couple who hosted Karen and the team were Dave and Leebeth Armon from the UK. They had a call to work among the tribal people of the area and were trusted by them. They had a home in Arusha and enjoyed meeting Christine and asked her if we would go out to spend time with them at some point, which we did the following year in May 1999.

We flew into Nairobi airport in Kenya and took a four-hour minibus ride through the Namanga crossing point to Arusha. It was clear to me that the minibus drivers drove at break-neck speeds to complete the journey as quickly as possible. We loved the time with Dave and Lee Beth and their children, having good fellowship and meeting some of the people they were working with. Also, we spent time in the beautiful Serengeti plains near Mount Maru with Kilimanjaro away in the distance.

We were amazed to hear how many missionaries were working in the area and they took us to the evangelical church on Sunday where most of these Christian men and women met. Dave and Leebeth felt rather frustrated in this atmosphere, as the services were conducted to the lowest common denominator in an endeavour to avoid any offence. This meant that they did not reflect what the Holy Spirit was doing around the world at that time and no one felt really edified.

Before we left Arusha to make the minibus ride back to the airport, we had been warned about the incredible number of fatal accidents along the route back to Nairobi. So I took up a seat towards the front of the bus close to the driver to keep a close watch along the way to make sure that he was fully awake all the time. However, there came a point where I could see he was struggling to keep his eyes open, so I asked him loudly that as he was tired would he like me to drive for a while. The whole bus broke out into spontaneous applause which ensured that he was fully awake for the rest of the journey and we arrived home safely.

- *Kenya* -

2011 saw my only visit to Kenya apart from the journey in transit to Arusha. This was strange because I have had quite a bit to do with the country through many friends who have lived, worked or travelled there over the years. The contact came about as a result of my friendship with Adrian and Pauline Hawkes who encouraged me to take a look at the work of Sammy Nawali, a church leader they were supporting in Nakuru. I asked Jim Holl's son, Derek, if he would accompany me and share the ministry, which he was very happy to do.

No long minibus rides this time as we were able to get a direct flight to Nakuru where Sammy picked us up, and we immediately felt comfortable with him. He took us to a guest house come hotel and we settled into our room which had a beautiful, uninterrupted, view across the landscape to the incredible Lake Nakuru in the distance. Many of you will know that this mighty soda lake situated in the Rift Valley, is home to huge flocks of Pink Flamingos which feed on the abundance of algae available in the shallows. Obviously, it was too far away to get much of a sighting of these magnificent birds, but I could see they were there. So it wasn't long before I rigged up my trusty telescope on its tripod, which I have carried all over the world for such moments, and there they were. For me the amazing bird life we found in so many of the places we visited was a special bonus. Apart from the joy of meeting and ministering among the people we went to serve, the birds and wildlife always provided an added incentive to travel.

It was great spending time with Sammy and his team and seeing the various projects he had up and running after just six short years he had been working in the area. He had an established school with a separate nursery and he also opened an orphanage where we heard some of the tragic stories of children they had taken in to care for. One lady in the church was looking into how they might look after autistic and handicapped children. There was a fully functioning car repair shop which was running so that they could offer apprenticeships to some of the lads at a loose end on the streets.

We were able to put an American brother who had joined up with Sammy in touch with Norman Barnes' Links International to get advice on a micro-enterprise project. We were truly impressed by all that the team had accomplished and it was a joy to share in the church. I made a note for Adrian, as he was soon to visit, that Derek gave an excellent talk on Jonah and I ministered from the book of Ephesians. I was also able to share a favourite word in the Sunday church meeting on *Jesus the Bridgebuilder* from the story of the woman at the well, as I felt this reflected much of what they were doing in reaching out to the marginalised of their community. So, all in all, it was a brilliant time in a church doing just what we're meant to do for the people around us who we serve.

- *Uganda* -

Our visits to Uganda came about through two contacts which took us into this beautiful country. The first invitation came through my long-time friend, Geoff Shearn, who we had worked with over the years to produce our worship recordings and music. He pioneered The Worship Trust which enabled Christian worship leaders and song writers to copyright their material and earn a well-deserved income. As such the Trust itself earned an income for administrating the service which enabled Geoff to invest in overseas work as he saw fit.

Geoff invited me to become one of his trustees and as a result we made a number of trips to see the work he was investing in there in Uganda. David and Valerie Crowhurst entered their missionary work later in life after they felt a call to Africa to serve underprivileged people. They built a beautiful home there in Uganda as their base and it was not long before they discovered how the Lord wanted to use them.

Valerie was visiting the home of a poor family with a large family and in the corner of the hut was a large wicker basket, the kind which often covered a brood of young chicks to keep them safe. She felt the Lord told her to kick over the basket which she did and to her horror there a was a disabled child underneath. Apparently, it was considered a shame on the family to have such a child and sadly they tended to hide them out of the way.

That was the moment that Valerie had a vision of the reason she and David were called to this place and thus Elizabeth House came into being which finally grew into a beautiful site with residential homes for around twenty disabled children. As a team we stayed in their lovely home and went to visit and spend time with the children. We also went to see a school which they funded in an underprivileged area and were amazed to see how much they achieved with their relatively small income.

We also visited, and were able to minister in, the local church in the area which adopted David and Valerie and they made it their spiritual home. God's Centre of Blessings Church in Bweyogerere led by Pastor Stephen Mugwanya was around 1000 strong and Geoff and the Trust were able to help the church with building projects and micro-enterprise initiatives. Pastor Stephen loved David and Valerie and gave them a great deal of support and encouragement.

Whist we were with them Valerie told us that David had made it very clear to her that he did not want to go back to the UK and said that when he died, he wanted to be buried there. You may feel it was strange of him to say such a thing. However, it happened that David was taking Valerie to a hospital appointment and on the way into the building he collapsed on the steps, had a massive heart attack, and died on the spot. Valerie remembered what he had said and so it was that David was laid to rest in the peaceful grounds of Elizabeth House where the children played.

On one of our trips, my daughter Sharon and her husband Michael at the time, were with us. Michael had set up a Christian Radio station in northern Uganda in the town of Gulu and we travelled together so that Michael could spend time with the man he employed to run the station. Gulu was a town which had seen a great deal of involvement from the Lord's Resistance Army (LRA), an extreme Christian network which terrorised the region.

The visit enabled us to visit churches and groups involved in the rehabilitation of the boy soldiers, thousands of whom were abducted by the LRA at an average age of 11. They were then brain-washed and forced into carrying out killings and control of the region. We were greatly impressed with the way these lads were cared for, retrained, and then helped to retrace their families. We were also welcomed by the mayor of Gulu at the time and had the opportunity to minister to church leaders in the town.

My other contact in Uganda was Pastor James Kato a delightful man full of love and grace. He was a friend of Simon and Bernie Trundle who led the VIA church in Wellingborough and later took on the leadership of the network from Tony Pullin. The church in Wellingborough under their leadership gained National acclaim and awards for the transformation of an estate area which had been run by gangs and drug dealers. Their efforts turned the whole community around and the pub which had been the hub of all criminal activity became a community centre and place of learning. Simon was also keen to reach out beyond the locality and as such began to support Pastor James' work in the poverty-stricken community which existed in the swamp area of Kampala. Against all the odds a church building was erected and soon a school was up and running. My connection came about after James attended the VIA conference. He invited me to visit the church and see what he was doing with the children in the school – I was impressed!

James' story:

In November 2000, the Lord visited me one night and in a loud voice asked me to leave a large church where I had been serving as an associate Pastor. In February 2001 I had a dream where the Lord appeared to me and asked me to build him a Church in Nateete, the swampy part of the small town. Having negotiated with the land owner, I bought the piece of land, before we had a single Church member.

In 2002, on the 3rd of February I planted 'The Jesus Worship Centre' after having had a 3-week open-air crusade where the Lord healed and saved many people from the area. The church began in rented premises but later moved onto the part of the swamp that we had reclaimed by earth backfilling.

On one of my visits to the UK, John gave me a book, 'Church at Community' by Ed Delph, a friend of his. On reading this book I felt the Lord challenge me to start a community school for poor pupils. By faith we started the school in our wooden church structure and 168 pupils turned up on our first day! What a challenging day that was! For teachers we had volunteers from the Church and the few shillings from our offertory is what we used to run the school until the Lord brought friends from the UK to give us support for the school. The love and kindness from our friends there carried us through over the years and today we have educated over 1000 pupils.

Since that time the church though has had its share of challenges, but it has continued to grow and we now have a permanent building for our worship and services.

I was also blessed to see how James was working with other pastors and church leaders in the city. Many of these men and women had become a little tired of the endless stream of American preachers who came to conduct healing campaigns which drew the people from the churches and did little to strengthen and build up the local work. So he invited this group to a series of sessions for me to share my heart and a little of what God was doing in the UK.

We had a great time together and I remember in one session where I was explaining that I didn't own a Mecedes Benz and I didn't have a great gift of healing which seemed to be essentials for any man or woman of God. While I was sharing a young lady put her hand up and asked if she could share her testimony.

She explained that I visited her church in Brazil and she asked me to pray for her. She asked for the ability to grasp the English language she needed in order to make her trip. She also asked for prayer to receive the finance involved to travel and work in Uganda and, finally, she asked for a door of opportunity to open. She went on to share that the Lord answered all my prayers and here she was in my meeting there in Uganda to give her testimony – I was blessed!

My great joy in Uganda was the amazing variety of bird life in the area where we stayed. I spent many happy hours up early in the morning wandering around watching the Hornbills with their incredible beaks and the colourful Turacos and listening to the almost mocking cries of the Hadada Ibis. I made hurried notes of tiny birds that I had seen flitting in and out of the bushes and then spent hours in the evenings trying to identify them only to find that there were often three or four almost identical species - frustrating! Nevertheless, bird watching is one of the things I miss the most as my travelling days are long since over.

- South Africa -

My first of many trips to South Africa took place in 1985 and it was a bit of a shock. Lesson one, when travelling always check what kind of climate you are entering! Africa = hot, so light clothing should be packed. Wrong! July in South Africa is just about mid-winter and it was perishing – you know, long johns, socks in bed and blankets at the meeting! At that time no home or meeting hall was equipped with heating, so it was a question of being prepared or spend your time jumping up and down whilst blowing your warm breath through clasped hands.

However, despite my foolishness I received an extremely warm welcome and my hosts, Albert and Maggie Gaisford, could not have treated me any better, they did me proud! We covered almost 2000 miles as we worked our way down from Johannesburg in the north, through Durban to Port Elizabeth, finally arriving in beautiful Cape Town in the south-west.

There were meetings every evening and sometimes during the day as we met a good cross-section of the many cultural groups which included English, Afrikaans, Indians, coloured and black people. My suspicions were confirmed as I could see that most people needed loving and firm involvement to help resolve the issues which remain under the surface even today. Thank God for those who were brave enough to risk all in their struggle to break down the prejudices to see a more tolerant society emerge. I found it a real privilege to share with so many who were willing to give me, a relatively ignorant Brit, a hearing.

Without reporting in detail on the visit, I felt that one of the most encouraging features of my time was watching reconciliation taking place between brothers and sisters who had been quite suspicious of one another. Kobus Swart, leader of his group in Halfway House, Waterfall City, prayed for me that there would be a special covering over me and that the Lord would give me a special grace for South Africa. He went on to humbly say that we here don't want to put the English on a pedestal but why should we reinvent the wheel if we can learn from our friends there.

Then, in 1990, Christine and I responded to an invitation to share in a Light From Africa (LIFA) conference which was to take place in Cape Town in February of that year. Paul Zink, one of the conference organisers, together with his wife Liesel, wanted to host us and our good friends, Ken and Maureen Rose who travelled with us, in a three-week trip which took us north as far as Durban.

They were incredibly kind, making sure that we had space to rest and relax and this was the visit which kicked off my passion for bird watching.

Ken was keen and was pointing out birds for me to check out. Then one day at a car stop, we saw a pair of majestic Crowned Cranes resting on top of two telegraph poles and I was smitten. I left South Africa with a strong desire to see 1000 different species on my travels, and so it was that on my final international trip to Brazil in 2013, I topped 1100 and was able to look back and thank the Lord for the endless hours of pleasure I had enjoyed.

The first few days before the conference were spent sharing with church leaders and fellowships in and around the Mitchells Plain area. It was so good to see how the saints were working into the townships, touching and changing lives with the message of the gospel and through all kinds of social projects. During these days we spent time with Derek Morphew who, at that time, was pastor of the Tygerberg Celebration Centre where Christine met and shared with Christ Light Christian Dance Company.

The conference itself, held in the Mowbray Presbyterian Church, carried the theme, *The Whole Church Taking the Whole Gospel to the Whole World*. Alongside Derek and me were Joseph Kobo and David Mniki who would both regularly feature in our future visits. Pastor Roger Petersen who, along with Paul Zink, organised the event, was also destined to become a special friend. The conference was a great success, nevertheless it was some years before I developed the contacts with these brothers and others who became such an important part of our lives.

After the conference we moved on from Cape Town stopping off at Swellendam and Port Elizabeth for meetings before going to Willowvale in the Transkei. Recently, Paul and Liesel wrote to share their memories of our time there which included a well-earned rest day:

> *We so enjoyed our trip into the Transkei area with you and Christine and Ken and Maureen. It was such a blessing to meet the local people and share in their joyous worship. We remember the dust rising from the carpet as they danced, it was so thick that we couldn't see from the back of the meeting place to the front.*

One elderly lady who received prayer for healing of her knees was immediately seen dancing with exuberance in the joy of the Lord. Most meaningful for us white folk, was sharing in a foot-washing ceremony which was extremely moving. Your interpreter, Chessy, not only spoke the words of the message but also followed all your movements to a 't'.

After the meeting we went on to spend the evening with one of the local chiefs who shared his meal with us. It was a tradition of theirs to offer their guests various delicacies from special parts of the sheep which was being served, for example the eyes. We noticed that you seemed to find a way to graciously pass on those. Then seeing the many children gathered, you told them a story and taught them your song 'If ever you see a Rainbow'. They were spellbound.

Also, while we were in the area, we made a visit to see a great work they were doing for the orphans. As we saw the carers at work, we could clearly see the love they showed to these needy children which visibly touched Christine's heart. Then there was time to relax in the cottage by the sea where you got busy with the fishing rod. This was obviously something you thoroughly enjoyed and one of the ladies took the trouble to cook your catch on condition she could have the bones which had been fried 'til they were crispy. Finally, we had the pleasure of meeting the mayor of Willowvale, enjoying his friendship and hospitality.

From Willowvale we carried on in the Transkei meeting up with David Mniki and his lovely wife Iris in Idutywa, sharing in the Kholo Centre meeting and seeing what they were doing in the area. Then on to Lujizweni with Joseph Kobo and his wife Mabel with more stories for the children, as well as speaking to his people who, with David's group, were always so open and responsive and ready to hear from us.

The final few days of our trip with Ken and Maureen who were such an encouragement to us throughout, were spent in Durban at The Church of the Good Shepherd. John and Wendy Heslop, who were leaders there at the time, welcomed us with open arms and had a series of meetings planned for us. Here, Christine and I shared our *What on Earth is God*

Doing? talks. She spoke on her passion, *What on Earth is God Saying About Women?* and I did two talks, *What on Earth is God Saying to Leaders?* and *What on Earth is God Saying to Youth?* We also took an early-morning breakfast having been asked to share on *Partnership in Marriage*. What a great way to finish a visit which remained fresh in our memories for years to come and created a platform for our future returns to the Rainbow nation.

Strangely, after the success of this 1990 trip, it was 1998 before I returned to South Africa. Furthermore, this was not to pick up on the great relationships I had made, but to accompany Gerald Coates and Noel Richards to a conference at Hatfield Baptist Church in Pretoria. However, team members Dave Matthews, Andy Au and Peter Butt followed me in 1992 to be with Joseph Kobo and his churches in Lujizweni after which they made regular trips to support him and his growing network.

The conference at the Hatfield church led by Francois Van Nierkerk was well attended with people from various parts of South Africa and other, mainly, African countries. There was a programme of seminars in which we took part and Gerald spoke in the evening meetings while Noel led worship, it was a special time. Francois pointed us to an art exhibition which he was excited about and I took time out to wander round during one of the meetings when there were few others there.

I was hugely impressed as Christine and I were both keen to see the arts strongly represented at all levels in the church. Indeed, she would often use artists to work with her when she was speaking or involved in worship. The organiser, Lucy Doran, had gathered a beautiful array of works by local artists and they were all for sale. I had time to chat with Lucy who shared our vision for the arts and we were both greatly encouraged. As a result, Lucy became part of the inspiration for a chapter in my book *The Shaking* entitled, *God's Amazing Technicoloured Dream Church* and Gerald and I both shipped a number of these paintings back to the UK.

It was from this time in Pretoria, when Gerald and Noel flew home, I went on to join Christine in the USA where she was about to have the hip replacement operation I spoke of earlier. Following this I made regular visits to South Africa between 1999 and 2008 to reconnect with the many friends I made during the trip with the Zink's and the Rose's.

After a short visit in 1999 I made a trip in 2001 which was hugely significant. A small team of four of us visited various churches between Cape Town and Idutywa in the Transkei. Dr Kate Walton (now Kate Forbes), Jim Holl and Ian Farr accompanied me and as a result we all became quite deeply involved in different ways and for Ian and Kate it was a life-changing experience.

Ian made a special link with David and Iris Mniki in the Transkei and soon after moved with his wife Gwen to be with them and connect with the other churches we were developing relationships with. After all these years Ian is still there having returned after losing Gwen to cancer to find love and companionship with beautiful Jesika, a lady he knew from a coloured community. I have watched Ian persist in his desire to make friends across the cultures and help to encourage genuine friendship and understanding across the divides.

Ian remembers:

> *At the end of that first trip with you, Jim and Kate I remember sitting in Cape Town with the brothers there for a feedback on the time. I recall saying, 'I have really enjoyed the time, would be willing to come again, but India is still my priority'.*
>
> *The next year we went out, taking our wives. Gwen and I went a little earlier than the rest of you and spent some time touring and spending a few days with the Mniki's in Idutywa. We then went down to Cape Town to join you and Jim and the ladies for a conference.*
>
> *After our return to the UK I was only there for a few days before flying off to take a team to work with Asha in the slums of Delhi. All the time I was there I just could not get South Africa out of my mind. After 2 weeks or so with the team, they all returned to UK*

and I flew down to Chennai where I was joined by Gwen. After a couple of days, I said to her, 'How would you feel if we moved to South Africa'. Much to my shock, she immediately replied, 'I think we should consider that'. She went on to remind me that when we had to leave India in 1985 she had felt the Lord say to her that there was one more culture we would have to live in before we were finished. She had felt when we were in Idutywa that the Transkei was it.

So it was that we moved to Idutywa to work and support David and Iris and the group there as much as possible. We also kept in touch with the other churches we had contact with including Roger in Cape Town, Glen Levendal in Plett and wherever doors opened for us. Willowvale being one such area where our very good friends Theo and Jesika had moved to live and work there.

Kate made numerous visits to serve and encourage David and the church in Idutywa and she also played an important role in the formation of a bridge of prayer between our friends in South Africa and the churches in the UK who were beginning to send teams and ministries in particular to Cape Town and the townships in the area working with Roger Petersen.

Kate tells her story;

I had taken a sabbatical in April 2000 and went on my first visit to South Africa with Peter Doherty and Andy and Nancy Charley and their family. We were going on behalf of Links International to undertake basic health care training with communities linked to Joseph Kobo in the Eastern Cape. Following this we travelled down to Cape Town to be with Roger and Jenny Petersen and their family and church.

I remember being completely bowled over by their care for us. So, when Roger and David Mniki visited the UK later that year, I went to see them when they were staying in Salisbury. It was then Roger gave me an open invitation to visit them again and you, in your generous and inclusive way, invited me to join you, Ian and Jim in New Year 2001.

We had a great time together over the two weeks we were there, connecting with the various groups which were beginning to develop relationships with our UK churches. Following that visit I went back to Cape Town, and then in August 2003 I travelled with a small team put together by Paul and Susannah Woodman with their family to David Mniki in Idutywa. Returning home I did a three-month diploma in Tropical Medicine in preparation to go out again the next year to Idutywa.

I mostly worked with the team at Kholo, David and Iris's church, doing health care training and teaching about HIV. I continued until 2010 spending 6 months each year in South Africa. During that time, I helped set up the charity ACET (AIDS Care Education & Training) and also undertook some training in Cape Town. However, at the end of the day, I feel that the most important thing that I did was make real friends and just be there with them. Indeed, David once said to me, 'Who you are is more important than what you do!' So it was that several ladies from Idutywa came to stay with us in Southampton, as well as the Mniki's, Roger and Jenny and other friends from Cape Town.

It was a precious and life-changing season for me and I am eternally grateful for the foundations laid and introductions made by both you and Christine – thank you!

Concerning the prayer bridge, Andy Horne, and his wife Sue, having moved from a Pioneer church in London to Cape Town to support Roger, also encouraged and served the growing prayer network. He writes:

Flowing out of the relationships that were developing with the UK, a bridge began to be built between the two countries which, from 2003 onwards, enabled several people from the UK to move to both Cape Town and the Eastern Cape. This, in turn, accelerated friends and family visits from local churches in Salisbury, Bromley, Southampton, Guildford and London, followed by ministry trips which opened a door. Then, what emerged was a very organic growth of friendship between individuals from different cultures and backgrounds who found Christ in the midst where love, hope and faith grew in fresh ways.

There was no specific strategy or structure in place but by putting relationships first as a foundation, many fruitful visits meant that partnerships developed whereby experiences, understanding, wisdom and skills were shared mutually.

This bridge has clearly been sustained and strengthened by prayer which began in early 2003 through the vision of Roger Petersen who arranged a joint telephonic prayer call between churches in Cape Town, Idutywa, Salisbury, Bromley and Southampton together with several other people joining in over the years.

In 2005 this became a monthly prayer call meeting most months of each year so that prayer needs have been shared, prophetic words have been given and churches have been strengthened as they sought to be good news in their communities. Also, not only has the technology grown from telephonic conference calls to video calls but also the sense of God's presence has also grown so that, on a regular basis, in each location, we feel the Lord amongst us encouraging us to continue beyond the last 20 years.

Jim Holl reports how his Jubilee Church became involved:

After my trip with John, Kate and Ian, I heard that the churches we had visited were asking John for help with training especially in the townships where there was such great need. As a result, I paid several visits with my wife Sylvia and this opened the door for Jubilee Church to send help.

First, Roger Petersen asked if we could help with some basic computer training for people in the local township. As a result, two of our young ladies – Jackie Mills and Caroline Kirk - put together a manual for every student who was able to join the course. However, due to some confusion in the booking of a venue they ended up at a Learn to Earn Centre in the huge Khayalitsha township with Roger and his pastors patrolling outside to ensure the safety of the ladies while they were teaching. When Roger came to our church some years later, he told us that what the ladies taught was the seed which led to a big RLabs course now successfully used in several other countries.

There followed various other training visits from people in the church including a team teaching first aid and another going to Plettenburg Bay to teach computer basics. Sadly, this latter group never accomplished their goal as the computers were of no use whatsoever. So, a quick change of plan and the team made themselves useful working with children and visiting homes in the area. A lesson in the need to be adaptable when seeking to work into some of the poorer areas of the world where things don't always meet our expectations.

More happy South African memories

Following the 2001 visit I made a further six visits often with Christine. Obviously, there is no way I could give detailed accounts of these nor would it be helpful. However, I am left with some lovely memories which come flooding back when I think about these times and the welcomes we received.

For example, we were so blessed by the way Roger Petersen and his wife Jenny made us feel so at home and cared for us whenever we were with them. Roger was a confirmed teetotaller but he made time to take us round some of the great vineyards in the area and ensured that we had the opportunity to sample some of the superb wines of the region. They also received us into the heart of their fellowship and went out of their way to welcome the many individuals and teams from the UK which came to work with them. And we must remember that that was against a background of hatred and abuse he, and the coloured people, suffered under the apartheid system for so many years. Thank God that the work there has gone from strength to strength.

Then there was Glen Levendal, the mayor of Plettenberg Bay, and his wife Anita and their family. Apart from the great times we had with them in their groups and churches sharing ministry and fellowship, it always felt like holiday time with them in that beautiful area. We stayed in top-quality accommodation overlooking a stunning golf course, one of a number I had the pleasure of playing in that beautiful country. I already mentioned the bird watching I took up in South Africa and the whole area around Plett and Knysna provided great opportunities to explore the hobby. How privileged we have been serving Jesus! Yes, there have been challenges and disappointments but so many wonderful surprises along the way.

In Idutywa we watched the school which David and Iris started grow from a couple of hundred to over 2000 and gain a badge of excellence as one of the best schools in the area. One year Christine had real fun as she was asked to take the older girls for their introduction to Shakespeare which, for African tribal girls in that area, could be a little daunting to say the least. However, Christine's love for the Bard and her knowledge of *A Midsummer Night's Dream* was inspirational and the girls absolutely loved their lessons with Christine. I think they would have gladly had her as a full-time teacher.

I guess it was probably the most moving moment I ever experienced in my travels and it took me completely by surprise. Iris was leading the meeting which was full of powerful praise and exuberant worship, typical of a black African church expressing its love and passion for Jesus. There was a pause and Iris called me to the platform and sat me down in a chair and next to it was a bowl of water and a towel. She signalled to one of the sisters to take off my shoes and socks. She then knelt and proceeded to weep as she washed my feet. I was utterly broken as I sensed that she was confronting the years of pain that white men had inflicted on her and her people and she was responding with forgiveness.

I was completely undone and stood up to ask her to take the chair so that in return I could wash her beautiful feet with my tears. The place went wild with joy and we knew that Jesus was doing a deep, deep work in all our lives as he washed away our sins and healed our crippled souls. What a saviour! What amazing grace! Only his suffering on that cruel cross could possibly enable the release of such a miracle. How our sad, sad and divided world needs a mighty outpouring of this amazing grace.

Finally, I must share a moment when the Lord came to Christine's aid in what could have been an unfortunate situation. I'm not sure where we were but Christine was speaking about the importance of maintaining unity and expressing tolerance towards those we disagree with when, suddenly, a lady stood up and almost ran to the front shouting and pointing at Christine. 'You don't know what it's like to have mixed races in your family!'

Christine was seldom lost for words but she had been taken completely by surprise and was almost overcome by the force of the woman's approach. Then she quickly recovered and found herself replying, 'Oh yes I do my dear! I have a mixed-race adopted daughter and one of my other daughters married an Indian gentleman and I have three mixed-race grandchildren!' At this the woman backed down and Christine was able to continue her talk in a much stronger position as she had grabbed everyone's attention.

We loved our times meeting and ministering among the black and coloured communities in South Africa and felt completely at home with them. Knowing that we were loved and accepted meant that we could be relaxed and have fun with the assurance that if we did make a mistake, it would not give offence and we could be corrected.

CHAPTER THIRTEEN

OTHER INTERNATIONAL VISITS

- Brazil -

I made it to Brazil on three occasions in 2001, 2003 and 2013. The first time I accompanied my friend Ian Farr, who had received invitations from contacts he had made on previous visits. Also, Peter Matthews, a young man from the Chadwell Heath Mission where Ian was in leadership, came along with us. The idea was to give him first-hand experience of overseas ministry – he was excited!

Unusually, I had made notes in my diary of all the places where we stayed covering around 2000 miles from Joao Pressoa in the north to Curitiba in the south - Brazil is a huge country. In between these two cities we went to Recife, Belo Horizonte, Sao Paulo and Sorocaba, covering many more miles travelling to the various churches and groups where we ministered.

Ian reminded me that when we got off the plane in Recife, he was immediately whisked away to a meeting with no idea what happened to us. That was typical of our friends there, who were always ready to change plans and adapt our schedule which made things exciting as we needed to be ready to share at the drop of a hat, sometimes on quite demanding subjects which would have benefitted with time for preparation.

Peter was most impressed, as was I, by the Lagoinha Baptist Church in Belo Horizonte. Ian had been invited there to speak at their missions conference by Carlos Gomez a friend who he met during his missionary travels. Apparently, they were rather disappointed that only 5,000 people had registered for the event out of the almost 20,000 members!

The Pastor, Marcio Valadao, became the senior leader of the church in 1972 when there were just 300 in the congregation, and since our visit it is said to have grown to around 50,000. He struck me as being a little like a Christian Mafia boss with his smooth button up overcoat with the collar turned up. Everywhere he went he commanded great respect be it in a restaurant or the shopping mall. What is more I don't ever remember him being presented with a bill for anything he ordered.

Nevertheless, he was a very humble man and his philosophy for church growth was to release people and support them in their chosen ministry. When someone in the church said they had a burden or a vision for some work or other, he asked them just two questions. When do you want to start, and what do you need? As a result, he had thriving ministries alive and operating into many areas of need across the city. He admitted his biggest problems were to train leaders fast enough to cope with the growth and the need for more car parking space with the continuous growth in the church!

On returning to the UK Peter felt the main impact on his life came from what he saw in the Lagoinha Church. He felt he would like to return there to spend some months with them observing and learning from the experience.

My second visit to Brazil in 2003 came about after some of our groups here made a connection with leaders from Salt and Light, a network with churches spread around the country. I'm afraid my memory of that visit is rather a blur as I made no record of the trip. However, I can say that my lasting memory of my time with those lovely people was the way in which I was received, taken in and welcomed as a member of the family.

I was not only included in all the activities of the church but also in every aspect of their lives. They knew how to live as loving communities, working hard and having fun together. I was taken to the local lido to swim and watch the vast array of beautiful birds and visit other attractions. It was clear that they not only enjoyed their worship but had also learned to live life to the full. It was great fun to be with them. I was also impressed with the quality of the leaders, many of whom had responsible jobs in areas of influence in the communities and beyond.

2013 saw my third and final visit to Brazil and I was delighted that my friend, Jim Holl, had kindly agreed to accompany me, on what was to be my final major international trip with Christine. By this time the symptoms of Christine's dementia were obvious. Furthermore, halfway through the visit she went down with a urinary infection and was delirious. This was rather scary as we were staying in a hotel at the time. However, I have to say that Harold Walker who invited us, together with his team, were fantastic in caring for us. They immediately took us to a hospital, where Christine was examined and underwent various tests to confirm what was wrong and a prescription was issued. All this within a couple of hours, I could hardly believe it. What is more, they covered all the costs over and above the generous gifts and travel expenses which we received at the end of our stay!

The events which led to Harold's invitation were quite remarkable. It happened, unbeknown to me, that in the late 1970's, Muir Gebbie and his friend, Bob Scheibe, working as missionaries in Montalvania, a small agricultural town in the state of Minas Gerais, had received a copy of my booklet *First Apostles Last Apostles* and translated it into Portuguese.

Following this Harold's father, John Mason Walker, together with Harold's elder brother, Robert, went to minister into the work Muir and Bob were doing. According to Harold, his father reprimanded the two of them, in his typically undiplomatic way, for giving undue importance to a politician who was also a rich landowner. He went on to rebuke them for their tardiness in the way they ran the meetings. As a result of John's preaching, whilst Bob resisted and tried to justify their position, Muir sincerely and humbly repented and the Holy Spirit came down and mini-revival took place as many people were saved and baptised.

My booklet was passed on to John who distributed it widely in their network of churches. Apparently, my words confirmed much of what they had been feeling and it was consistently referred to over the years. So it was that I felt I had achieved celebrity status as I was introduced as '....the man who wrote *First Apostles Last Apostles*'. I just hope that my ministry during my visit lived up to their expectations and thank the Lord I had Jim and Christine with me!

The main focus of the trip was a conference to which all the churches in the network were invited. It was held in a beautiful Catholic retreat centre, Vale da Aguia, translated Eagle Valley, which is located in Sorocaba about an hour from the capital city Sao Paulo. This was run by Fr Pedro Arruda, a lovely Catholic priest who had formed a close relationship with Harold and he attended almost all the meetings. Before we left Fr Pedro came forward and knelt before us asking for prayer. We were deeply impressed by his openness and humility.

Many of the church leaders shared how they loved the fact that we joined in fellowshipping round the meal tables. Apparently, other *big named* Americans who came to minister among them, left after each session and shut themselves away until they emerged to share at the next gathering. We explained that we believed friendship was at the heart of church and leaders were not to be aloof and set apart. It was also encouraging to see that, despite Christine's dementia, she was able to move out in her prophetic ministry on occasions which was a real blessing.

Jim reminded me that there was a great interest in the idea of organic church, and we shared our understanding on the fluid nature of a living church which was able to adapt and become effective in any and every situation. Harold remembered that Jim spoke about the transition of passing on the leadership of their church over to his son. He made a mental note of how important it is to retain the relationship and to draw on the knowledge and experience of 'fathers' in the church.

Jim also reminded me that after the conference was finished, the leaders stayed on to have a couple of lengthy sessions where they grilled us with all kinds of questions. He graciously said that he felt I did a great job which I really appreciated as I have always enjoyed being put on the spot in that kind of situation. I feel at such times we get to the heart of the issues which concern the leaders the most.

After the conference Jim and I were able to split up and get around to visit quite a few of the churches and we were encouraged by the welcome and acceptance we received. We loved the intensity of their worship and openness to our ministry. I felt that in just the short time we were with these lovely people, we found ourselves among friends and very much at home. Furthermore, on top of all the hospitality we received and all our expenses covered, we were the recipients of generous love gifts to send us on our way home rejoicing!

- Thailand -

Thailand was another of our favourite destinations - it is an incredible place. Apart from its natural beauty, the great welcome and hospitality of the people, the air is alive with a cacophony of sound and full of the aromas of delicious foods. I also observed that the shops and many markets for the most part displayed the fine work of skilled craftsmen and artists.

Christine and I made five trips together between May 1998 and June 2003. Christine made a final visit in 2005 without me as she took Nancy Daugherty, the wife of the surgeon who worked on her hip, on a team with Bev Webb. At the time we made our visits things were very inexpensive which made travel and shopping a delight. We made these visits in order to support Dave and Carole Summers and their daughter Rebecca who were engaged in a variety of different initiatives.

Recollections from Dave and Carole Summers:

> *It was in the early 80s that we first met you and Christine, and we soon came to value you both very much. After returning to the UK from Thailand you invited us to link up with 'Team Spirit'. It was clear to us that the Lord wanted us to learn from you and others with you, and be a part of what was happening in the house church/new church movement. Through that involvement, our respect and appreciation for you and Christine grew. Not only did you become good friends that we enjoyed spending time with, doing things like playing golf, bird watching, enjoying the beauty of flora and fauna as we travelled together later in Thailand, but we valued the fact that we shared much in terms of heart and vision together.*
>
> *During our time in Cambodia, though we were far apart, our friendship and relationship with you continued, you were a great encouragement to us and a great source of strength and support.*
>
> *Jumping ahead a few years we joined with a new YWAM ministry that was focusing on training church planters for work in China. The plan was for Carole and I to return to Thailand and set up a base of operations there in Chiang Mai. While in Harpenden we ran a School of Frontier Mission and you, along with other friends like Norman Barnes and Pete Lyne, came to do some teaching and ministry during the three-months' training. You and Christine also helped with the first missions training programme that we ran at the Providence Hotel in Chiang Mai shortly after we moved back there.*
>
> *After this time, as the second group of workers moved into China, we encouraged you to go to Kunming to spend some time ministering to different co-workers that we were linked with there. Sometime later Christine and you led the first team to come and work with us amongst the Shan people in Fang District. We were working at that time with a young Shan man called Ou. Ou loved to lead people to Jesus!*

OTHER INTERNATIONAL VISITS

You and Christine were able to minister to those who were responding to the Lord and join in some of the baptisms that took place in the lake up above Suan Chaa village. The team that you brought out with you that year were from City Life Church in Southampton and it was Bev Webb's first trip. We remember that Bev had a fear of flying and Christine dragged her on to that first flight which completely changed Bev's life, as after that she led two teams a year for some years working in the villages amongst the refugees and their children.

On one of your trips we found a place called 'Amala's House' that was a small resort with a lovely garden. Amala was a great cook and could speak some English so you both used to love to stay there especially because you could do some bird watching in the early morning and evening, and Christine loved the unusual shrubs, flowers and trees in the garden. The price was very great too, just around three or four pounds a night all in!

You and Christine also travelled with us to Mae Sot which is further south on the Burma border. This is where the Maela refugee camp is situated. It was the home of many thousands of Karen refugees displaced from Burma. We were able to visit the camps together and you both ministered there. Our friends amongst the believers there were most hospitable and loved the fact that you and Christine could be with them. Tho Lay and Saw Tho were the ones who opened the doors for us to minister to believers in the church there.

You both made several subsequent visits to support us in the work in Thailand and to encourage us and to stand with us. We were very aware that you would always be ready to help with counsel, encouragement and wisdom. We knew that you would respond immediately with real care and love.

It's difficult to measure the impact and influence that you and Christine have had on us and on lots of people in Thailand, Burma and China, but we are sure it's significant, and we are so thankful for it.

We so loved visiting with Dave and Carole who both had a quiet and deep faith in Jesus which carried them through many challenges. The people were very aware of their love and the real connection they had with them.

I remember that one year it was near Christmas time. Carole was home here in the UK and waiting for Dave to come back for the break. She phoned me to say that Dave had gone down with cerebral malaria, a severe disease which could be fatal. She asked what I thought she should do. Should she wait and pray or should she immediately go to be with Dave. I said, 'Carole, you are a woman of faith, I believe you can trust what your heart is telling you!' She said that she believed Dave would be healed and didn't feel she should travel at that time to be with him.

So I agreed with her and we stood together for Dave's healing and safe return home. I am glad to say that our prayers were well and truly answered and Dave was home for Christmas.

- Ethiopia -

It was Christine who found herself drawn into the two trips she made to Ethiopia as a result of our friendship with Phil Izatt. Phil, together with his wife Jean, were part of the leadership of the Petersfield Church which we visited regularly at the time. Phil was also working with Tear Fund on a number of projects which were serving the Kale Hiwot (Word of Light) Church in Ethiopia which, in the 1990's, was 5 million strong and has since doubled its numbers to 10 million. It happened that Tear Fund were looking for a woman to work on a report looking into the controversial subject of FGM – Female Genital Mutilation – which was still widely practised even within the church at that time. Phil recommended Christine and Tear Fund were delighted and suggested that she should accompany Phil on his next visit.

OTHER INTERNATIONAL VISITS

Phil writes:

On that trip, commissioned by Tear Fund, Christine was truly amazing! Eight of us, Christine, me and six Ethiopian men, travelled for five days into the bush over dust and rocky tracks to find evidence of the outcomes of a project I had worked on. Remember, it was culturally unacceptable for 7 men 1 woman in close proximity overnight. Think of the toilet stops! No facilities, just men going left into the trees and Christine, with no embarrassment, going right. This went on for days and she related to us men as a confident equal - a big deal, but in it she remained respectful of being there at my invitation.

We arrived at a clearing in the bush to see a wonderful, locally-resourced, designed and project-managed community centre built by the church for the community to use, as an outcome of the consultancy. Here, Christine and I were invited to a meeting of about 30 district church leaders. After the normal courtesies the meeting began and Christine whispered to me 'Where are the women? Let's decline to take part unless they bring the women in!'.

Although she was there at my invitation and I was responsible to Tear Fund for our work being culturally sensitive, I trusted her judgement and asked her question. The room of men were visibly shocked and the senior leader explained firmly that the women were necessarily preparing the food and looking after the children. You can guess what happened next, Christine jabbed me in the ribs urging me to repeat our refusal to take part. So, while choosing more diplomatic language, I conveyed our 'request' - more silence!

Finally, one of the junior men was sent to bring back a small group of timid women who hid themselves in the darkest corner of the hall. Christine whispers, 'Ask the senior leader to give me permission to speak Philip'. Although this might risk the consultancy, it felt right to me. Christine remained seated, though a man would have stood, and she quietly but firmly asked the fearful women how their lives were going. The atmosphere was electric as Christine repeated her question.

Eventually one of the Ethiopian women spoke...very quietly and Christine encouraged her to speak up, looking to me to see if she should press on. Then one of the women spoke up, telling them everything in her life, and that of her children, was going backwards into the dark past and she was scared of the future. Another then another echoed this point and the atmosphere noticeably shifted from shock to humility as the Holy Spirit moved.

Ethiopian men must be the strong ones, in contrast Kale Hiwot men were actually very humble as I experienced many times during the 10 years I worked with them.

Christine, with my agreement, turned to the senior men, asking: 'What do you feel about this?' There followed a full two-hour discussion which included the women!

This was clearly the Holy Spirit at work within the consultancy enabling better engagement with women and girls. Eventually, around two years later, I learned that Kale Hiwot had turned all its thousands of church buildings into weekday literacy schools, with evangelists becoming teachers using the English bible as their teaching material, with pupils numbering tens of thousands and being predominantly women and girls from the church and the local community. This also led to the gospel reaching deeper into Ethiopian society transforming the relationships of men and women into partnerships - a true mark of the kingdom.

I feel privileged to have known such a brave person as Christine and feel honoured to have experienced working with her on this occasion. Furthermore, it seems there were no lasting cultural insensitivities from this breakthrough event, but many thousands found freedom as a result, surely this is a mark of the Holy Spirit's revolution of love.

When Christine returned from her trips she shared with me a couple of the things which she was really excited about. On the first visit, after travelling with the men in the van, before she left, one of the guys came up to her with tears in his eyes and said, 'Christine, I want you to know that my little girl will never be cut'. That one thing alone made her feel that the whole trip was worthwhile.

On her second visit she returned to a church with a congregation of 1200. During her first stay, the pastor had explained that, as he didn't have a school building, his girls had to walk some kilometres to school every day. This meant that they were often accosted and even raped by young men on the way.

Christine pointed to the beautiful church building and asked why he couldn't use that for the school during the week. The pastor was clearly shocked as he considered the church building to be a holy place. Christine took her time and went on to speak about her understanding from scripture was that it was the people who were the church and the building, beautiful though it was, was just a building. You can imagine her delight on returning to find that in the short time since her last visit, the church building was full of happy children receiving their school lessons!

- *Christine in France and Romania* -

Christine also made trips to France and Romania. In France she connected with Andrew and Sarah Paine, a lovely couple who were facing the challenge of church planting there in Saint-Sauvant, a commune in the Charente-Maritime region in south-western France. Apart from the incredible amount of paper work and red tape, there is little interest in evangelical Christianity with less than 2% of Christians involved. However, Andrew and Sarah were there for the long haul and Sarah, being an artist, gave them a different opening into the community. Thus, Christine, with her interest in the arts, was able to encourage and support them through several visits which were greatly appreciated.

Richard and Emily Bailey were friends who were involved with Pioneer People, the local church in Cobham at the time. They lived quite close to us in Leatherhead, and Christine particularly enjoyed getting together with Emily as the couple were starting their family and, of course, Christine loved spending time with Emily and their children.

Local church leader David Taylor had launched a local community project called Cobham Romania Aid (later Heart for Romania) which took teams to work on projects in Romania. He later became the Director of the Princess Margareta of Romania Trust in the UK which was supported by the exiled King Michael and Queen Anne. David had frequent contact with the ex-Romanian royal family and later introduced church leader, Gerald Coates, to the family. Queen Anne listened to Gerald's story and clearly responded to the gospel message.

Richard Bailey travelled out with David and the teams. After Richard and Emily were married, they both went to live in Romania for a short period. Richard, who had been in contact with a poor gypsy community there, knowing Christine had a heart for such people, invited her to travel there with him. His desire was to encourage them by sharing the good news and providing clothing and other material support.

Christine was immediately drawn to this needy group who were rejected by the local community. And, despite the language difficulties, she was able to connect with them and demonstrate God's love for them and their outcast children. Typical Christine! Somehow, time and time again she managed to reach people whatever their identity or background.

- *Other visits to European countries* -

I made numerous visits to Europe, other than those mentioned thus far, including many trips because of my growing relationships with charismatic leaders' groups over the years. I must say that some of memories of the earlier trips are quite sketchy as I didn't keep records.

For example, I clearly remember spending time in France with Bill and Sophie Kapituniuk, in Billy-Montigny, but I have no recollection how that came about or what was achieved. We also spent many happy fellowship holidays in a tiny village in the French alps with Dudley and Gill Ward. They were an interesting couple who were restoring a village of half a dozen or so houses called Entrepierres, near the town of Sisteron. It was a beautiful area where we all camped in a field and enjoyed traipsing around the hills looking at butterflies, finding fossils and fishing in the little lakes. Apparently, their son Jonathan, just a young boy when we were there in the early seventies, now runs the place as a tourist centre.

In Germany, Pioneer held a successful international conference in the church of Rudolf Pinke in Frankfurt, where some of our team were developing relationships there and in other parts of the country. Ultimately, a number from the network made frequent visits and some ended up living and working in Berlin.

I was also invited to minister to a large Lutheran charismatic group in Stuttgart. The leaders kindly took me to visit one of the many castles there where they fed the birds of prey by throwing food from a tower. We were enthralled as we watched the birds swoop to catch the food before it reached the ground.

In the evening, I was asked to speak and a lovely English lady was translating for me, chosen as being the most experienced. I started by thanking them for their hospitality and said how much I enjoyed watching the spectacle of the eagles swooping down to catch their food from the tower. I was rather bemused as to why the congregation burst out into howls of laughter. Of course, I do like to crack the odd joke. However, I was completely unaware of what I had said which caused such amusement until it was explained to me that the German word for eagle is 'adler' and 'igel' is the word for hedgehog! The prospect of flying hedgehogs was just too much for my listeners to ignore.

Just one trip to Spain as far as I can remember, which we made to visit Peter and Carol Armon. They were the parents of Dave mentioned earlier when we spent time with him and his family in Tanzania. Peter and Carol worked for World Horizons and had pastoral oversight of various people in the Spanish team and in North Africa. Peter also worked in Gibraltar as a locum in the government hospital, and occasionally in the naval hospital. Later, he went on to work full time in the government hospital which we saw as God's provision because he was able to help the Morocco team with hospital appointments. I am always thrilled to see how people who are called to *live by faith* find creative ways to trust God for their income and aspects of their work. We loved spending time with them and sharing with them.

Apart from multiple journeys to Italy in connection with my work with the Catholics, I made a couple of visits to spend time with Pietro Evangelista and his wife Sandra. He is the Italian representative for the American publisher Destiny Image and he also looked after several groups and fellowships which I enjoyed visiting with him and sharing ministry. I see now that he has expanded his business and is helping Christian leaders and ministries to publish their books with many titles in his portfolio.

CHAPTER FOURTEEN

FINAL WORDS ON THE LOVE OF MY LIFE

A tribute from Sue Rinaldi at the time of Christine's passing:

Christine Noble was a gifted and passionate Christian leader who fought for other women to be free in their callings.

I remember the day I met her. I was 19, maybe 20. I had already seen this mighty enigma of a woman from afar speaking at various conferences and discussing challenging issues such as women in leadership. She did all this in a style that was as agile and as adept as an Olympic champion who had clearly dedicated themselves to a mission.

Surrounded by predominantly male church leaderships, or contexts where females were simply the 'spouses', she had stature in abundance, and alongside her husband John, modelled a refreshing and redemptive equal partnership of differing gifts. As a radically thinking young woman, I was relieved. Actually, more like ecstatic!

So when Christine Noble first visited the house church I attended in Southampton, I was ready! Ready to listen. Ready to learn. This began many years of being an extremely grateful recipient of her influence and inspiration, where I was not only privileged to call her a role model, but also to call her a friend and to serve alongside her at many events and conferences.

With forthright clarity, she confronted the religious boundary lines that prevented women from taking their rightful place in God's plan, essentially because Christine loved God, loved freedom and loved people! She wanted all people to know the love and freedom only God can bring.

She would speak passionately about the Kingdom of God and about living free from all that would impede or corrupt our Christ-won freedom; she would leave trails of Spirit disturbance as she ushered in heavenly touchdowns after discerning powers and principalities that were not welcome, and she would lucidly communicate her weighty and wildfire passion to see women reach their full potential in Christ in life and in ministry. For me and for countless others, women and men, her shaking of the 'role defined by and according to gender' tree was where she shone as bright as a laser beam.

Her book, 'What in the World is God Saying About Women?' published in 1990 by Kingsway, created tidal waves of response. I can imagine shouts of 'Hallelujah' and 'About time' being punctuated by appeals for calm and dutiful devout reticence. Yet, in true Christine fashion, the book boldly and prophetically unravelled centuries of dogmas and prejudice towards the XX of our species, and with forthright clarity, she confronted the cultural, historical and religious boundary lines that prevented women from taking their rightful place in God's plan. She was not recruiting foot soldiers for a Christian battle of the sexes, but rather she was leading the charge 'for a fresh understanding of what God's word truly says and of the dignity which Jesus brought to all creation'.

Those words, quoted from her book, afford us precious insight into her heart. Her desire to confront centuries of damage and distortion, particularly where women have been silenced and subjugated, and her intrepid ability to war in the spiritual realm against forces of evil that seek to corrupt and contaminate, was awesome.

After battling dementia for many years, Christine finally went to be with Jesus on Saturday. Her husband John and their family have been amazing and indefatigable in their devotion, care and adoration of her. Tributes have poured in from people around the world, giving voice to her impact and influence upon them, affirming her legacy will live on in countless lives and, indeed, across generations.

She was a warrior. A mother (both spiritual and actual). A wife. A role model. An agent provocateur. She axed down trees of limitation and foliage of restriction so others could roam free on clearer, cleaner and never-say-never lands. She climbed ladders to pull down the low ceilings that were shielding our eyes from bigger destiny skies.

But she was also a little scary! It's true... sometimes we feel intimidated by those who are more akin to being a force of nature. There were times when she was blunt and extremely straightforward. There were times when she was leading seminars with John, when they resembled a comedy duo rather than seasoned, serious church leaders!

I remember her sitting on many an event platform party or in a conference, and there she was...crocheting! How marvellous! I remember my first ever trip to the USA was with John and Christine. Being rather scared of air travel and especially turbulence, I will never forget her response when I timidly admitted my fear. 'Oh, it only starts to get exciting when turbulence happens.' (How very Christine of her.) And then I remember a conversation espousing the wondrous fruit smells of shower gels and hand creams. Obviously not charmed by these products, Christine defiantly remarked, 'Who wants to smell like a strawberry!?'

For all these memories and more... for everyone she's influenced... for every church she has served and shaped... for every nation she has embraced... we honour you as a freedom-fighter... our very own statue of liberty!

Also, Christine's friend and colleague Linda Harding writes a brief tribute which recalls the great Into Focus women's weekends they did together to encourage and release women to realise their full potential.

Linda writes

When Christine joined Pioneer, she brought such understanding and encouragement to me in the lonely path that I was walking as a single woman in leadership in Pioneer with no role models. Christine was such an inspiration and became a dear friend. Although we were very different in our giftings and personalities and life circumstances, we enjoyed many special memorable moments on the development of 'Into Focus' - with a shared desire to see women empowered and released to be their unique selves!

With a wonderful team of equally unique women, we ran many hugely significant weekends ministering together …. seeing countless women challenged, healed, and transformed – many of whom continue to be leading in countless different spheres of life today! Working with Christine was always fun – although often unpredictable - her passion, her directness and her freedom to be her unique self, meant the schedule sometimes changed but certainly ensured we always kept in step with the Holy Spirit – and we saw women wonderfully set free! Christine and I also had the joy of ministering together in Norway to many beautiful Norwegian friends there - a special time together.

Christine's life of generosity and love was always an inspiration to me, and so many women. She, together with John, trail-blazed a way for women and men to follow. The younger generations of today will never have to face the giants and fight the battles that Christine fought for women… and for men.

- Signing off -

I can't close without sharing a little more about my dearest Christine and the last few years we spent looking after her. The only way I can describe the loss of a loved one to the evil disease of dementia, is like experiencing multiple bereavements. To lose the one you love is always going to be an horrendous heart-wrenching experience followed by a period of grieving. However, with dementia, every stage along the way you lose a piece of your beloved and each time there is a feeling of bereavement and grieving.

First, facing and accepting the diagnosis felt like a knockout blow. I could see how Christine struggled with that and I suffered deep emotional hurt as I tried to help her come to terms with it. Then came the moment when I had to explain to her that she was no longer allowed to drive and that was hard for both of us.

Later, I remember going to our annual Pioneer conference and Christine was not well enough to join me. I struggled from the start as I met many of the 500 delegates who, obviously, all wanted to know how my lady was. By the time I got home I felt as if I'd experienced a bit of a nervous breakdown.

The only positive thing about that weekend was that Wayne Drain came in to see Christine on his way back to Sidcup with the group who he brought from Arkansas. Amazingly, Christine perked up and prayed and prophesied over each one of Wayne's team and we were all in tears. That was the last time she did anything like that. Furthermore, Wayne gave me a $20 bill and prophesied that I would prosper financially, after which my stamp business took off and our mortgage was cleared and the business has gone on from strength to strength.

I could go on, but would just say that releasing Christine into the care home after her increasing deterioration when she struggled at times to believe that I was her husband, was both an incredible pain and at the same time a relief. Also visiting her every day for five years, apart from during lockdown, was a test but not something I would have missed. Lockdown itself brought challenges as trying to communicate through a window when I wasn't allowed in left me traumatised, and at one point I had to walk away as it was too painful.

Her last few days were hard to watch as she went through 'nil by mouth' but, thankfully, I don't think she knew much about that. Strangely, the day she did finally leave us to be with Jesus, and that after me pleading with her to go (which, of course she knew nothing about), was a relief after all the pain of watching her at the end. I must thank my lovely Sharon who, with some help from Ruth, sat with her day and night holding her hand, something I just could not have done at the time.

- Looking on the bright side -

In 1 Thessalonians 5:18 (NIV), Paul commands us to *Give thanks in all circumstances; for this is God's will for you in Christ Jesus.* Most Christians struggle with this instruction, particularly when we are facing serious challenges in our lives. How is it possible to say, 'Thanks, Lord' when we are suffering? However, it is only when we realise that the Lord uses everything that happens to us, be it good or bad, to shape us. So that as we embrace our circumstances and thank him, we mature and grow more like him.

As I pondered this during my struggles with Christine, I realised that every circumstance which we face will result either in bitterness springing up, if we continually resist God, or blessing if we choose to respond with thankfulness. As I sought to examine what was happening to me, I found that little by little my heart was being softened. I began to understand the pain that others felt who were facing similar issues to me and I felt empathy growing, the depth of which I had not experienced before.

As a result, I found that opportunities were coming my way to sympathize with others and comfort them. Apart from individuals, I spoke with groups of men, and on one occasion was able to counsel the wife of one key church leader who was at her wit's end with her husband and all his strange behaviour. It also happened that my Facebook posts began to reach others who were suffering. Then, later, I became an ambassador for the charity Embracing Age and was able to serve them in a variety of different ways. So, all in all, I found that in the twilight of my life I had developed an entirely new side to my ministry – thank you Jesus!

FINAL WORDS ON THE LOVE OF MY LIFE

So with so much more that could be said about my life with Christine and her many exploits, I feel this is a good place to draw our story to a close. It is impossible to say how grateful I am to God for bringing Christine into my life and for giving us such wonderful opportunities, over so many years, to serve him and his wonderful *Pure Church!*

The end

APPENDIX ONE

Rich Robert's reply to dad's letter

Dear John

Thank you for sending me a copy of your father's letter regarding the Baptism in the Holy Spirit. It appears that your dad was influenced by the Holiness Movement.

The Holiness Movement started with John Wesley and the Methodists. It then spread to other parts of the Church and influenced major Christian leaders, including Charles Finney. Its stronghold was in the USA and it gave rise to several denominations, such as the Church of the Nazarene. Holiness teaching also influenced the Salvation Army and other Christian movements in the UK, such as the annual Keswick Convention. Some Holiness Churches became Pentecostal in the early twentieth century.

Holiness teaching envisages the Christian life as a two-stage process: the first stage is conversion and the second stage is what is called 'entire sanctification'. This is also known as sinless perfection, an experience whereby the believer loses all desire to commit sins (historically, smoking, dancing and listening to popular music were regarded as sins). The Holy Spirit was seen to be the author of this experience and the phrase 'Baptism in the Spirit' is sometimes used by Holiness teachers to describe 'entire sanctification'.

In contrast, most Pentecostal and Charismatic believers think of the Baptism in the Holy Spirit in terms of empowerment for service, as in Acts 2, rather than it being an experience of purification from sin. This is often accompanied by a heightened awareness of God and a new love for the Bible. Of course, the Holy Spirit is the Spirit of holiness. The disciples experienced 'tongues of fire' at Pentecost and the implication of fire is purification – the refining fire - so your dad did have a point in linking the oncoming Spirit with purity.

APPENDIX ONE

Your dad argued against a three-stage Christian experience - conversion, entire sanctification followed by a subsequent Baptism in the Spirit. He rightly saw this as overly complex, but I would consider that the idea of 'entire sanctification is the dubious element in this scheme. He does mention power for service and the impartation of spiritual gifts, so his views are not as polarised as they could be. However, his main emphasis, in keeping with the Holiness Movement, seems to be cleansing from sin to reach a state of perfection.

It is often the case that an initial or fresh infilling of the Spirit will increase our devotion to God and make us less likely to want to sin, but the idea of sinless perfection seems more of a theory rather than reality. For one thing, we are enjoined to pray daily that our trespasses be forgiven - why would we need to do this if we had ceased to sin?

In fact, several sections of the New Testament are difficult to square with the Holiness Movement. Paul's account in Galatians suggests that Peter's withdrawal from the Gentile believers was regarded as a lapse into sin, despite his powerful experience(s) of the Spirit. In addition, 1 John reassures us that confession leads to forgiveness and again; this would not be needed if we were in a state of sinless perfection. Scripture does not suggest we reach a stage of perfection until we 'see him as he is', at which point 'we will be like him' (1 John 3:2).

It is clear that your father had a love for Scripture and was immersed in particular passages, many of which are my favourites! You have a good and godly heritage.

Blessings

Rich

Richard Roberts
www.newcharismatic.com

APPENDIX TWO

House church Bibliography

Booklets:

Forgive us our Denominations, John Noble, self-published

First Apostles Last Apostles, John Noble, self-published

Not Under Law, Gerald Coates, self-published

Sunday and the Rest, Nick Butterworth, self-published

The Church in the House, George Tarleton, self-published

The Gospel According to St George, George Tarleton, self-published

Books:

5.5.55, Maurice Smith, 1969 CLC

Tilgi oss alle vare Kirkesamfunn, (Norway Forgive us our Denominations) 1977 Ansgar

The Battle of the Sexes, John Noble, 1978 self-published

Hide & Sex, John Noble, 1981 Kingsway

Go and Make Apprentices, Phill Vogel, 1986 Kingsway

Man's Inhumanity to God, David Matthews, 1986 Kingsway

My Life for my Wife, Rod Boreham, 1987 Kingsway

God Gave me a Dream, Norman Barnes, 1988 New Wine Press

House Churches – Will they Survive? John Noble, 1988 Kingsway

The Turning Tide, Brenda Robson, 1989 Marshal Pickering

APPENDIX TWO

What in the World is God Saying About Women? Christine Noble, 1990 Kingsway

City Vision, Stuart Murray, 1990 Darton, Longman & Todd

The Forgiveness Equation, John Noble, 1991 Marshall Pickering

Past Perfect, Christine Noble, 1991 Marshall Pickering

Everyman's Guide to the Holy Spirit, the End of the World and You, John and Christine Noble, 1991 Kingsway

The Ladies Aren't for Silence, Joan Martin, 1991 Word Books

Breaking the Mould, Edited by Gerald Coates, 1993 Kingsway

Is Leadership Male? Joan Martin, 1996 Nelson Word

The Shaking, John Noble 2002, Monarch Books

L'equation du Pardon, (French The Forgiveness Equation) John Noble, 2002 rdf

Rystelsen, (Norway The Shaking) John Noble, 2002 Prokla-Media

In the Valley, Mary Matthews, 2013 What's Your Story?

Making Disciples – How did Jesus do it? Tony Pullin, 2014 CWR

At the Beginning Mary Matthews 2017 New life Publishing

Pentecost Released, Peter Butt, 2019 self-published

Our Journey, Peter Butt 2022, self-published

Eternity Calls: Grace Barnes. She Lived Her Dream, Norman Barnes, 2023 self-published

Pure church